# Rock Climbing
# The
# Flatirons

Richard Rossiter

**CHOCKSTONE**

FALCON®
HELENA, MONTANA

## A FALCON GUIDE ®

Falcon® Publishing is continually expanding its list of recreational guidebooks. All books include detailed descriptions, accurate maps, and all information necessary for enjoyable trips. You can order extra copies of this book and get information and prices for other Falcon® books by writing Falcon, P.O. Box 1718, Helena, MT 59624 or calling toll free 1-800-582-2665. Also, please ask for a free copy of our current catalog. Visit our website at FalconOutdoors.com, or contact us by e-mail at falcon@falcon.com.

© 1999 by Richard Rossiter
Published by Falcon®Publishing, Inc., Helena, Montana
Printed in Canada


1  2  3  4  5  6  7  8  9  0  TP  04  03  02  01  00  99


Falcon and FalconGuide are registered trademarks of Falcon® Publishing Inc.

Library of Congress Cataloging-in-Publication Data
Rossiter, Richard, 1945-
    Rock climbing the Flatirons / by Richard Rossiter
        p.   cm. -- (A FalconGuide)
    ISBN 1-56044-918-7 (pbk.)
    1. Rock climbing--Colorado--Boulder Region Guidebooks.  2. Boulder Region (Colo.) Guidebooks.   I. Title.   II. Series: Falcon guide.
    GV199.42.V62B6876   1999
    796.52'23'0978863--dc21                                      99-38035
                                                                 CIP

**CAUTION**

Outdoor recreational activities are by their very nature potentially hazardous. All participants in such activities must assume responsibility for their own actions and safety. The information contained in this guidebook cannot replace sound judgment and good decision-making skills, which help reduce risk exposure, nor does the scope of this book allow for disclosure of all the potential hazards and risks involved in such activities.

Learn as much as possible about the outdoor recreational activities in which you participate, prepare for the unexpected, and be cautious. The reward will be a safer and more enjoyable experience.

♻ Text pages printed on recycled paper.

# Table of Contents

# Preface

It's Bike Week in Daytona Beach, Florida, and a warm ocean breeze billows the curtains beside the open glass doors of my condo. Morning sunlight sparkles and shimmers on the waves of the Atlantic as they roll into shore, filling the room with the sound of breaking surf. Spellbound at my PowerBook, I drag my attention back to the monitor and recall that I am writing the sixth edition of *Boulder Climbs*, and that if I don't get with it, I'll still be writing it in the next millennium. Ah yes, the Flatirons.

The Flatirons could be said to run from Eldorado Canyon, or even the West Bank on Eldorado Mountain, to Flagstaff Mountain—though the name usually refers to the crags along the east sides of Boulder Mountain and Green Mountain; even then, only the first five on the northeast quadrant of Green Mountain are actually named "Flatirons." All the Flatirons, by any name, are part of a sedimentary uplift called the Fountain Formation, which consists of a very hard, conglomerate, metamorphic sandstone that is excellent for climbing. Uplift and erosion have left in place a stunning array of buttresses, slabs, towers and fins, wildly ranging in shape and size. Enchanting trails wind among the canyons and ridges, providing easy access to these magnificent crags. The Flatirons by any measure are a rock climber's paradise.

# Acknowledgments

I would like to thank the following people for contributing information, participating in on-site photo sessions, holding poses in the midst of difficult moves, and for making the task of writing the sixth edition of *Boulder Climbs* a lot more fun, meaningful and enlightening: Gerry Roach, Bill DeMallie, Dan Hare, Steve Dieckhoff, Steve "Crusher" Bartlett, Bonnie Von Grebe, Kath Pyke, and the staff at Boulder Mountain Parks who have taken time from their busy schedules to meet with me and to provide information and maps regarding their efforts to balance preservation and use.

# BOULDER AREA MAP

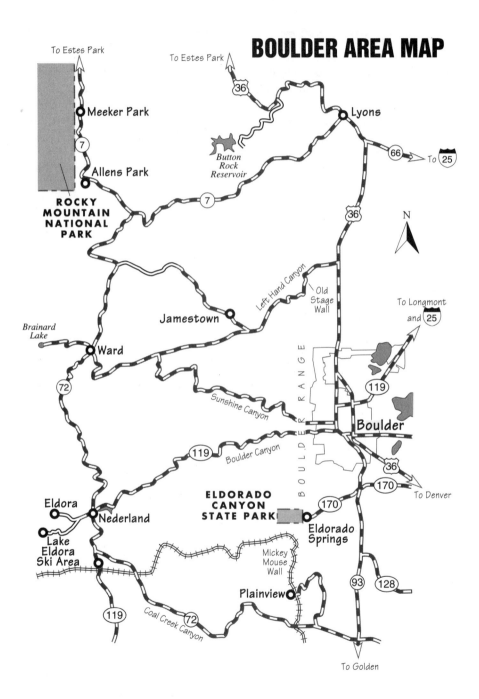

# Introduction

## WILDLIFE CLOSURES
## by Kath Pyke of The Access Fund

The Access Fund is a national non-profit organization that works to keep climbing areas open and to conserve the climbing environment. The Access Fund supports land and recreation management based on objective analyses, information on critical resources and how climbers affect these resources. The climbing environment provides crucial habitat for many kinds of plants and animals, some of which are rare or quite sensitive to disturbance from humans.

For this reason the Access Fund supports seasonal climbing restrictions to protect nesting raptors at over 70 climbing locations in the United States. These are targeted to protect endangered or threatened species such as peregrine and prairie falcons and golden eagles. Typically, restrictions start in early spring and run through early to mid-summer; the critical nesting period when birds are raising their young. By working in partnership with biologists and land managers, the Access Fund strives to help provide the necessary protection for the nesting birds without excessive climbing restrictions. We encourage lifting restrictions early if nest sites are not established and the flexibility to change restricted areas if birds vary their nest site from year to year.

Support from local climbers is vital to the success of the raptor program. Resource managers, with limited budgets for monitoring, welcome raptor sightings or reports of unusual behavior. Equally, the Access Fund needs your feedback. If you need more information or have a concern about a raptor closure, please call the Access Fund. The Access Fund exists to help climbers and will be able to coordinate local meetings to take up issues on your behalf.

Nest sites and management considerations may vary from year to year; keep an eye out for signs at parking lots and trailheads which give current information, or call the responsible agency listed on our web site: http://www.accessfund.org.

## RAPTORS AND THE BOULDER FRONT RANGE

The City of Boulder implements seasonal closures on Mountain Parks and Open Space lands. Signs are posted at parking lots and trailheads. Closures may vary from year to year.

The unique geography and abundant cliffs of the Boulder Front Range make ideal conditions for cliff nesting raptors and thus support some of the highest population densities in Colorado. However, given its close proximity to a growing urban area and the high recreational demands placed on these same areas, resource managers have a major task in trying to balance wildlife protection with recreation opportunities.

City of Boulder staff carry out the following measures as part of their annual education and outreach program to provide information on climbing restrictions and conscientious use:

*   signing at parking lots and trailheads

- Distribution of seasonal closure details to local climbing gyms, stores and organizations
- Presentations and open question sessions at local venues
- A telephone hot line service with the latest update on wildlife closures
- Internet access through web site: http//bcn/boulder.co.us/boulder/
- Coordination of an annual raptor monitoring program for volunteers and City of Boulder staff
- Annual meetings with Access Fund representatives to review wildlife closures and management practice

## 1999 CLOSURES IN BOULDER MOUNTAIN PARKS

Note that the following closures may vary from year to year:

- The entirety of Shadow Canyon, including The Matron and all crags listed in the text. One is still allowed to walk up the Shadow Canyon Trail, but don't stray off the path.
- The entire north side of Fern Canyon to Seal Rock, which includes the first thirteen crags listed in the Nebel Horn chapter of this book.
- Bear Creek Spire and the surrounding terrain within a 100-yard radius.
- The entirety of Skunk Canyon, including the north side of Dinosaur Mountain and the Sacred Cliffs. Ridge One is open.
- Bluebell Canyon area, including the Third Flatiron, Queen Anne's Head, W. C. Fields Pinnacle, East and West Ironing Boards, The Fin, Green Thumb and Jaws.

**FYI Line.** For Information on wildlife closures and other restrictions, call the FYI number at 303-441-4060, extension 420.

**Boulder Mountain Parks:** To speak with a staff member call 303-441-3408.

# MAP LEGEND

| | | | | |
|---|---|---|---|---|
| Interstate | | Cabins/Buildings | | |
| US Highway | | Topography | | |
| State or Other Principal Road | | Gate | | |
| Interstate Highway | | Mine Site | | |
| Paved Road | | Railroad | | |
| Gravel Road | | County Line Boundary | | |
| Unimproved Road | | Continental Divide | | |
| Trailhead | | | | |
| Main Trail(s) /Route(s) | | Fence Line | | |
| Bushwhack | | | | |
| Parking Area | | Powerline | | |
| River/Creek/Waterfall | | National Park | | |
| County Road | CR | | | |
| Forest Road | FR | Map Orientation | | |
| Forest Trail | FT | | | |
| Four Wheel Drive | 4WD | Scale | | |
| Two Wheel Drive | 2WD | | | |
| Campground | | | | |

## AUTHOR'S PERSPECTIVE

Some readers probably have old, dog-eared copies of the original *Boulder Topographics, A Pictorial Guide To Boulder Climbs* published in 1981. Two years later, the title was abbreviated to *Boulder Climbs*. Back then, the biggest issue in climbing was whether or not it was ethical to use gymnast's chalk on the hands. By 1985, the French had rap-bolted Verdon Gorge and the idea of free climbing the blank expanses of rock between crack systems was spreading around the world like wild fire. Boulder (and most climbing areas) became a war zone between those who chose to drill and those who didn't. Some climbers looked to government agencies to intervene and stop the bolting, and in most places, that is just what happened. But when you ask the government to do something, they almost always do way more than you want—or could even imagine. A case of shooting yourself in the foot.

Most land managers had paid little attention to the sport of climbing and were largely unaware of its rapidly growing popularity, much less that climbers were drilling little holes in the rock and placing bolts in them. When irate "traditional" climbers began storming the desks of park managers, demanding that rap-bolting be stopped, they triggered an avalanche of government intervention and regulation that has yet to reach the bottom of the valley.

It is ironic that some of the climbers who complained, chopped routes and wrote letters to editors, eventually bought drills and started putting up their own bolt routes, only to find themselves restrained by the very limitations they had sought for others. Even stranger is that the debate for many climbers was not over bolts, but whether bolts should be placed "on the lead" or from a toprope—an issue that completely evaded the comprehension of non-climbers.

It is now fall of 1999, and the issue is not about stopping the bolts, but about stopping the government from taking away your right to climb on public lands. Most agencies have found ways to stop or severely limit the use of bolts and pitons. Some, such as Boulder County Open Space, have even set about mutilating fixed anchors in their jurisdiction. The biggest threat to your freedom, though, is the ever-expanding imposition of "wildlife closures," which has become nationwide policy.

Boulder Mountain Parks (the venue covered in this book) began enforcing closures in the late 1980s when it was discovered (likely through one of my books) that a golden eagle was nesting on Ridge Two in Skunk Canyon. Since then, the closures have multiplied and expanded to include many of the best crag areas in the park.

If nesting continues to increase, it follows that under current policy, more and more crags will be closed. This means that climbing in the Flatirons will effectively be eliminated except in the fall and early winter. Other areas have seen the same fate. Vast sectors of the South Platte are closed each year and cannot be entered. The entirety of Mickey Mouse Wall is closed and the area cannot be entered. Crags at Lumpy Ridge are closed. Crags in Boulder Canyon and Eldorado Canyon State Park are closed. Even the west shore of Boulder Reservoir is closed.

Dale Goddard on *Beware the Future* (5.14a),
Skunk Canyon. Photo by Dan Hare.

Questions: Should Boulder Mountain Park (a front-country park—not a wilderness area) become an exclusive wildlife sanctuary, or should it be shared with the public? Will people be allowed only to hike on major trails, as per the current closure in Shadow Canyon? Should access be limited to ranger-guided tours? If the birds want the park, should humans abdicate? Would it be better if we all just stayed at home and watched wildlife specials on TV?

There is no argument that some level of protection is needed for nesting raptors. It is, however, my observation that the current closures go well beyond what is actually required to protect the reproductive cycles of these birds. For example, could climbers on the Ironing Boards (especially on the west sides) disrupt a bird nesting on the south side of the Third Flatiron? Could climbers on the west side of the Sacred Cliffs possibly have an adverse effect on an eagle nesting hundreds of yards away, beyond sight or hearing, on Ridge Two in Skunk Canyon? How close would humans need to be to cause a bird enough stress that it would abandon its nest and leave its young to die? Is the frequency of passersby a factor? How many birds are actually nesting in Boulder Mountain Parks? Not all of the closed areas actually have nests.

Raptors have little fear of humans, or even the movement of large objects such as automobiles, as they will nest in the noise and chaos of New York City as well as in the wilderness. Peregrine falcons have for centuries been domesticated and used for sport hunting. Golden eagles and falcons have flown casually beneath my heels as I worked my way up a climb. There is evidence to indicate that raptors will habituate to a variety of environments and that they do not avoid areas frequented by humans. Such behavioral patterns are exhibited by many other animals such as bear, raccoons, many species of birds, rodents and deer.

During 1991, two climbers were apprehended by rangers for entering a closure at the Matron in Shadow Canyon. A *Daily Camera* (newspaper) article covering the bust explained that humans within 50 feet of a nest could cause the adult birds to abandon the nest and newly hatched chicks. A week later, in the same section of the paper was a photograph taken with a flash camera of the tiny chicks inside the nest, who had been banded by a wildlife agent! What is more, the agent had hired two climbers from the International Alpine School to get him to the nest.

My point is this: Raptors are not as sensitive to human beings as would be indicated by the duration and extent of current closures, and that these closures could be pared down considerably without adverse affect to the raptor population. Urban life with all its rules and conformity is a stifling affair. Humans need the parks too.

I have included the position of the Access Fund as well as the policies and current restrictions of Boulder Mountain Parks. The Author's Perspective represents those people (including myself) who feel that the closures are too long and too broad and must be reduced to something considerably more exact.

## OTHER ENVIRONMENTAL CONSIDERATIONS

To preserve the natural beauty and ecological integrity of our climbing environment, a few suggestions are offered (by the author): Use restrooms or outdoor toilets where possible. Otherwise, deposit solid human waste far from the cliffs and away from paths of

Jim Michael on *Death and Transfiguration* (5.11b),
Green Mountain Pinnacle. Photo by Dan Hare.

approach and descent. Do not cover solid waste with a rock but leave it exposed to the elements where it will deteriorate more quickly, or better, carry a small garden spade and bury it. Carry used toilet paper out in a plastic bag or use a stick or Douglas fir cone. Do not leave man-made riffraff lying about. If you pack it in, pack it out. Take care to preserve trees and other plants on approaches and climbs. While travelling in scree gullies and talus fields, seek sections that are more stable; thrashing up and down loose scree causes erosion and destroys plant life. Always use trails and footpaths where they have been developed and demonstrate consciousness by removing obstructions, stacking loose rocks along trail sides, and picking up trash. Dogs are best left at home as they cannot be attended while one is climbing. Unattended dogs are often a nuisance or even a hazard to others, especially in high-use areas.

## FIXED PROTECTION

Fixed protection has become a major point of contention with park managers and powerful wilderness lobbies. The very concept of "climbing management" and resultant closures and restrictions has developed around climbers' use of bolts and other forms of fixed anchors, especially in high profile areas. If we are to have access to public lands and preserve the freedoms we have enjoyed in the past, it is critical that we promote a sensible and responsible public image. Climber organizations such as the Access Fund do much to help this cause, but our actions in the field are even more important.

Bolts, pitons, and slings that can be seen from the ground (or through binoculars) are easy targets for complaint. Dangling slings are highly visible and should be eliminated. Bolt hangers should be camouflaged. For those in the first ascent business, always place bolts in the most useful possible position for someone leading the route. Bolt anchors are best fitted with threadable hangers such as the Fixe rappel anchors (with rings) because they are permanent and much less visible than slings or chains.

Knowing that every bolt and piton we place will be counted and documented by some regulatory agency or wildlife organization, it is obvious that some restraint on our part is necessary. As for new free climbs requiring bolts, only the very best lines should be developed. Contrived and mediocre routes should be left to obscurity. When the decision is made to place bolts on a new route, only the best gear should be used so that it is reliable and permanent. Bolts should not be placed on the lead. The emphasis should not fall on the style of the first ascent, but on the resultant route. Knowing that a good route will be climbed many thousands of times and that holes drilled in the rock will last for millennia, it is obvious that the quality and positioning of fixed hardware must take precedence over other considerations.

**Note:** Placement of any new fixed protection is banned in Boulder Mountain Parks. A new policy allows for the replacement and upgrading of existing fixed protection, but requires a review by Boulder Mountain Parks staff. For information, call: 303-441-3408.

## EQUIPMENT

Appropriate climbing hardware can vary drastically from one route to another and what a climber chooses to carry is a matter of style and experience. So-called sport climbs obviously require only quickdraws unless otherwise noted. There is on other climbs an array of devices that most parties would want to carry. Thus, a "standard rack" (SR) for the Boulder area might consist of the following gear:

A set of RPs

Wired stoppers up to one inch

Various camming devices up to 2.5 inches

7 or 8 quick draws (QDs)

3 to 5 runners long enough to wear over the shoulder

I double-length runner

6 to 8 unoccupied carabiners (usually with the runners)

## RATINGS

The system used for rating difficulty in this book is a streamlined version of the so-called Yosemite Decimal System. The class five designation is assumed, so that 5.0 through 5.14 is written as 0 through 14 without the 5. prefix. The Welzenbach grades Class 3 and Class 4 have been retained. The Roman numeral grades I through VI for overall difficulty are not used.

The potential for a long leader fall is indicated by an "s" (serious) or "vs" (very serious) after the rating of difficulty. A climb rated "s" will have at least one notable run-out and the potential for a scary fall. A climb rated "vs" typically will have poor protection for hard moves and the potential for a fatal or near-fatal fall. The absence of these letters indicates a relatively safe climb providing it is within the leader's ability. However, the process of book production can occasionally result in errors and omissions. It is vital that every climber use common sense and acknowledge responsibility for themselves before stepping off the ground and starting up any route.

Remember that the rating of a climb is not absolute, but represents an informal consensus of opinion. Some of the routes in this book may never have been repeated which makes their ratings extremely subjective. But even the ratings of long-established routes are debatable—all of which should serve as a warning to not rely entirely on numbers. Look at the route up close and use your best judgment before proceeding.

### Arrangement of Text

All crags and routes in this book are catalogued from left to right as they are normally viewed on approach. I have used this format simply because books published in western languages, such as English, are paginated from left to right. This lends a visual logic to the information as one leafs through the text and drawings. Thus, the text begins with crags normally approached from the south end of the Mesa Trail and finishes with Gregory Canyon at the north end of the Flatirons. Features such as Bear Canyon are listed east to west along the south (Nebel Horn) side and west to east along the north (Dinosaur Mountain) side. The Sacred Cliffs of Green Mountain face west and are catalogued from north to south (left to right).

# BOULDER MOUNTAIN

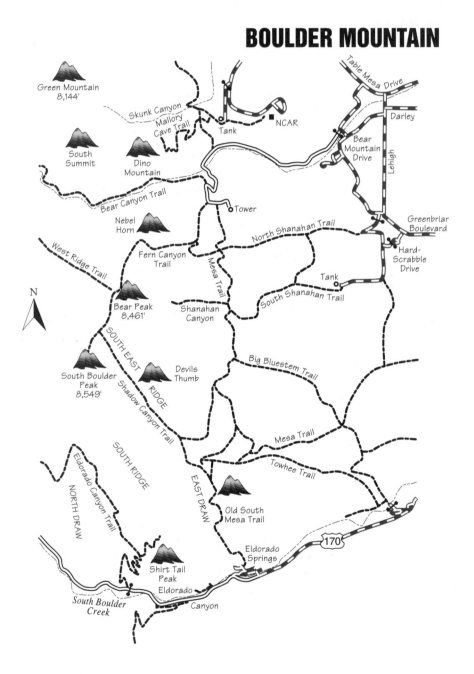

Green Mountain
8,144'

Skunk Canyon

Mallory
Cave Trail

Tank

NCAR

Table Mesa Drive

Darley

Bear
Mountain
Drive

Lehigh

South
Summit

Dino
Mountain

Bear Canyon Trail

Nebel
Horn

Tower

North Shanahan Trail

Greenbriar
Boulevard

West Ridge Trail

Fern Canyon
Trail

Mesa Trail

Hard-
Scrabble
Drive

Tank

South Shanahan Trail

Bear Peak
8,461'

Shanahan
Canyon

SOUTH EAST RIDGE

Big Bluestem Trail

South Boulder
Peak
8,549'

Devils
Thumb

Shadow Canyon Trail

Mesa Trail

Eldorado Canyon Trail

SOUTH RIDGE

Towhee Trail

NORTH DRAW

EAST DRAW

Old South
Mesa Trail

170

Eldorado
Springs

Shirt Tail
Peak

Eldorado

South Boulder
Creek

Canyon

# PART I. BOULDER MOUNTAIN

Viewed from Downtown Boulder, the skyline south of Green Mountain is graced by the pointed, rocky summit of Bear Peak (8461 feet). This is the northern twin of double-summited Boulder Mountain, which lies between Bear Canyon and Eldorado Canyon. The southern and higher twin summit is South Boulder Peak (8549 feet). A craggy subsidiary summit called the Nebel Horn rises up along the northeast shoulder of Bear Peak, and with Dinosaur Mountain to the north, forms the entrance to Bear Canyon. The Nebel Horn is separated from the main peak by a broad, sandy col that marks the top of east-lying Fern Canyon. The south ridge of Bear Peak is separated from the south ridge of South Boulder Peak by the forested draw of Shadow Canyon. A beautiful trail ascends this canyon to the broad col between the twin summits.

Perhaps the more significant aspect of Boulder Mountain, however, is the South Ridge, which runs from the summit of South Boulder Peak, south-southeast all the way to Shirt Tail Peak, then dives steeply in a miasma of towers, ramps, and ridges to the green waters of South Boulder Creek. Among its ramparts are Sobo Buttress, Diamond Head, Physical Crag, the Veil, the Matron, Shirt Tail Peak, Cadillac Crag, Rincon, the West Ridge, Redgarden Wall, the Wind Tower, and the rest of famous crags on the north side of Eldorado Canyon. The easiest approach to any of these features but the Matron is from Eldorado Canyon, thus the south ridge of Boulder Mountain is described in the out-of-print *Boulder Climbs South,* soon to be replaced by *Rock Climbing Eldorado Canyon.*

## TRAILS

Those who dislike hiking would do better visiting Eldorado Canyon or Boulder Canyon as Boulder Mountain offers no drive-up crags, and the nearest routes are 30 minutes from the road.

**Mesa Trail**— This important trail runs north and south for 6.9 miles along the east faces of Green Mountain and Boulder Mountain and is crossed or traveled upon in the approaches to all crags in this section of the book. There are several ways to access the Mesa Trail along Bear Peak: Mesa South, the southern trail head along Highway 170 (Eldorado Springs Drive), the Old Mesa Trail that begins in Eldorado Springs (beware of access problems), the Shanahan Trail, the Bear Creek service road, or from NCAR. One may also reach the Mesa Trail from Chautauqua Park or from the Bluestem Trail, but these add distance and are less useful for reaching crags on Bear Peak. See maps.

**Shadow Canyon Trail**— This trail branches left from the southern Mesa Trail at about 2.0 miles, then winds its way up the floor of Shadow Canyon through giant boulders and evergreens to the saddle between South Boulder Peak and Bear Peak. The trail is 1.3 miles long and climbs about 1800 feet. From the saddle, short trails lead to either summit. The Shadow Canyon Trail may also be reached from the Old Mesa Trail, which climbs up an open valley of wild grasses and sumac from the town of Eldorado Springs.

**BOULDER MOUNTAIN,**
from the southeast

Shirttail Peak

The
Matron

South
Boulder Peak

Bear Peak

Nebel Horn

SHADOW
CANYON

ELDORADO
CANYON

**North Shanahan Trail**— This trail provides the most efficient approach to Fern Canyon and the Slab. From South Broadway, turn west on Greenbriar Drive, continue for about a mile, and turn left on Hardscrabble Drive. At the west end of this street is a circle with a few parking slots. Hike a short way west, then take the north branch. The trail eventually crosses the Mesa Trail and leads directly beneath the northeast corner of the Slab. In another 50 yards, the North Shanahan Trail intersects the Fern Canyon Trail (1.5 miles in all).

**South Shanahan Trail**— This trail may be used to reach any feature from Shanahan Crags to the Maiden. Begin from the same trail head as the North Shanahan Trail, but take the south branch after the first 100 yards. After about one mile, stay left at a junction and continue for another mile to a junction with the Mesa Trail. Here a less-developed path continues up Shanahan Canyon (the wooded draw that descends from between South Shanahan Crag and the Sphinx) and ends in the talus beneath the south face of South Shanahan Crag.

**Fern Canyon Trail**—This trail may be used to reach the Slab, the Goose, Fern Canyon, and the summit of Bear Peak. Reach this trail via the Bear Creek service road (see Bear Canyon Trail) or the North Shanahan Trail. From the Bear Creek service road, continue north on the Mesa Trail about 60 yards past the Bear Canyon Trail junction to the signed trail junction (on the right). It is about one mile from here to the col at the top of Fern Canyon.

**Harmon Cave Trail**— This unmarked trail provides the easiest approach to Seal Rock and Gnome Wall. Its beginning is indistinct and climbs abruptly to the west from the service road (Mesa Trail) about midway between the junctions to the Bear Canyon Trail and the Fern Canyon Trail. See map.

**Bear Canyon Trail**—This trail affords access to the north slope of the Nebel Horn, the south slope of Dinosaur Mountain, and at length leads to the summit of Bear Peak. To reach the trailhead from Broadway, go west on Table Mesa Drive, left (south) on Lehigh Street, right (west) on Bear Mountain Drive, and right on Stoney Hill Road to a cul de sac at its end. Walk through a wooden gate, cross Bear Creek, and hike west on a service road for about 0.7 mile to its junction with the Mesa Trail. Continue on the service road (now the Mesa Trail) for another half mile as it winds around to the south. Find the Bear Canyon Trail at a switchback below some powerlines. One may also park along Bear Mountain Drive (before reaching Stoney Hill Road) and pick up a path though a field that also leads to the service road. See Bear Canyon Trail under Green Mountain.

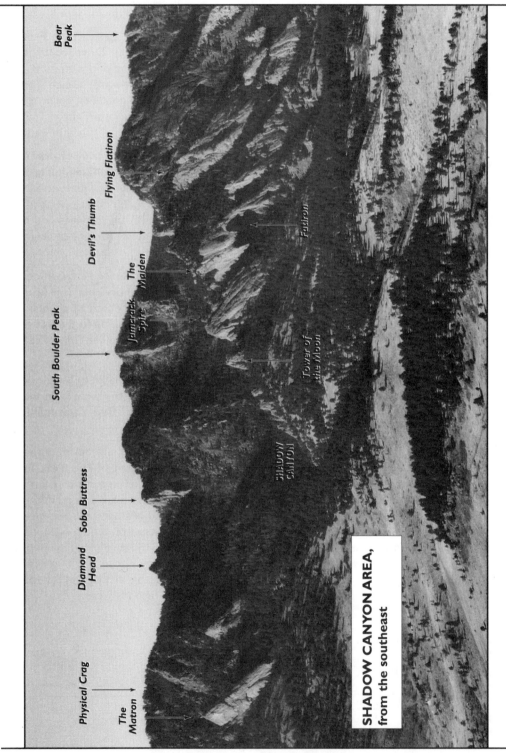

Bear
Peak

Flying Flatiron

Devil's Thumb

The
Maiden

South Boulder Peak

Jamcrack
Spire

Flatiron

Tower of
the Moon

Sobo Buttress

SHADOW
CANYON

Diamond
Head

Physical Crag

The
Matron

**SHADOW CANYON AREA,**
from the southeast

# SHADOW CANYON

Shadow Canyon is the broad, U-shaped draw between the south ridge of South Boulder Peak and the southeast ridge of Bear Peak. Remember that these "peaks" are the twin summits of Boulder Mountain. The canyon begins as a grassy gulch near the south end of the Mesa Trail, but becomes deeper and densely forested above 6600 feet. The top of the canyon is the saddle between the two summits (8200). Crags approached from Shadow Canyon are listed from south to north along the west side of the canyon and from north to south along the east side. All features are approached from the Shadow Canyon Trail.

## THE MATRON

The Matron is an enormous rib of rock on the lower west side of Shadow Canyon. Viewed from the east, it may be seen to resemble a forearm with a clenched fist. Matronly references are somewhat more difficult. Perhaps, compared to the Maiden, one could imagine its "west overhang" to have fallen off. To reach The Matron, hike the Mesa and Shadow Canyon Trails for about 2.3 miles, then cut left (west) on a signed path that leads directly to the bottom of the buttress. The terrain along the north side of the crag is the easiest to hike. To descend from the summit, rappel 60 feet west from an eye-bolt to another eye-bolt at a small ledge along the north side of the west face, then rappel 100 feet to the highest ground at the bottom of the west face.

### 1.  EAST RIDGE 5 ★
FA: BILL EUBANKS, BRAD VANDIVER, STAN BLACK, 1948.
This classic is mostly a scramble after the first pitch. Access onto the lower east ridge is barred by a large overhang. Begin about 50 feet up along the north face from the low point of the rock. Work up onto a smooth wall, follow a crack around to the left, then go straight up to a tree on the east face (5, 70 feet). The summit is gained in three long pitches with the last being the most difficult along the right side of the face (4).

### 2.  NO STRANGER TO DANGER 9 S
FA: CARL HARRISON AND MIKE BROOKS, 1982.
Begin about 250 feet (?) up along the north face from the bottom of the east ridge, beneath a greenish waterstreak high on the wall. Climb directly up to the water streak and up a poorly protected groove to the East Ridge.

### 3.  QUICHE ON A LEASH 10
FA: CARL HARRISON AND MIKE BROOKS, 1982.
Find a left-facing dihedral about 100 feet down and east from the North Face route. Climb the dihedral for 20 feet, then go left to a tree. Climb the face back into the dihedral and undercling to its top. Pass an overhang and follow a squeeze chimney to the top of the wall.

### 4.  PASTA MAN 9 S
FA: CARL HARRISON AND AL TORRISI, 1982.
Begin beneath the large boulder that leans against the face to the east of the North Face route. Climb a left-angling crack through a small roof, up a poorly protected face to the left of an arête, and finish on a ridge to the right of a small pine tree.

THE MATRON—North Face
1. East Ridge 5 ★
5. North Face 6 ★
8. Northwest Crack 10b/c

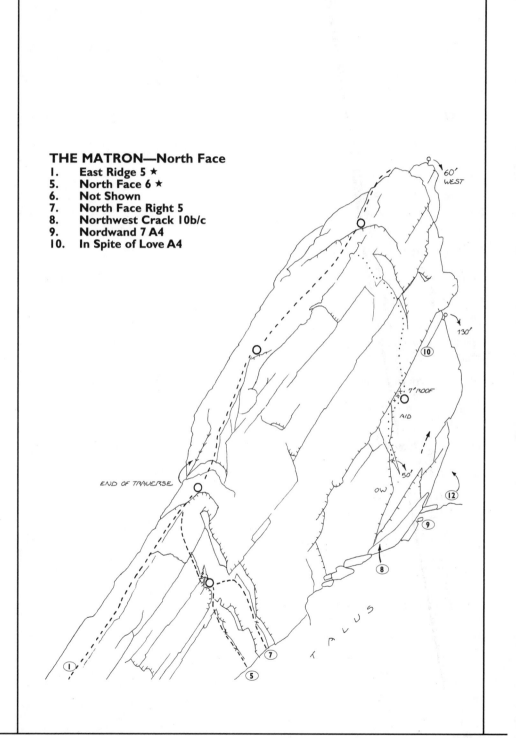

**THE MATRON—North Face**

1.    **East Ridge 5 ★**
5.    **North Face 6 ★**
6.    **Not Shown**
7.    **North Face Right 5**
8.    **Northwest Crack 10b/c**
9.    **Nordwand 7 A4**
10.   **In Spite of Love A4**

60'
WEST

130'

10

7' ROOF

AID

50'

END OF TRAVERSE

OW

12

9

8

1

T A L U S

7

5

### 5.   NORTH FACE 6 ★
FA: KARL GUFSTAFSON AND SKIP GREEN, 1951.
A couple hundred feet up from the low point of the rock, scramble up a short chimney formed by a leaning block to gain a bench at the base of the route. Climb about 15 feet up the left of two cracks, then up to the right to a recess formed by an overhang. Power up through the overhang and belay on a ledge with a tree. Climb a left-leaning crack and join the East Ridge route.

### 6.   NORTH FACE CENTER 5
FA: GEORGE LAMB AND ROBERT SUTTON, 1953.
Begin about five feet left of a large, left-facing dihedral, go up 20 feet to a stance and on to a crack. Go up the crack for about ten feet, up a slightly rotten wall, and straight left to the belay ledge on the regular North Face route.

### 7.   NORTH FACE RIGHT 5
Begin about 40 feet right of North Face. Climb a large, left-facing left-leaning dihedral to an overhang, then traverse left to the belay on North Face Center.

### 8.   NORTHWEST CRACK 10B/C
FA: ERIC ALDRICH, MASON FRISCHETTE, JIM GARBER, 1977.
Climb a short, right-leaning off-width crack 150 feet up and right from the North Face route.

### 9.   NORDWAND 7 A4
FA: LAYTON KOR AND T.J. BOGGS, 1964.
Begin to the right of a huge flake. Nail up and left to the top of the flake. Continue on aid up and right beneath a seven foot roof, out over the roof, left, then right, and up along a left-leaning, left-facing dihedral to easier ground.

### 10.   IN SPITE OF LOVE A4
FA: ERIC DOUB AND KEN SHELDON, 1980.
Climb the first pitch of Nordwand to a belay under the roof, then follow the stratum beneath the overhang all the way to the eye-bolt at the edge of the west face.

### 11.   SOUL SURVIVOR 11
FA: CHARLIE FOWLER, c.1982.
Step off the top of a flake to the right of Nordwand and work up to the edge of the west face.

### 12.   WEST FACE 8 S ★
FA: MIKE O'BRIAN AND PARTY, 1955.
This excellent route ascends the left side of the west face on small holds and pebbles. Two or three old bolts can be supplemented with RPs and stoppers. Begin at the bottom of the face just right of a small overhang. Diagonal up and left past a bolt, out over a roof, straight up past two more bolts, then up to large eyebolts at the left edge of the face. A second pitch goes up a right-facing corner and on to the summit.

### 13.   SUNDAY COMIX 9+ S ★
FA: JEFF LOWE AND KERRY SHROYER, 1980. RACK: DOUBLE SET OF RPS, TRI-CAMS, AND A FEW LARGER PIECES.
This exciting route climbs nearer the middle of the west face.

### 14.   NEW AGE SLAB 9 VS
FA: ED WEBSTER AND CHESTER DREIMAN, 1983.
Climb to the fixed pin on Sunday Comix, then up and right to belay. Continue along the right edge of the upper west face.

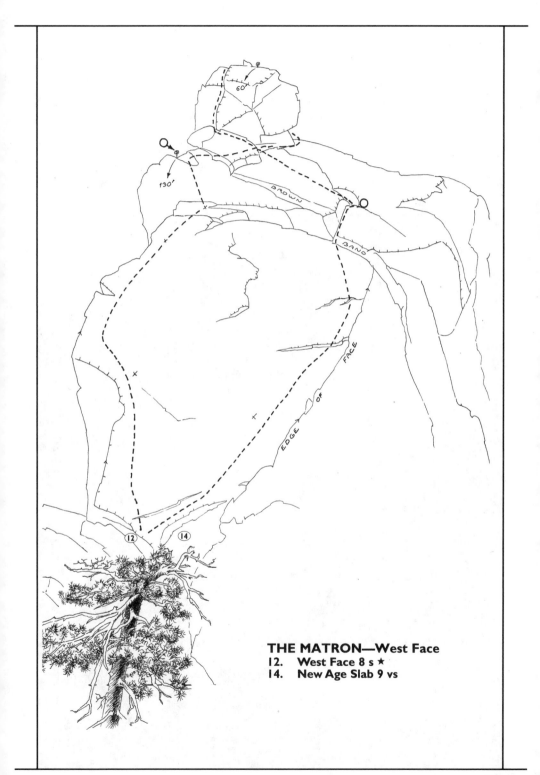

**THE MATRON—West Face**

12.    **West Face 8 s ★**
14.    **New Age Slab 9 vs**

**THE MATRON—South Face**

1. East Ridge 5 ★
16. South Face 6 ★
18. Lower South Face 11d s A0

\* DESCEND VIA RAPPEL :
FROM EYE-BOLT ON SUMMIT,
60° WEST TO SECOND BOLT,
THEN 100° WEST OR NORTH.

## THE MATRON, from the
### southeast
1.    **East Ridge 5 ★**
5.    **North Face 6 ★**
16.   **South Face 6 ★**
17.   **Direct Start 10d**
18.   **Lower South Face 11d s A0**
19.   **Warlocks 12a ★**

SHADOW CANYON
TRAIL, CIRCA
50 METERS

### 15.  INTENSIVE CARE 10A VS

Climb the right edge of the west face to a bolt anchor. Work up and left and join one of the other routes.

### 16.  SOUTH FACE 6 ★

FA: DALE JOHNSON AND PHIL ROBERTSON, 1952.

Begin at the lower south corner of the west face. Scramble east down a ramp to a large tree and rope up. Descend a fourth-class ramp to a low point beneath the overhanging south face of the summit tower, then work up to the east a short way to a good belay niche. Climb a groove up to the east and belay in a hollow with some bolts. Traverse right around an exposed bulge (crux), then up the right to join the East Ridge route.

### 17.  DIRECT START 10D

FA: LARRY DALKE AND PAT AMENT (7 A3), 1965. FFA: ART HIGBEE AND JIM ERICKSON, 1977.

Begin on a ledge with a small tree. Wander up and left to a stance beneath a headwall (7). Pass the headwall on the right (crux) and traverse 20 feet left to a marginal belay. Hand traverse about 10 feet right (9), then climb straight up to the traverse on the South Face route.

### 18.  LOWER SOUTH FACE 11D S A0

FA: LAYTON KOR AND BYRON DIEHL, 1965. FFA: UP TO POCKET, ROGER BRIGGS AND CHRIS REVELEY, 1974. FFA: OF ROOF ABOVE POCKET, JOHN BRAGG, 1975.

Begin about 50 feet up to the west from the bottom of the south face. Climb a steep, left-facing flake and crack to a belay at the bottom of a long, diagonal inset ramp (10a). Climb the ramp to a pocket beneath an A-shaped overhang and belay. Climb out the right side of the roof and up the bulging wall to the east ridge.

### 19.  WARLOCKS 12A ★

FA: CHIP RUCKGABER AND SKIP GUERIN, 1982. SR UP TO A #4 FRIEND.

Begin from a large block a few paces down and right from the preceding route and 25 feet or so up from the low point of the face. Jam up a left-arching fist to finger crack and step right at the top. Rappel 70 feet.

## SHADOWFAX

Across the canyon to the southwest from Devil's Thumb and about 400 feet above the trail are two spires and a squarish block. The block, known as Cubical Crag, is a bit below the spires and is host to the following routes. Both routes by Dave Kozak and Mark Lane, 1981.

### 1.  MAGNIFICENT MADNESS 9

Begin on the north side. Climb the right side of a crack system to a ledge, traverse 15 feet left and follow a dihedral to the top.

### 2.  ELMER FUDD 6

Climb a pair of cracks up the south face.

**Note:** The following crags are located on the east side of Shadow Canyon (Bear Peak) and are listed from north to south (left to right).

## SUNSET WALL

Sunset Wall is located roughly midway between the col at the top of Shadow Canyon and Devils Thumb. The southwest-facing wall is easily 300 feet high but is interrupted by ledges and gullies and has not caught on as a climbing objective. A Wind Ridge type of route was climbed near the left edge of the wall by Bruce Spozi and Steve Matous about 1980. Dave Kozak and partners also visited the area around 1981 and did several climbs, records of which are not available at this time. To reach the wall, hike to the top of Shadow Canyon and contour around to the base of the cliff.

## DEVILS THUMB

Devils Thumb is the familiar and provocative spire seen on the south shoulder of Bear Peak. It was allegedly known by local indians as Toponas. The east side of the Thumb is slabby, and an ascent would present little challenge but for a broad overhang just below the "distal joint." An early scene of industrial tourism, the 15 to 20-foot overhang was brought down to size by the installation of an iron ladder. The ladder is gone now but a large iron bar that apparently served as an anchor is still in place just above the top of the overhang on the Left Side route. The west side of Devils Thumb presents an enormous overhang, perhaps the biggest in Boulder.

The easiest approach to Devils Thumb is probably to hike the Shadow Canyon Trail until one can gaze east up a vast talus field to the awesome west overhang of the Thumb. Hike directly up through giant blocks and dwarfed trees to the objective. East face routes are most easily reached from the notch on the south. To approach from the east, hike the Mesa Trail to a point just north of the Fatiron, then go west (cross-country) up a broad draw to the base of the Thumb. To escape from the summit, down-climb the east face to the iron bar on the Left Side route and make a short rappel to the slab below.

### 1.    REPRIEVE 10D

FA: MIKE MUNGER AND BILL FEIGES, 1979.

Begin at the southwest corner, just right of the main overhang, and climb a crack up and right to a belay. Work diagonally left past a fixed pin to a belay at the west edge of the face (10d). Climb straight to the top (9).

SHADOW CANYON, east side

### 2.   LEFT SIDE 7

Scramble up the east face slab, then climb an obvious crack through the middle of the big roof. Scramble to the summit.

### 3.   TOPONAS 8

Also known as Right Side. Climb a wide crack through the right side of the east face overhang and scramble to the summit.

### 4.   HANGNAIL 4 AI

FA: KYLE COPELAND AND SCOTT SOUNDERS, 1983.

Begin at the northwest corner. Climb past two bolts (free switching to aid), hook up to a left-leaning open book, and up to a sling belay at two bolts. Move right over funky rock to a seam. The final 20 feet are apparently unclimbed.

## THE PYRAMID

Just south of Devils Thumb is a pyramid-shaped formation with a moderate crack on the northwest ridge.

## JAMCRACK SPIRE

The next major feature south of Devils Thumb, normally approached from Shadow Canyon, is Jamcrack Spire. From the east, it appears as a large flatiron south of The Maiden, but all the routes are on the steep west face and the namesake north tower. To reach the west side of Jamcrack Spire, follow the Shadow Canyon Trail to a point near a huge boulder on the right. A faint path branches off to the right in this area and may be followed up into talus below the west face. To escape the summit, scramble off to the east and back around north, or rappel west from a tree between the north and south summits.

### I.   RIGHT FOR GRAPENUTS 9 +

FA: ERIC DOUB, TR, 1979.

Climb the arête along the left side of the north face.

### 2.   LEFT CRACK 8

Climb the left of the two diagonal cracks on the north face of the spire.

### 3.   RIGHT ONE 10A

FA: JIM ERICKSON, 1978.

Climb the right of the two diagonal cracks on the north face of the spire.

### 4.   RECKLESS ENDEARMENT 10A/B

FA: GLENN RANDALL AND DAN HARE, 1982.

Begin down and right from the spire and left of Big Dog. Climb a right-facing dihedral about 30 feet to a rotten flake that leads left to a slab. Climb the right side of the slab (9vs) to a small roof, then left over the roof (10a) to a sling belay at a flake. Climb a flake/corner (10a), then jam a crack the top.

### 5.   MONSTER OF ROCK 10

FA: ALEC SHARP, DAVE LOVEJOY, TOM WHITTAKER, 1979.

Climb the left of two wide cracks through a roof.

### 6.   BIG DOG 11

FA: ALEC SHARP AND DAVE LOVEJOY, 1979.

Begin with a moderate crack (8), then take the right of two wide cracks through a roof.

Jamcrack Spire

Tower of the Moon

### 7.   HOLEISTIC 10B/C

FA: ALEC AND MURIEL SHARP, 1979.

Climb the first pitch of Fear of Flying. Climb a left-facing dihedral to a roof that is turned on the right.

### 8.   FEAR OF FLYING 10 ★

FA: JIM ERICKSON AND CINDY STANLEY, 1975.

Begin beneath a big overhang at the south (right) side of the west face. Climb an easy pitch for 100 feet to a ledge. Climb up for 20 feet, then hand-traverse right and take a leaning dihedral to the top (one hard move).

## TOWER OF THE MOON

Tower of the Moon is located just south of Jamcrack Spire. The southwest face is broken and unappealing, but the west buttress is beautiful, with routes to match. The tower may be seen through the trees to the east after hiking about 300 feet above a spring on the Shadow Canyon Trail. Hike directly up to the tower from the trail. To escape from the main summit, scramble off to the east, then back around to the north.

### 1.   MOON SHADOW 12C/D ★

FA: DAN HARE AND JIM LE SUER, 1989. NOT REDPOINTED.

This route ascends the blunt arête that forms the left margin of the northwest face. Begin up and left of the arête, even with a sloping ledge above a long roof. Move out onto the ledge and belay at a small left-facing dihedral. Step up and right to a bolt, go straight left, then and up past several bolts to a rest stance. Go right and up the difficult arête past more bolts, then up and right to an anchor.

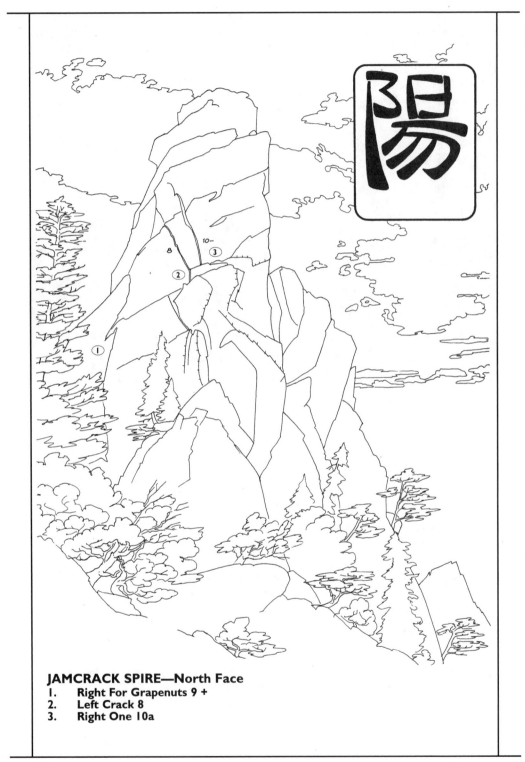

**JAMCRACK SPIRE—North Face**

1.  **Right For Grapenuts 9 +**
2.  **Left Crack 8**
3.  **Right One 10a**

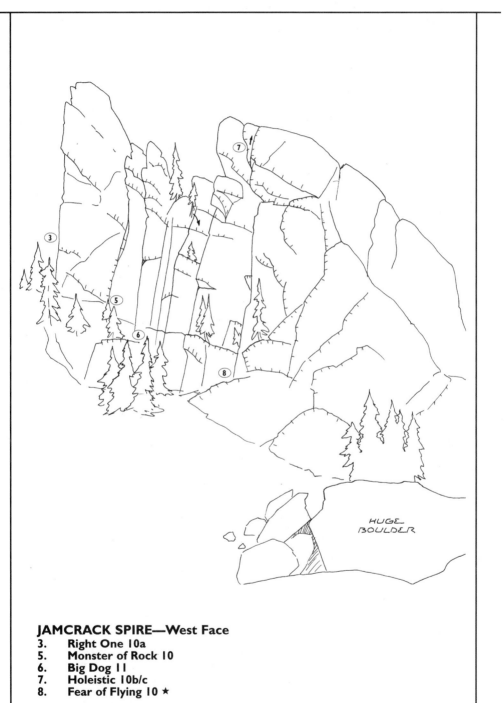

**JAMCRACK SPIRE—West Face**

3.  **Right One 10a**
5.  **Monster of Rock 10**
6.  **Big Dog 11**
7.  **Holeistic 10b/c**
8.  **Fear of Flying 10 ★**

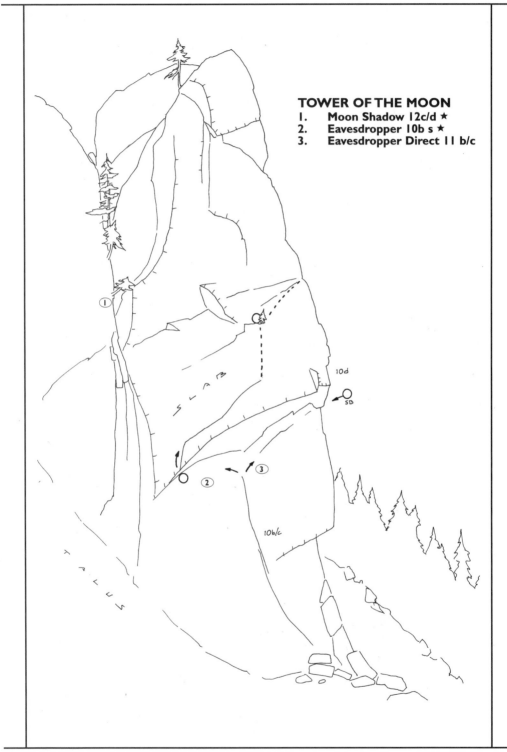

**TOWER OF THE MOON**
1. Moon Shadow 12c/d ★
2. Eavesdropper 10b s ★
3. Eavesdropper Direct 11 b/c

## 2.   EAVESDROPPER 10B S ★

FA: SCOTT WOODRUFF AND DAN HARE, 1975.

Begin at the bottom of the northwest face. Climb thin cracks (crux) up to a huge roof and traverse left to a belay at the edge of the face. Move straight up and gain a crack that goes right just above the roof, then go up a slab to a belay ledge. Angle up and right to the arête, which is followed to the summit (poor pro).

## 3.   EAVESDROPPER DIRECT 11B/C S ★

FA: JEFF ACHEY AND CHIP CHASE, 1982.

Climb to the roof as for Eavesdropper, then traverse right to the arête and belay. Climb the overhang directly on the arête (crux) and join the upper section of Eavesdropper.

**BEAR PEAK, east side**

Nebel Horn

The Slab

FERN CANYON

Shanahan Crags

Sphinx

Wings

Devil's Thumb

Flying Flatiron

The Maiden

SHADOW CANYON

BEAR CANYON

# BEAR PEAK

Bear Peak (8461 feet) is the north summit of Boulder Mountain. The broad east face of Bear Peak presents a magnificent array of slabs and buttresses with many routes of low to moderate difficulty. These are the Southern Flatirons. Fern Canyon and the Nebel Horn, located along the northeast shoulder of Bear Peak, offer some of the best modern climbs in Boulder Mountain Parks. Bear Canyon to the north, is no less interesting. The following crags are located along the broad east face of Bear Peak.

## THE MAIDEN

Viewed from the east, this famous crag has such a narrow profile, one must look hard to make it out between the Fatiron and Jamcrack Spire. Seen from vantage points to the south, it resembles the head of an eagle with its beak protruding to the west. The Maiden has the most famous free rappel in Colorado and was also the scene of early bolt wars. More significant, this unusual crag is host to a number of engaging and historical routes, and is worth a visit.

**Approach**— Hike the south Mesa Trail and locate an old, open water tank at the northern junction with the Shadow Canyon Trail, due east of The Maiden. From the vicinity of the water tank, hike up to the north edge of an old quarry and follow a faint trail to the base of the east ridge. The gully below the north face is an easy hike all the way to the top of the slope and affords easy access to the East Ridge, all north face routes, and the famous Standard Route. The gully along the

**BEAR PEAK, The Maiden area**

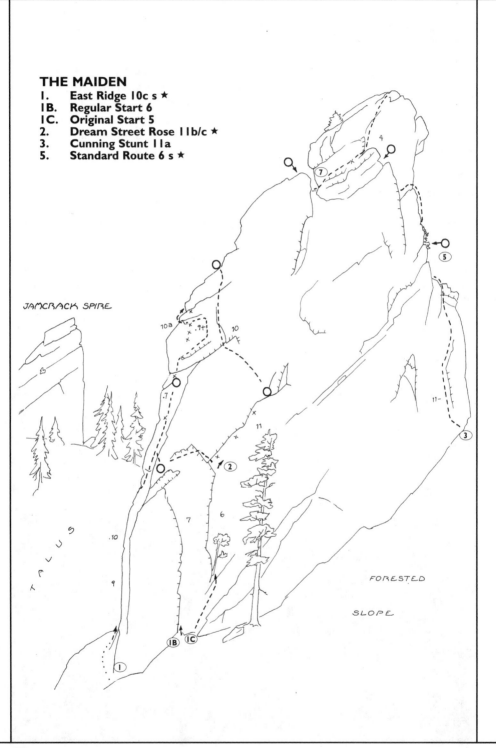

**THE MAIDEN**
1. East Ridge 10c s ★
1B. Regular Start 6
1C. Original Start 5
2. Dream Street Rose 11b/c ★
3. Cunning Stunt 11a
5. Standard Route 6 s ★

JAMCRACK SPIRE

FORESTED

SLOPE

south side of the Maiden may also be hiked but requires a bit of navigating due to some enormous boulders along the way. The west end of the Maiden may also be reached from the Shadow Canyon Trail by hiking east up the steep slope to a notch just north of Jamcrack Spire. To descend from the summit, rappel 115 feet west to a narrow platform called the Crow's Nest. From here, rappel 120 feet to the south from an eye-bolt.

### I.   EAST RIDGE 10c s ★
FA: DALE JOHNSON, PHIL ROBERTSON, CARY HUSTON, 1953. FFA: STEVE WUNCH AND DIANA HUNTER, 1970.

Begin at the low point of the crag. 1. Step in from the right and climb a vertical hand crack for about 65 feet to a belay on a steep ramp (10a). 2. Climb the ramp for about 60 feet to a belay at the base of an overhanging wall with a line of bolts (7). 3. Work up to the first bolt and go right to the edge of the face, up a few feet, then hand traverse back left past the top of the bolt ladder to the left (south) edge of the face and up to a belay (10b/c, 70 feet). 4. Climb up along the south side of the arête to a notch (optional belay), move right beneath an overhanging wall, then up a ramp on the right to belay in an alcove (5, 110 feet). 5. Climb a slot, then scramble up the east ridge to the summit (4, 100 feet).

### IA.   ROWLAND'S HORN 10?
FA: ED WEBSTER AND PETE WILLIAMS, 1984.

Begin about 20 feet left of the direct first pitch. Follow a "weakness" in the rock until it is obvious to join the regular line.

### IB.   REGULAR START 6
Begin about 20 feet up and right from the bottom of the east ridge. Climb a right-facing dihedral and belay on a small ledge. Join the main route (10b/c).

### IC.   ORIGINAL START 5
FA: GEORGE LAMB, DAVID ROSE, DALLAS JACKSON, 1952.

Climb a crack just right of the Regular Start and traverse left to the same belay.

### 2.   DREAM STREET ROSE 11b/c ★
FA: JEFF ACHEY AND PAUL MEYERS, 1980.

Begin with the right variation to the East Ridge, but where it goes left to join the main line, break right along a steep ramp with three pitons and belay on a small ledge. Angle left and jam a hand crack through a roof, continue up a steep wall, and join the East Ridge a short way above the main overhang.

### 3.   CUNNING STUNT 11a
FA: JIM ERICKSON AND NANCY MCNEIL, 1975.

Jim Erickson...always handy with a crack or a play-on-words. Begin 100 feet or so up and right from the preceding route. Lieback/undercling along the left side of a flake, then go up and right to join Direct North Face.

### 4.   DIRECT NORTH FACE 9 s
FA: ART HOWELLS AND MIKE BORGHOFF, 1960. FFA: JIM ERICKSON AND CINDY STANLEY, 1975.

Almost directly beneath the Crow's Nest along the lower north face, a huge flake has detached from the wall. Climb the right side of the flake (9) and belay on top. Work up and right through a roof (9s), and back left to the Crow's Nest.

### 5.   STANDARD ROUTE 6 s ★
FA: ROY PEAK AND MARK TAGGART, 1944.

Also known as the North Face, this is the most popular route on the crag. Begin at the far west end of the Maiden, climb a short wall to get up onto the west ridge (3), and belay. Scramble down the ridge to the east and belay at the low point (the Crow's Nest). Follow the strata down across the north face,

## THE MAIDEN, from the northwest

1. **East Ridge 10c s ★**
3. **Cunning Stunt 11a**
4. **Direct North Face 9 s**
5. **Standard Route 6 s ★**
6. **West Overhang 11a ★ or 11d ★**

RAPPEL FROM CABLE AROUND BLOCK, 120° TO THE CROW'S NEST THEN SOUTH, 120° TO GROUND.

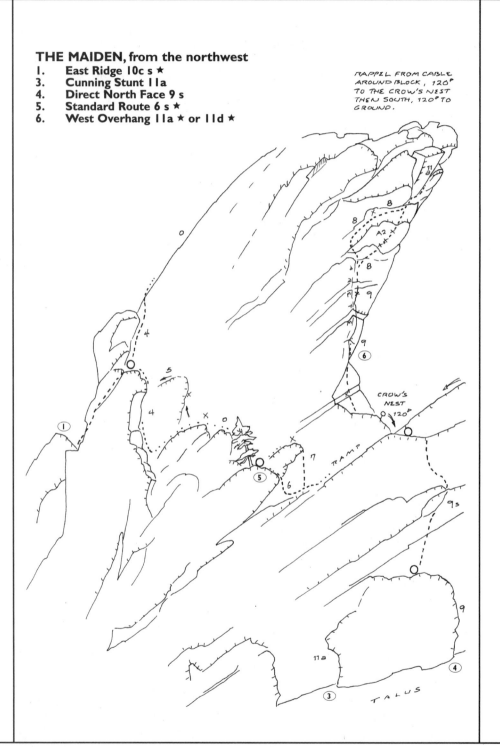

climb a short corner (6 s) or up the face to a ramp (7 s), and move left to belay at a tree. Traverse left and slightly down into a right-facing dihedral, then step around to the east and climb the wall at its left to a good belay in an alcove. One may also climb the dihedral (7). Or, take the first right-facing corner (just before angling downward), followed by an exciting traverse into the alcove (5, the Walton Traverse). From the alcove, climb an easy slot (0), then scoot up the east ridge to the summit.

### 5A.  HIGH NORTH 7
Begin at the base of the Walton Traverse and follow the strata up and right to the north side of the west overhang.

### 6.    WEST OVERHANG 11A ★ OR 11D ★
FA: DALE JOHNSON, PHIL ROBERTSON, CLEVE MCCARTY, 1956. FFA: STEVE WUNCH AND KEVIN BEIN, 1977. ORIGINAL LINE: FA: DALE JOHNSON, DAVE ROBERTS, CARY HUSTON, 1953. FFA: HARRISON DEKKER AND RANDY LEAVITT, 1981.

This dramatic route ascends the overhanging west side of the summit tower. There are two versions of this route, both of which begin at the Crow's Nest and climb a thin crack (9) to a precarious belay beneath the main roof. The original aid line provides the hardest free climbing and goes straight up through the middle of the big roof (11d), then up a slot to the summit (11a). The original free version follows another aid line and sneaks around the left side of the big roof (8), crawls out right to a "belay foothold," then climbs the slot (11a) to the summit. Either version can be done in one pitch from the Crow's Nest.

### 7.    GATES OF GALAS 10D
FA: BOB HORAN AND SUE PATENAUDE, 1982.

Below and slightly west of the Crow's Nest, a huge flake leans up against the wall. Climb the east edge of the flake, traverse right, and climb a left-facing corner to the Crow's Nest.

THE MAIDEN, from the northwest
3.    Cunning Stunt 11a
5.    Standard Route 6 s ★
6.    West Overhang 11a ★ or

**THE MAIDEN—South Face**
1.     East Ridge 10c s ★
6.     West Overhang 11a ★
9.     South Face 8 s ★
10.    South Crack 11c ★

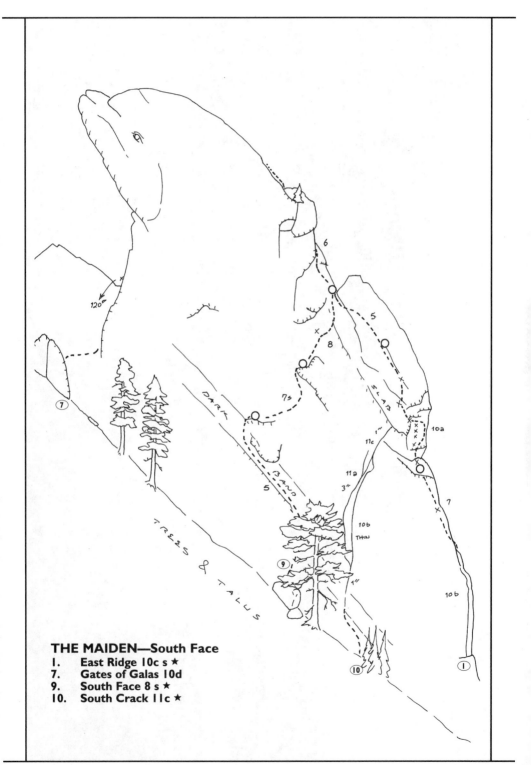

## THE MAIDEN—South Face

1. **East Ridge 10c s ★**
7. **Gates of Galas 10d**
9. **South Face 8 s ★**
10. **South Crack 11c ★**

**BEAR PEAK, Devil's Thumb area**

The Pyramid

Devil's Thumb

Flying Flatiron

South Wing

Tiny Tower

Devil's Advocate

Apostle

### 8.  HIGH SOUTH 7 A3
FA: LAYTON KOR AND LARRY DALKE, 1966.

The exact location of this route is unknown. Diagonal up and left across the south face to a steep crack that leads up to the Crow's Nest (7s). This crack may be the upper half of Gates of Galas. Climb a slab and go around the arête on the right. Traverse straight right to a couple of bolts, then directly up to a belay. Follow a ramp up and left to the summit (7s).

### 9.  SOUTH FACE 8 s ★
FA: HARVEY CARTER AND CLIFFORD SMITH, 1953. FFA: GERRY ROACH AND JEFF WHEELER, 1958.

Begin a short way up and left from South Crack, near a big block and a huge pine. Work right and up to a stance at a flake (optional belay), then mostly straight up to join the East Ridge route.

### 10.  SOUTH CRACK 11c ★
FA: ROGER BRIGGS AND LUKE STUDER, 1972. FFA: STEVE WUNCH AND JOHN BRAGG, 1975. SR TO A 3.5 FRIEND.

Begin about 60 feet up and left from the bottom east ridge, beneath a crack system that arcs up to the right. Mostly hands and fingers with the crux near the top.

## THE FATIRON

Just north of the Maiden, a stumpy flatiron rises up to a blunt summit, then drops off on the west and swoops up again to form a higher but less distinct summit. Approach as for the Maiden (above). To escape from the stumpy east summit, down-climb 100 feet to the west and south and rappel 20 feet from small trees to the slab that leads up to the west summit. To get down from the west summit, rappel 40 feet west from a tree or climb off the north edge of the face about 150 below and east of the summit.

### 1.  LITTLE MURDERS 9
FA: JIM ERICKSON AND CINDY STANLEY, 1975.

Begin up along the south face of the Fatiron. Climb a crack and chimney system up and slightly right. The crux is just off the ground.

### 2.  EAST FACE 5 ★
FA: GERRY AND BARB ROACH, 1972.

Scramble up to the notch behind a small, broken flatiron that leans against the main east face and run the rope out to some trees (cl4). Climb the smooth face right of an incipient crack and arrive at a sturdy tree. The face to the left of the crack may also be climbed (5). Stay with the crack, then tackle a steeper section followed by a couple hundred feet of easier ground and gain the east summit. Escape the east summit as described above and scramble 350 feet to the west summit.

## FLYING FLATIRON

Immediately northeast of Devils Thumb, a triangular flatiron sweeps up to a narrow summit that is pierced by a large hole. This hole creates the "flying buttress" or natural bridge for which the feature is named. So far, the only known route climbs the east face to the inside of the arch and does not reach the actual summit. Approach as for the Devils Advocate. The low point of the east face is just south of this feature. Descend from the arch by tying a 20-foot sling around the eastern pillar of the arch and rappelling about 50 feet north to the ground.

### 1.  EAST FACE 6
FA: GERRY ROACH, STEVE ILG, DIANE VENUTO, 1986.

This 1000-foot route gains the arch, but does not continue to the summit. Close, but no cigar. Hike to the lowest point of the west rib, 100 yards south of the Devil's Advocate and below a 30-foot roof. Begin a few feet to the south. Turn a three-foot roof and gain the steep wall above, then head up and right to a large tree. Five more 160-foot pitches, mostly easy, lead to the base of the summit ridge. On the sixth pitch the ridge narrows dramatically. The final pitch to the arch takes on a steep wall. Rappel or continue as described below.

## 2.   EAST FACE COMPLETE 7 ★

FA: ROB CASSADY AND JEFF NADING, 1994.

This route climbs to the summit, above the arch. Begin from the bottom of the east face, 20 feet left of a smooth, steep dihedral. 1. Climb a left-angling ramp to a tree (3, 140 feet). 2. Continue up the ramp to a big ledge (6, 130 feet). 3. Cross the ledge and climb a depression up the middle of the face. Ascend a corner for 15 feet, then go right to a ledge with a tree near the right edge of the face (6, 120 feet). 4. Angle up and right past a tree to an "A-shaped chimney." Climb along the right side of the chimney to another tree (3, 150 feet). 5. Climb straight up to the right edge of the face (2, 120 feet). 6. Angle left across a depression, past a couple trees, to a steeper wall. Climb a "ladder of huecos" to a ledge (1, 150 feet). 7. Cross to the left edge of the face and climb to a tree (2, 155 feet). 8. Climb a slot through a steep wall, then continue up the narrow ridge to slings around the east side of the arch (6, 100 feet). 9. Step carefully around a large, loose block and climb an east-facing ramp with a finger crack along the south side of the west pillar of the arch, then step back a few feet east to the summit. Rappel 65 feet north from blocks, five feet west of the summit.

## THE APOSTLE

This formation is located almost straight east of Devil's Thumb. Approach via the Mesa Trail and head west up an old trail at a drainage that is several hundred yards south of the junction of the South Shanahan Trail. This draw is about 150 yards north of a water tank along the Mesa trail. A couple hundred yards west from the Mesa Trail there is a stone shelter beneath a large boulder; the bottom of the Apostle is another 200 yards above this. To descend from the summit, scramble about 90 feet down to the west.

## 1.   SOUTHEAST RIDGE CLASS 4

The east face is separated into two sections by a small south-facing wall. Begin at the lowest point of the north section and climb the ridge crest past trees to the top (550 feet).

## 2.   NORTHEAST RIDGE 6

Begin at the low point of the rock. Go up a low-angle slab, and right to some trees at the north side of the rock. Climb the north face for about 40 feet past the big overhang at the bottom of the east face (crux), and belay on a ledge about 30 feet higher. Scramble 250 up the northeast ridge to the summit.

## DEVILS ADVOCATE

This formation sits below and northeast of Devils Thumb, near the bottom of the Flying Flatiron, and a few hundred feet south of Tiny Tower. Its south face is dead vertical and curves out to overhang near the top. Approach as for Tiny Tower. To descend from the summit, scramble north, then west through a hole to a broken ledge west of the summit. Descend a deep crack to the west and escape a final overhang via two dead trees that lean against the wall.

## 1.   NORTHEAST RIDGE 5

FA: GERRY ROACH, 1984.

The east face of the Devils Advocate is guarded by large overhangs; however, there is a way around them. Begin at the low point of the rock. Work up and right over a slab to some large trees on the north side of the rock. From the trees, climb west up a small ramp and work around onto the north face, then climb 40 feet up a steep wall and regain the east face (northeast ridge) above the overhangs. Continue to a good belay in about 30 feet. Another 250 feet of easier climbing leads to the summit.

## TINY TOWER

Tiny Tower is located low on the southeast ridge of the Flying Flatiron. To reach Tiny Tower, hike the Mesa Trail to a point some 200 yards south of the junction with the South Shanahan Trail. Leave the trail and hike west-southwest through an open meadow, then work left into a draw that leads directly to the base of the rock. To descend from the summit, scramble down the east face for about 15 feet, turn north along a crack, and scramble west down a 30-foot chimney to the ground. Hike down along the north side of the crag to reach the base.

### 1. EAST FACE 6 OR 7 ★

FA: GERRY ROACH AND STEVE ILG, 1986.

Locate a fin that forms the bottom of a large right-facing dihedral high on the face. Begin at the low point of the east face. Work straight up easy slabs, then head up and right around the low end of the fin (4, 155 feet). Climb the dihedral and belay at a stump in a patch of scrub juniper. Move left from the belay and climb a steep corner in the left wall of the dihedral (6). Climb a steep slab, then move right and follow a chimney to a notch with a tree. Traverse left along a crack , then climb a final slab 15 feet to the summit. One may also begin about 70 feet up along the right side of the east face: Traverse left across a red slab, then lieback a flake to gain better holds. Continue straight up to the bottom of the fin mentioned above (7, R. Rossiter, solo, 1998).

### 2. WEST RIDGE 0 ★

"Ornate...should not be missed." Climb the short but ornate west ridge to the summit.

## THE WINGS

North of Devils Thumb and reaching to the crest of the ridge, are two enormous slabs, South Wing and North Wing. These provide excellent slab routes for those who don't mind a long approach.

## THE SPHINX

This fierce little crag is located high on the south side of Shanahan Canyon across from the south face of the Southern Shanahan Crag. Its profile from the north may account for its name. Approach as for Shanahan Crags.

### 1. LOWER EAST FACE 7 s

FA: GERRY ROACH, 1985.

Begin at the low point of the rock and climb a 90-foot slab to a ledge. Climb a bulge at its north side, and after another 90 feet, arrive at a broad ledge that runs across the face. Hike up this ledge to a point near the south edge of the rock. Climb a deep chimney for 120 feet (4) to a large tree on the lower south face, then up a steep, exposed 60-foot wall (7 s) to a small tree on a higher ledge. Scramble north along this ledge to the bottom of the Upper East Face route. It is possible to walk off from this route at any of three ledge systems on the lower face.

### 2. UPPER EAST FACE CLASS 3

FA: GERRY ROACH, 1985.

Begin by climbing the Lower East Face route or by walking out from the north onto a big ledge that is above the overhangs of the preceding route. Climb up a gully for 110 feet to a notch on the northeast ridge, then continue up the east face to the summit. 350 feet.

## THE KEEL

This is the long, narrow rib of rock that climbs to the southwest out of upper Shanahan Canyon. The crest can be scrambled for 1000 feet from bottom to top. The small flatiron just to the north of the Keel is called the Rudder.

**SHANAHAN CRAGS, South Face**
1. Leonine 11a ★
2. South Face 4 ★
3. Southeast Ridge 3rd Class

## SHANAHAN CRAGS

North across a wooded gully from the Sphynx are two small flatirons known as North and South Shanahan Crags. There is also a smaller East Shanahan Crag on the north side of the draw, about 100 yards east of South Shanahan Crag. South Shanahan Crag has two summits with all but the first route arriving at the higher south summit. Only routes on the South Crag are described in this guide.

Approach via either branch of the Shanahan Trail. Where the South Branch crosses the Mesa Trail, head west up the draw into Shanahan Canyon and follow a faint trail up into the talus field between the Sphynx and South Shanahan Crag. Descend from the summit by scrambling about 100 feet down to the north.

### 1.   LEONINE 11A ★
FA: RICHARD WRIGHT AND S. MOORE, 1988.
Begin at the upper left side of the south face. Climb a blocky left-facing dihedral and belay after about 60 feet. Continue up the dihedral to a small roof and climb the headwall above past four bolts. 200 feet.

### 2.   SOUTH FACE 4 ★
FA: GERRY ROACH, 1985.
From the low point, hike up along the south face past an arête and dihedral to a smooth, dark face that is less than vertical. Farther to the west the face becomes quite steep. Climb an obvious crack straight up to the ridge crest. 140 feet.

### 3.   SOUTHEAST RIDGE CLASS 3 ★
Begin at the low point and follow the ridge to the summit. The route is about 600 feet long.

## THE SLAB

The Slab is a very big rock, easily among the largest of the Flatirons. But unlike the First and Third Flatirons (which it likely dwarfs), it is wide instead of tall. The east face is about 2000 feet long and 500 feet high and hosts several interesting slab routes. The northwest face is vertical to overhanging and offers an array of excellent bolt-protected face climbs.

**Approach**— To reach The Slab, hike the north branch of the Shanahan Trail, which passes below the lower right side of the east face. The northwest side is accessed by a footpath that leads south from the Fern Canyon Trail. Reach the Fern Canyon Trail via the Shanahan Trail or the Bear Canyon Trail (see under Boulder Mountain).

**Descent**— There are several ways to escape the summit ridge: 1. Rappel 75 feet west from a bolt. 2. Farther along, down-climb a tree to the west. 3. Rappel west from trees. 4. At one point it is possible to walk off to the west. 5. Traverse the entire ridge crest from north to south to where it merges with the east slope of Bear Peak. Lower off or rappel from all "sport climbs."

## East Face

The following routes are located along the massive east face. Aside from the few established routes, there is vast potential for innovation and the creation of entirely new lines. Like most Flatiron slab routes, protection is somewhat sparse.

### 1.   KEYHOLE ROUTE 8
FA: GARY NEPTUNE AND JIM GLENDENNING, CIRCA 1982.
This isolated route is located about 50 feet to the right (north) of a huge left-facing dihedral that marks off the southern third of the east face. Start just left of a smaller, left- facing, left-leaning dihedral that arcs south forming an overhang just below the "keyhole" (a slot with flakes jutting into it, about 300 feet up the face). Climb straight up to the overhang, turn the roof, and belay on a small ledge. Continue up through the keyhole and on to the summit ridge.

## 2. Syzygy 0

The face to the south of the dihedral of Left 'n Up is reminiscent of big, choppy swells out at sea. One way to do this route is to begin at a large hollow between swells, then sail straight up through rough water to ports of call on the summit ridge. One may navigate by a large tree on the skyline.

## 3. Left 'n Up 0

Ascend the face just left of a discernible left-facing dihedral system, about 200 feet south (left) from the northeast arête. Five or six pitches.

## 4. Bulges 0

Begin this line about 100 feet south from the northeast arête and climb directly up to the summit ridge.

## 5. Northeast Arête 5 ★

FA: RICHARD ROSSITER AND LYNN HOUSEHOLDER, 1977.

This route ascends the far right edge of the east face. Climb a couple of easy pitches just left of the arête and belay beneath a large wing-like flake that hangs in space above the north face. Climb under the wing and back onto the arête, then run the rope out to where the angle eases off on the summit ridge.

## North Side

The following climbs are located on the very steep north and west sides of the Slab. Hike the Fern Canyon Trail until just northwest of the Slab, then break south on a footpath that leads to the wall.

## 6. Just Another Boy's Climb 11d ★

This is the farthest left of the "sport climbs" on the north face. Climb a slab to a stance and belay (8). Climb jugs up a water streak and pull to the left, then make a strenuous hand traverse out under the roof. Heelhook and crank up to an anchor. Bring mid-range cams (1.5 and 2.0 Friends). Eight bolts to a two-bolt anchor, 100 feet.

## 7. Nasty Boys (?)

This route goes right from the third bolt on Boy's Climb. It is not known if this route was ever completed.

## 8. Boys with Power Toys 12b ★

FA: CHRIS BEH AND KURT SMITH, 1989.

Begin about 50 feet right of Boy's Climb. Ascend a vertical wall to a difficult overlap and continue with face climbing on the right wall of an open corner. Nine bolts to a two-bolt anchor, 70 feet.

## 9. Face Line (?)

A steep face climb may exist a short way right of Power Toys.

## 10. Whipping Post 11d ★

Begin up to the right of Power Toys, where the roof fades. Climb up and hand traverse left, up past a ring bolt (crux), then up fine black rock (9) toward the crest. Eight bolts to a two-bolt anchor, 90 feet.

## 11. Undertow 12b ★

FA: ERIK FEDOR AND ROB CANDELARIA, 1989.

"Jug dyno paradise." About 100 feet south of Whipping Post, follow a line of bolts up the awe-inspiring, overhanging wall. A 2.5 or 3.0 Friend may be placed in a pocket after the sixth bolt. Seven bolts to a two-bolt anchor, 80 feet.

**THE SLAB—north side**
6.    Just Another Boy's Climb 11d ★
8.    Boys with Power Toys 12b ★
10.   Whipping Post 11d ★
11.   Undertow 12b ★

## ADVISORS

The Advisors are three obscure flatirons on the south side of Fern Canyon, west of The Slab. Each one provides an interesting slab climb in the Class 4 range. The farthest west Advisor is perhaps the best and provides an excellent view of the crags on the north side of Fern Canyon. Approach via the Fern Canyon trail and look for a faint footpath once above The Slab.

# BEAR PEAK

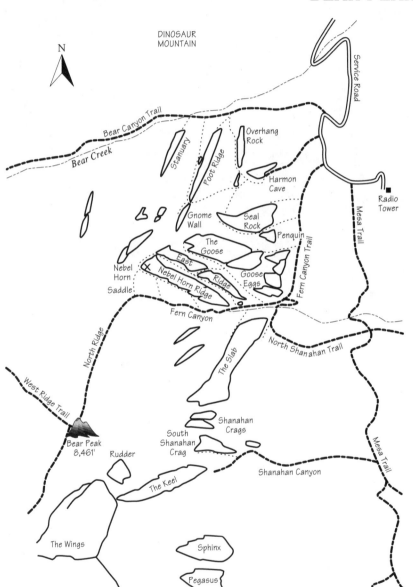

DINOSAUR MOUNTAIN

N

Service Road

Bear Canyon Trail

Bear Creek

Overhang Rock

Statuary

Poot Ridge

Harmon Cave

Radio Tower

Mesa Trail

Gnome Wall

Seal Rock

Penquin

The Goose

Fern Canyon Trail

Nebel Horn Saddle

East Nebel Horn Ridge Ridge

Goose Eggs

Fern Canyon

North Ridge

North Shanahan Trail

The Slab

West Ridge Trail

Bear Peak 8,461'

Rudder

South Shanahan Crag

Shanahan Crags

Mesa Trail

Shanahan Canyon

The Keel

The Wings

Sphinx

Pegasus

# NEBEL HORN

· · · · · · · · · · · · · · · · · · · · · · · · · · · · · · · · · · · · ·

The Nebel Horn is a subsidiary summit about one-half mile down along the southeast ridge of Bear Peak. It is separated from the main peak by a broad, sandy saddle from which Fern Canyon descends to the east. Significant features include the Fern Canyon Ridges, the Goose, Seal Rock, Overhang Rock, Gnome Wall, Poot Ridge and the Sanctuary. The craggy summit of the Nebel Horn may be reached by a short class 3 scramble up the west side and provides a magnificent view of the surrounding terrain. This summit is also the top of a long spine of rock called the Nebel Horn Ridge that is host to several excellent rock climbs (see below).

**Trails**— Important trails for reaching crags on the Nebel Horn include the North Shanahan Trail, Fern Canyon Trail, Harmon Cave Trail and Bear Canyon Trail (see under Boulder Mountain). From the west end of the Bear Canyon Trail, a rugged path continues up the northwest ridge to the summit of Bear Peak , but it is of little use for purposes of rock climbing.

## FERN CANYON CRAGS

Heavily forested Fern Canyon is nestled between the southeast slope of the Nebel Horn and the northeast slope of Bear Peak. Its narrow entrance lies between the north end of the Slab and the Southern Goose Egg. The north side of Fern Canyon is characterized by two long spines of rock that rise to the northwest and present an excellent array of climbs including easy slabs, steep cracks and radical arêtes and roofs protected by bolts. Several smaller features in this area also provide engaging climbs. Note that climbs and crags are listed from left to right and front to back from the sandy saddle at the top of Fern Canyon.

### Mars Block

The Mars Block is a small buttress located 300 feet north of the saddle atop Fern Canyon. A path leads from the saddle to its base.

**1. CREAM PUFF 12D**
FA: LANTZ, PEMEROY, ROBINSON, 1989.
Follow six bolts up the right edge of the north face.

**2. THE SCHOOL 12C**
FA: MARK ROLOFSON AND STU RITCHIE, 1989.
Climb the very steep west face past four bolts around to the right from Cream Puff.

**3. THREE MUSKETEERS 7**
FA: MICHAEL MASSARI, SOLO.
Three separate lines slant up and left to a common finish on the left of three west-facing sections. These were named Athos, Porthos, Aremis.

**4. SNICKERS DIHEDRAL 4**
Climb the short dihedral between the left and middle sections.

**5. DEVIL DOGS 13 TR**
Climb the very smooth face just left of Plain or Peanut. This is the first route to have been climbed on the Mars Block.

**NEBEL HORN, from the southeast**

Seal Rock

Goose Eggs

The Goose

East Ridge

Southern
Goose Egg

Nebel Horn Ridge

Fiddlehead

Onoclea

Pellaea

FERN
CANYON

### 6.   PLAIN OR PEANUT 11A
FA: CHERRY AND MASSARI.
Follow four bolts up the center of the middle section of the Mars Block.

### 7.   ALMOND JOY 8
FA: MASSARI.
Climb an undercling up and left to a stance and on to the top.

### 8.   MOUNDS 5
FA: MASSARI.
Climb a water groove to ledge and on to the top.

### A QUICKIE 11A
FA: TRIPP COLLINS AND RICHARD WRIGHT, 1989.
This route is located on an independent feature downhill to the east, but uphill from Mentor. Climb a thin face with four bolts.

### MENTOR 12B
FA: LANTZ, POMEROY, ROBINSON, 1989.
This route is on an isolated outcrop about 150 yards uphill from Superfresh just right of the Fern Canyon Trail. Climb the obvious, overhanging, pocketed wall past four bolts.

## NEBEL HORN RIDGE

The Nebel Horn Ridge begins along the Fern Canyon Trail, about 50 yards west of a giant boulder (Superfresh) and culminates in the summit of the Nebel Horn. It consists of three distinct sections separated by gaps or notches, the lower two of which are large flatiron-like formations with fine east face routes. These are called Pellaea and Onoclea in ascending order. The upper section of the ridge has several excellent climbs on its steep southwest face.

**Approach**— To reach the upper southwest face, hike the Fern Canyon Trail to the first northward switchback above an overhanging, pocketed wall with the route Mentor. Branch right (north) on a footpath, go through a small notch, and enter the rocky, wooded gully that runs beneath the face. This area may also be reached from the saddle at the top of Fern Canyon: Follow a path north around the west face of the Mars Block, then head back to the east beneath the Nebel Horn summit block. To reach routes on the northeast slabs, hike the Fern Canyon Trail about 150 feet past the huge, square boulder of Superfresh that rises on the right. Branch right and follow a path into the rugged gully between the Nebel Horn Ridge and the East Ridge.

### 1.   NEBEL HORN ROUTE CLASS 3
From the sandy col at the top of Fern Canyon, hike north past the Mars Block, then scramble up steep, broken rock to a grassy trough on the east side of the ridge crest., below the summit tower. Climb south along a groove/ramp, then ascend a final step to the summit. The summit may also be reached from the gully between the Nebel Horn Ridge and the East Ridge or from the notch just west of Onoclea (class 4).

### 2.   RAINBOW BRIDGE 9 ★
FA: RICHARD AND JOYCE ROSSITER, 1988.
At the top of the ridge, directly below the summit of the Nebel Horn, a clean buttress leans out to the south. Scramble up a short slab and belay behind a tree. Climb the overhang (crux) and the face above near to the arête. Four bolts to a two-bolt anchor.

Nebel Horn Ridge

East Ridge

Iron Cross .11a

Ilga Grippeur .11b/c

Fluorescent Gray .11c

Onoclea

Fiddle Head

Pelaea

**NEBEL HORN RIDGE**
2. Rainbow Bridge 9 ★
3. Ruby Slipper 11c ★
5. The Violator 13c ★

East Ridge

The Goose

To Routes
1-10

Nebel Horn
Ridge

Fiddlehead

Pellaea

**EAST RIDGE**

**Stealth Slab**
13. **Ilga Grimpeur** 11b/c ★
18. **Fluorescent Gray** 11c ★
**Fiddlehead**
24. **Chains Of Love** 12b ★
25. **Stemadilemma** 11d ★
27. **A Shadow Sickness** 9 ★

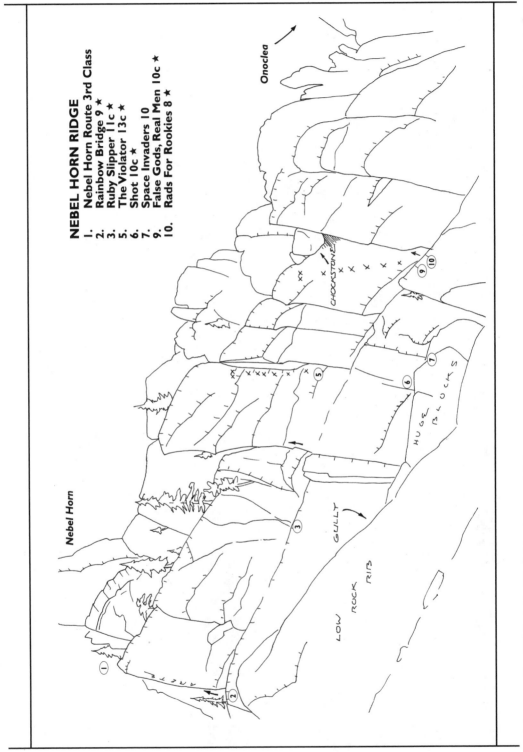

**NEBEL HORN RIDGE**
1. Nebel Horn Route 3rd Class
2. Rainbow Bridge 9 ★
3. Ruby Slipper 11c ★
5. The Violator 13c ★
6. Shot 10c ★
7. Space Invaders 10
9. False Gods, Real Men 10c ★
10. Rads For Rookies 8 ★

*Nebel Horn*

*Onoclea*

CHOCKSTONE

HUGE BLOCKS

GULLY

LOW ROCK RIB

### 3. RUBY SLIPPER 11c ★

FA: JEFF ACHEY AND BILL BRADLEY, 1981.

Begin up on a ledge about 200 feet down and right from Rainbow Bridge. Climb a thin crack in a smooth red slab. Rack up to one inch.

### 4. EARACHE MY EYE 10

FA: ERIC DOUB AND ERIC GOUKAS, 1981.

Climb a steep wall followed by an overhanging off-width crack, just right of Ruby Slipper.

### 5. THE VIOLATOR 13c ★

FA: COLIN LANTZ, 1989.

Begin about 100 feet down and right from Ruby Slipper. Climb a slab past several bolts to the base of an overhanging arête and belay (10b). Climb the arête past seven bolts and lower off. Rack: QDs only.

### 6. SHOT 10c ★

FA: JEFF ACHEY AND CHIP CHASE, 1981.

This route ascends the left of three similar features just right of The Violator. Climb a steep face into a right-facing dihedral and finish with a slot through a roof.

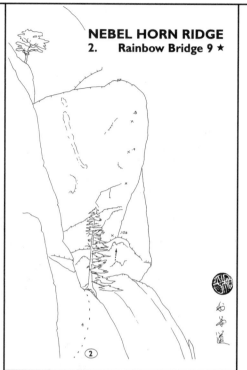

**NEBEL HORN RIDGE**
**2. Rainbow Bridge 9 ★**

### 7. SPACE INVADERS 10

FA: CHIP CHASE AND JEFF ACHEY, 1981.

Begin to the right of Shot. Climb a short left-facing dihedral and finish with a fist crack through a roof.

### 8. ON THE CONTRARY 11d TR

Begin five feet left of False Gods. Lieback steep ramps to better holds and pass a small roof from the left.

### 9. FALSE GODS, REAL MEN 10c ★

FA: LANTZ, BEH, MASSARI, 1989.

Climb the left wall of a deep cleft with a chockstone. Six bolts to a two-bolt anchor.

### 10. RADS FOR ROOKIES 8 ★

FA: KATHY LANTZ AND MICHAEL MASSARI, 1989.

Climb the right wall of the cleft past four bolts to a two-bolt anchor.

## Onoclea

Onoclea is the middle section or flatiron of the Nebel Horn Ridge and culminates in an airy summit. To escape from the summit, downclimb to the northeast and make a short rappel in the gully.

### 11. WEST FACE 7

Hike up the gully to the east of Pellaea and Onoclea until it is possible to scramble southwest to the notch between Onoclea and the upper "horn" section of the ridge. Climb the steep, smooth west face to the summit of Onoclea.

**NEBEL HORN RIDGE**
2. Rainbow Bridge 9 ★
3. Ruby Slipper
5. The Violator 13c ★
7. Space Invaders 10
9. False Gods, Real Men 10c ★

**Onoclea**
11. West Face 7

*Nebel Horn*

*Onoclea*

## 12.   EAST FACE 3

Hike up the gully to the gash that separates Pellaea from Onoclea. Climb the south edge of Onoclea's east slab (just right of the gash) all the way to the summit.

# Pellaea

Pellaea is the lowest section of the Nebel Horn Ridge and host to a single slab climb up its east face. To escape the summit, make a short rappel into the gash to the north, then scramble off to the south and west.

## 14.   EAST FACE 5

Begin near the low point of the east face. Work up and left to the south edge and pass a bulge (crux), then climb straight up to the top passing another bulge on the last pitch. 500 feet of beautiful rock.

### SUPERFRESH 12C ★

FA: LANTZ, POMEROY, ROBINSON, 1989.

This route is located on a giant boulder (the Superfresh Block) a short way downhill from the bottom of the Nebel Horn Ridge and on the right side of the trail. Climb the overhanging east arête past five bolts and lower off.

### OUT OF AFRICA 13A

This route is located on the Slab Overlook, a giant block at the narrow entrance to Fern Canyon, on the left side of the trail and immediately north of the Slab. Climb the overhanging southeast arête past three bolts to a two-bolt anchor.

# EAST RIDGE

The East Ridge begins in the trees to the north of the giant boulder of Superfresh, some 200 yards west of the narrow entrance to Fern Canyon. It then climbs 1,500 feet to a minor crest just north of the summit of the Nebel Horn. The East Ridge consists of two long sections divided by a deep notch or gap. The upper section is characterized by a series of clean dihedrals and the smooth Stealth Slab. The lower section is known as the Fiddlehead. Note that routes along the southwest faces of both sections are described from left to right.

**Approach**—Hike the Fern Canyon Trail about 150 feet past the huge, square boulder of Superfresh that sits on the right. Branch right on a path that leads into the rugged gully between the Nebel Horn Ridge and the East Ridge. The upper section of the ridge may also be reached by hiking around the west end of the Nebel Horn.

## 1.   KENT'S KRACK 12A TR

FA: KENT LUGBILL.

This climb is on a separate block at the far west end of the East Ridge. Start up a corner with some loose blocks at the bottom, follow a crack across the overhanging wall, then dyno up the arête.

## 2.   BABYBACK 5

Climb a short left-facing dihedral near the top (west end) of the East Ridge.

## 3.   UNITY 9

FA: ROGER BRIGGS, SOLO, 1974.

Climb the next dihedral right of Babyback. A tree grows partway up the corner.

## 4.   GALACTIC WARRIOR 7

FA: DAN HARE AND JOEL SCHIAVONE, 1981.

Climb a crack just right of the arête that forms the right margin of the Unity dihedral.

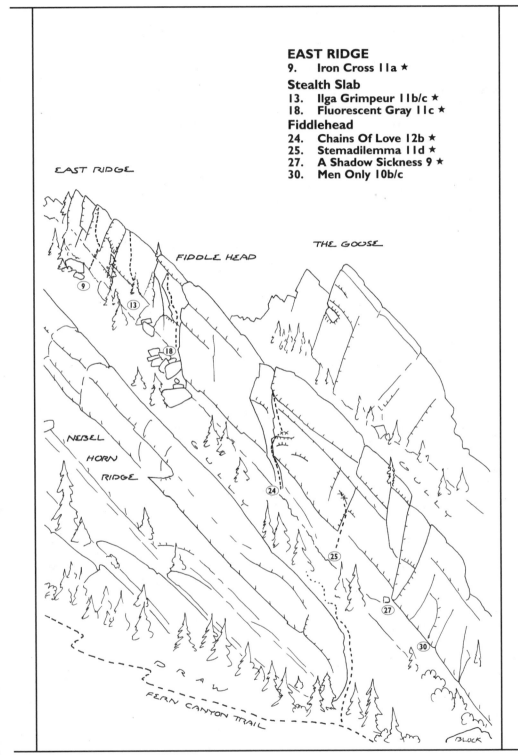

**EAST RIDGE**
9.    Iron Cross 11a ★
**Stealth Slab**
13.   Ilga Grimpeur 11b/c ★
18.   Fluorescent Gray 11c ★
**Fiddlehead**
24.   Chains Of Love 12b ★
25.   Stemadilemma 11d ★
27.   A Shadow Sickness 9 ★
30.   Men Only 10b/c

EAST RIDGE

FIDDLE HEAD

THE GOOSE

NEBEL
HORN
RIDGE

GULLY

GULLY

DRAW

FERN CANYON TRAIL

BLOCK

Dihedrals

**UPPER EAST RIDGE**
3.   **Unity 9**
6.   **Fountain of Youth 10b** ★
8.   **Lightning Bolt Arête 11b** ★
10.  **Superguide 9** ★

Fiddlehead

### 5.   THE KNACK 6
FA: Dan Hare, solo, 1981.
Climb the next left-facing dihedral to the right of Unity.

### 6.   FOUNTAIN OF YOUTH 10B ★
FA: George Hurley and Bill DeMallie, 1989.
Climb two-thirds of The Knack, then break right and climb the arête past three bolts.

### 7.   HAYWIRE 9+
FA: Healy, Schiavone, Hare, 1981.
Climb an easy left-facing corner (The Knack) to a ledge, angle up and right, then climb a slot through a roof and continue to the top of the ridge.

### 8.   LIGHTNING BOLT ARÊTE 11B ★
FA: Bill DeMallie and George Hurley, 1989.
Begin just left of a bow-shaped tree. Climb a short, left-facing dihedral past a pin and move left to belay on a ledge with two rings. Follow bolts up the arête above. Six bolts. SR.

### 9.   IRON CROSS 11A ★
FA: Bill DeMallie and George Huley, 1989.
Climb a left-right-left, flip-flop dihedral past a pin and belay at two ring bolts. Move left and follow bolts up the steep face. Seven bolts. Rack up to a #3 Friend.

### 10.   SUPERGUIDE 9 ★
FA: George Hurley and Bill DeMallie, 1989.
This route takes the farthest right of the arêtes, just uphill from Sporofight. Climb a left-facing dihedral a few feet right of Iron Cross, work up through a slot, then move out right and climb the arête past a pin and a bolt. 80 feet. SR.

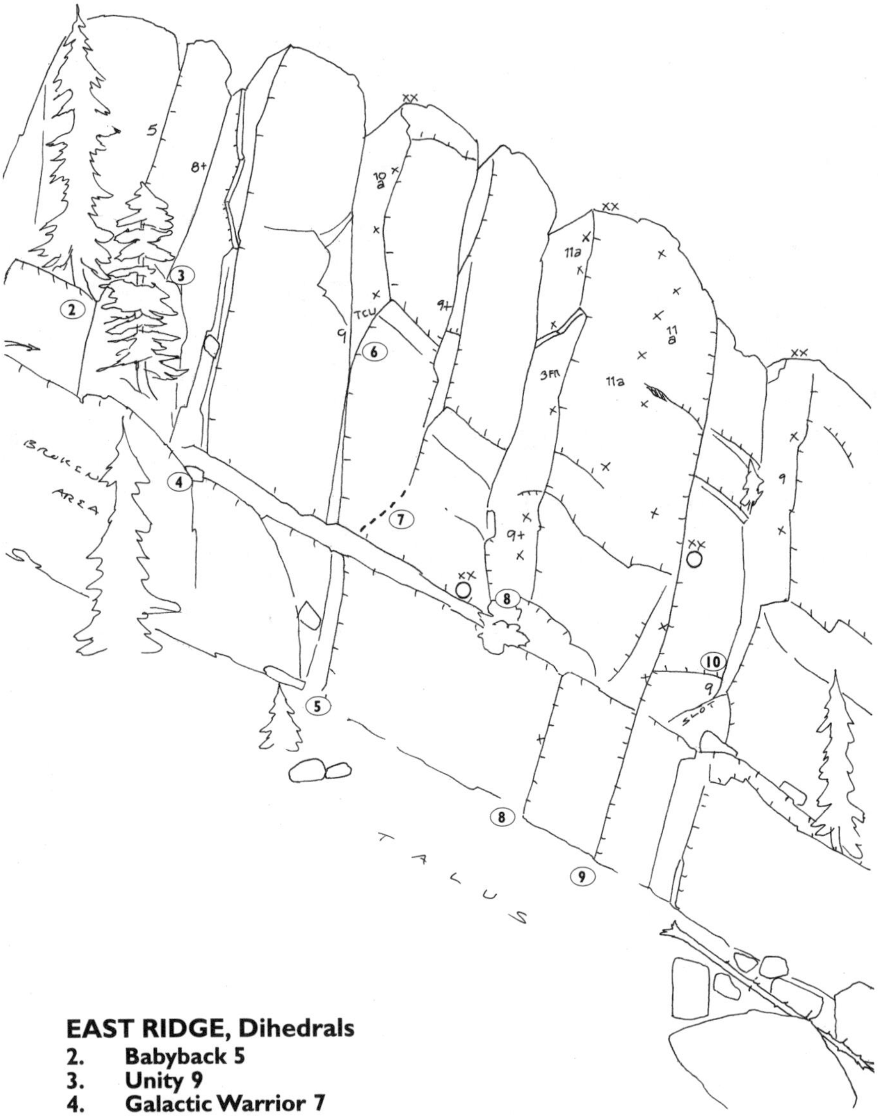

**EAST RIDGE, Dihedrals**

2. Babyback 5
3. Unity 9
4. Galactic Warrior 7
5. The Knack 6
6. Fountain of Youth 10b ★
7. Haywire 9+
8. Lightning Bolt Arête 11b ★
9. Iron Cross 11a ★
10. Superguide 9 ★

**Stealth Slab**

11. **Sporofight 10 s or 11s**
12. **A Blessing In Dick's Eyes 10c vs**
13. **Ilga Grimpeur 11b/c ★**
14. **Slabmaster 12a ★**
15. **Edgemaster 10c ★**
16. **Downclimb 6**
17. **Everpresent Lane 10d ★**
18. **Fluorescent Gray 11c ★**
19. **Exile 12a ★**

## Stealth Slab

To the right of the dihedrals and left of Everpresent Lane is a smooth slab with the following routes. Begin from a ledge about 20 feet above the talus.

### 11.  SPOROFIGHT 10 s or 11s
FA: BRET RUCKMAN AND MARCO CORNACCHIONE, 1989.

Climb an obtuse right-facing, right leaning dihedral. It is easier to exit left before reaching the top of the wall.

### 12.  A BLESSING IN DICK'S EYES 10c VS
FA: BRET AND JUDY RUCKMAN AND PAM RANGER, 1989.

The name is a reference to Richard DuMais' enthusiasm for the route being established without fixed protection; but as Bill DeMallie put it, "If he (Richard) didn't have a heart attack on the approach, he'd have one trying to lead this pitch." Begin a short way right of Sporofight. Climb a seam past a "shitty pin," and continue up the unprotected wall to finish as for Sporofight.

### 13.  ILGA GRIMPEUR 11B/C ★
FA: MARCO CORNACCHIONE AND BRET RUCKMAN, 1989.

Begin beside a tree well down and right from A Blessing. Follow a line of seven bolts up and left along a water streak.

### 14.  SLABMASTER 12A ★
FA: DAVE CRAWFORD AND BILL DEMALLIE, 1989.

Originally named Stealth Bomber. Follow a line of eight bolts up the middle of the slab.

The Goose
(behind 14, 15)

**Stealth Slab**
14.   Slabmaster 12a ★
15.   Edgemaster 10c ★
17.   Everpresent Lane 10d ★
18.   Fluorescent Gray 11c ★
**Fiddlehead**
21.   Leprechaun Promenade 10b ★
24.   Chains Of Love 12b ★
27.   A Shadow Sickness 9 ★

The Slab

Fiddle Head

### 15. EDGEMASTER 10c ★

FA: BILL DEMALLIE AND GAIL MCCLANHAHAN, 1989.

Follow a line of nine bolts up the right side of the slab.

### 16. DOWNCLIMB 6

The far right side of the Stealth Slab presents a beautiful moderate route.

### 17. EVERPRESENT LANE 10D ★

FA: DAN HARE, JOEL SCHIAVONE, PAT HEALY, 1981.

Begin just right of the Stealth Slab and 70 feet left of the gap in the ridge. Climb a shallow, right-facing dihedral with a fixed pin and belay from a tree.

### 18. FLUORESCENT GRAY 11c ★

FA: BRET RUCKMAN AND TIM COATS, 1989.

Begin about 40 feet right of the preceding route, just before the big gap in the ridge. Follow bolts along a steep, zigzag arête. Seven bolts to a two-bolt anchor, 85 feet. Bring nuts up to one inch.

### 19. EXILE 12A ★

FA: BRET RUCKMAN, 1989.

Locate a line of bolts on the east-facing wall of the gap, about 75 feet to the right of Fluorescent Grey. Six bolts and a pin to a two-bolt anchor, 60 feet. Bring a 0.5 Tricam.

## Fiddlehead

The following routes are located on the lower section of the East Ridge, below the gap. The first four of these ascend the flat west face of the Fiddlehead.

### 20. LEFT EDGE 7

FA: ROSSITER, 1989.

Scramble up onto a huge block at the lower left side of the west face. Climb the left edge of the west face and finish with a rounded left-facing dihedral.

### 21. LEPRECHAUN PROMENADE 10B ★

FA: CHRISTIAN GRIFFITH AND SKIP GUERIN, 1981; OF SECOND PITCHES: ROSSITER, 1989.

Also known as Left Joint. Begin at the bottom of the flat west face beneath a giant boulder. Climb the left side of the wall past three bolts and belay on an in-cut ledge. A second pitch takes the face to the left (7) or the roof at a left-facing flake (10c). QDs only for first pitch; rack up to #2 Friend for the second pitch.

### 22. LUCKY CHARMS 10D ★

FA: GRIFFITH AND GUERIN, 1981.

Also known as Rip This Joint. Begin as for the preceding route. Climb straight up past a bolt to a shallow hole, then move up and right (crux) to gain a short crack.

### 23. IRISH SPRING 9

FA: SKIP GUERIN, 1981.

Begin as for the preceding route. Move up and clip an old bolt, then climb along the right edge of the face.

### 24. CHAINS OF LOVE 12B ★

FA: LANTZ, POMEROY, ROBINSON, 1989.

This route ascends a big roof about midway between Irish Spring and Castles Made of Sand. Climb a crack up to a good ledge with a two-bolt anchor, then master a huge roof with six bolts and a two-bolt anchor. Bring mid-range gear for the first pitch.

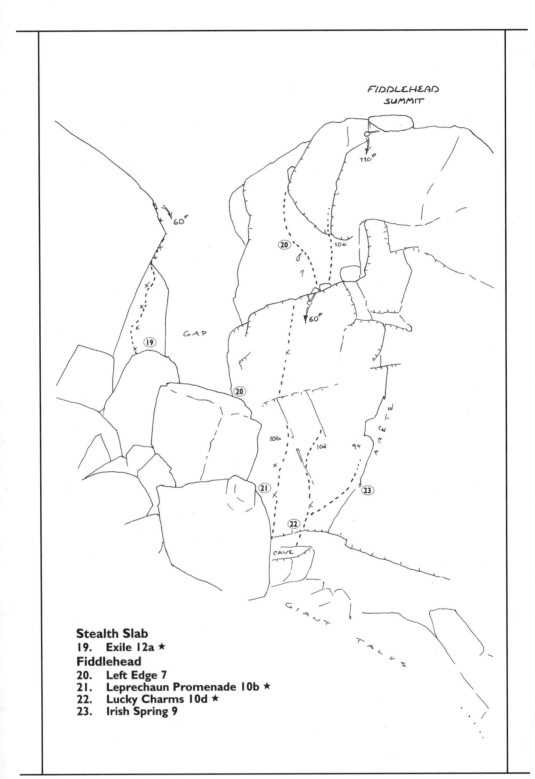

**Stealth Slab**
19.   Exile 12a ★
**Fiddlehead**
20.   Left Edge 7
21.   Leprechaun Promenade 10b ★
22.   Lucky Charms 10d ★
23.   Irish Spring 9

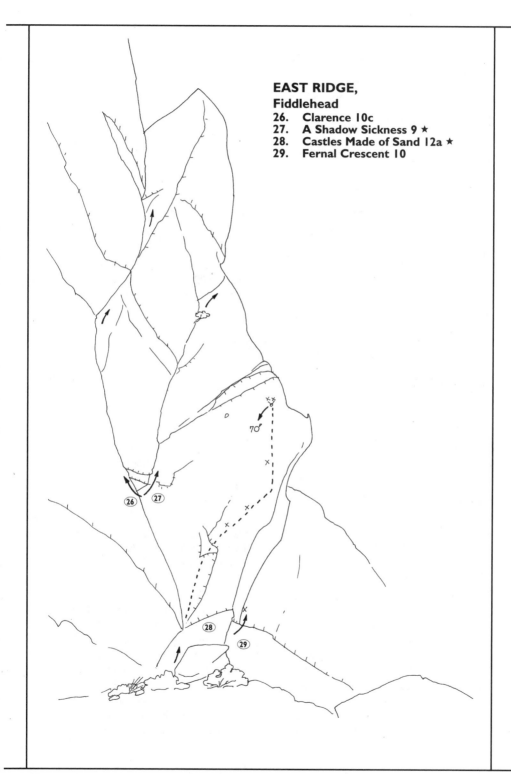

**EAST RIDGE,**
Fiddlehead
26. Clarence 10c
27. A Shadow Sickness 9 ★
28. Castles Made of Sand 12a ★
29. Fernal Crescent 10

### 25. STEMADILEMMA 11D ★
FA: TIM COATS AND BRET RUCKMAN, 1989.

Begin a short way down and right from Chains Of Love. Climb a short, steep right-facing dihedral and lower off from two pins. Rack up to a #2 Friend.

### 26. CLARENCE 10c
FA: JEFF ACHEY

Begin about 90 feet down and right from Chains Of Love. Climb a big dihedral and take the crack on the left through the head wall.

### 27. A SHADOW SICKNESS 9 ★
FA: JOEL SCHIAVONE AND PAT HEALY, 1980.

Climb directly up the huge left-facing corner of the preceding route, and belay under a roof. Take the crack on the right past a small tree.

### 28. CASTLES MADE OF SAND 12A ★
FA: DAN AND JIM MICHAEL, 1988.

This route is located on the smooth right wall of a huge dihedral about 200 feet northeast of the Superfresh Block. Follow a line of four bolts up the wall near the arête. 65 feet to a two-bolt anchor.

### 29. FERNAL CRESCENT 10
FA: ERIC DOUB, ERIC GUOKAS, CHRISTIAN GRIFFITH, 1980.

Begin at a right-arching, right-facing dihedral just right from Castles Made Of Sand. Climb up the corner past a fixed pin and continue to the crest of the ridge.

### 30. MEN ONLY 10B/C
FA: JEFF ACHEY AND KENT LUGBILL, 1980.

Begin 70 feet or so down and right from Castles Made Of Sand beneath a long, low overhang. Step off a block and move left in the more imposing of several cracks.

### 31. EAST FACE 4

Begin well up in the gully between the Fiddlehead and the Goose. Climb the east slab, staying mostly to the left and gain the summit of the Fiddlehead.

## THE GOOSE

The Goose is the massive flatiron between Fern Canyon and Seal Rock, straight east from the summit of the Nebel Horn. That the crag resembles an actual goose is subject to debate; that it is host to a variety of excellent routes...well, no one will argue that. The Goose has a north and a south summit. The north is higher and may be reached by an easy scramble. The south summit, and the knife-edged ridge leading from it to a notch on the north, is the high point of three great faces, each having fine routes.

**Approach**—To reach the west or south sides of the Goose, hike the Fern Canyon Trail about 50 yards beyond Slab Overlook, then break right and walk north up open forest and talus between the Goose and the back side of the East Ridge to the base of the rock. One may also reach this area from by scrambling through the big gap in the East Ridge. To reach the east face, hike the Fern Canyon Trail until a bit northeast of the rock, then hike west, passing north of the Goose Eggs.

**Descent**—To escape from the south summit, rappel 120 feet down the west face from the more northerly of two anchors, just south of the highest point. Or rappel 165 feet down the vertical southwest face from the more southerly of the two bolt anchors. It is also easy to traverse the knife-edged ridge to the notch between the two summits and down to the alcove beneath the west face.

**THE GOOSE—South Face**

5. Raging Bull 11a or 12b ★
7. Sweet & Innocent 10a ★
8. South Face 4

## 1. NORTH SUMMIT CLASS 4

Begin in the alcove between the north and south summits. Climb without difficulty up a broken gully to the notch between the two summits. Scramble to a platform on the north side of the summit tower and climb straight to the top.

### 1A. VARIATION 4

Climb an east-facing slab 20 feet left of a tunnel.

### 1B. VARIATION 6 OR 8

Climb an east-facing slab just left of the tunnel, followed by a south-facing wall beside an overhanging groove. One may also turn a roof just south from the top of the tunnel (8).

### 1C. TUNNEL CLASS 4

Climb a tunnel inside the summit blocks, then go ten feet north and up to the top.

## 2. LOVE'S LABOR LOST 10A ★

FA: RICHARD WRIGHT AND KAREN KUDDES, 1989.

Begin in the alcove between the north summit and west (northwest) face and scramble to a ledge that runs out across the wall to the right. Follow six or seven bolts up and right across the smooth west face. Bring a #2 and #4 Friend.

## 3. DESERTED CITIES OF THE HEART 9 ★

FA: RICHARD ROSSITER, SOLO, 1988.

Begin in an alcove at the bottom of the west face. Climb 50 feet to the largest tree on an incut ledge. Turn a roof at a thin crack (9), then climb straight up staying a few feet right of a shallow, crackless, right-facing dihedral. Finish at the south summit. Nine bolts were placed on this route by Richard Wright during 1989.

## 4. ARÊTE 8 S

FA: R. ROSSITER, SOLO, 1988.

This route ascends the right edge of the northwest face. Begin in a little alcove at the bottom of the face. Climb up and right and follow the arête all the way to the south summit.

## 5. RAGING BULL 11A OR 12B ★

FA: RICHARD WRIGHT, A. BLONDENBURG, 1988. PITCH TWO: ROB CANDELARIA, WRIGHT.

The first pitch (previously known as Cub) is fairly popular. Begin on a pedestal near the left edge of the southwest face and follow a line of bolts to a big ledge (11a, 7 bolts, 90 feet). Climb up and right over the bulging headwall. 14 bolts, 165 feet. Rack: QDs and wired stoppers.

## 6. WILD HORSES 13A ★

FA: ROB CANDELARIA, RICHARD WRIGHT, 1989.

Begin as for Sweet and Innocent, but break left out of the dihedral and follow a line of bolts up and over the bulging headwall. Nine bolts to a two-bolt anchor, 145 feet. Rack up to a #1.5 Friend.

## 7. SWEET & INNOCENT 10A ★

FA: JOEL SCHIAVONE AND DAN HARE, 1982.

Begin from a ledge at the bottom of a left-facing, right-leaning dihedral. Climb the dihedral and pass a bulge (crux, #2 Friend) near the top. Finish as for South Face.

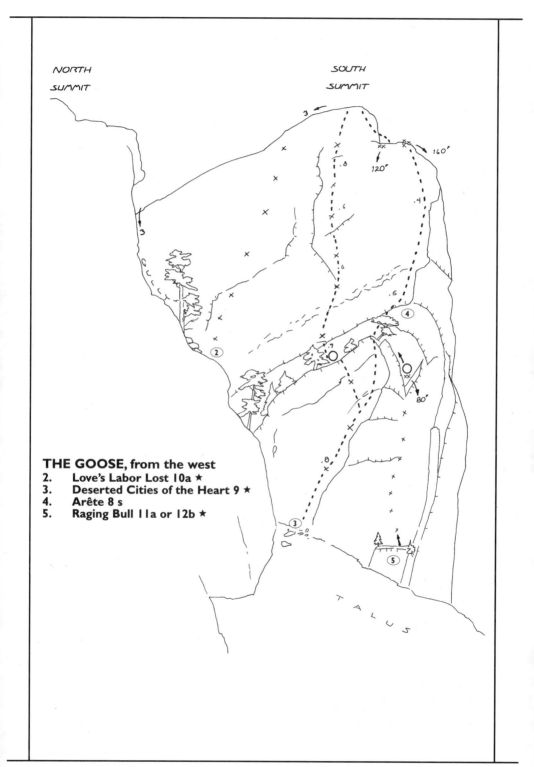

**THE GOOSE, from the west**

2. Love's Labor Lost 10a ★
3. Deserted Cities of the Heart 9 ★
4. Arête 8 s
5. Raging Bull 11a or 12b ★

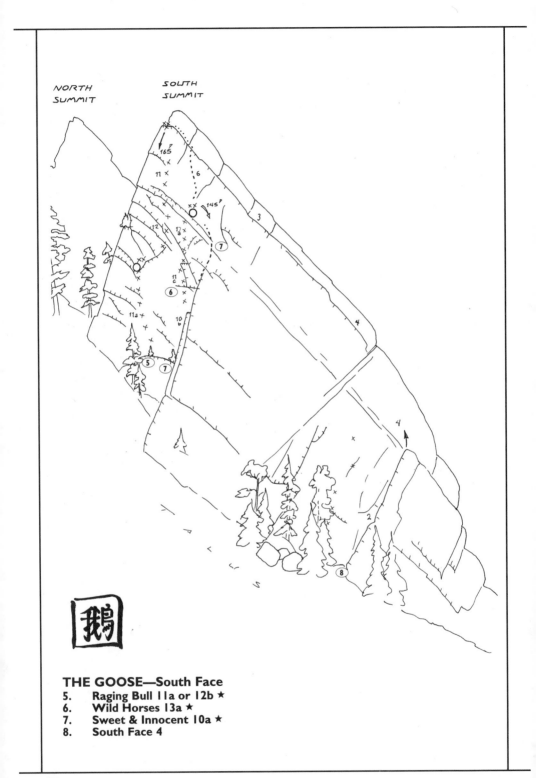

NORTH
SUMMIT

SOUTH
SUMMIT

165°

11

6

145°

3

12

7

11
c

6

11a

10
b

4

5   7

4

2

8

鵝

## THE GOOSE—South Face

5.    **Raging Bull 11a or 12b** ★
6.    **Wild Horses 13a** ★
7.    **Sweet & Innocent 10a** ★
8.    **South Face 4**

## 8.  SOUTH FACE 4

Begin at a blocky, low-angle, left-facing dihedral near the middle of the south face. Climb the dihedral followed by a short southeast-facing wall (crux) and gain a long ramp just below the south edge of the east face. Follow this ramp for a couple of hundred feet to the exhilarating south summit.

## 9.  MOTHER GOOSE 7 ★

FA: ROB CASSADY JIM SINCOCK, 1994.'

This ingenious route finds an unlikely passage through the gigantic roofs that bar access to the main east face (south side). From the Fern Canyon Trail, hike west past the two middle Goose Eggs, then scramble up a gully (class 4) until it is possible to angle left beneath the big roofs. Continue left (south) past some big boulders to a small pedestal with a tree. 1. Climb up and right for 30 feet, then traverse 50 feet left to a ledge with some loose rocks (optional belay). Climb 10 feet, then follow a ledge up and right (poor rock) that leads through an offset in the big roof and "belay at the last crack in sight" (7, 130 feet in all). 2. Climb straight up for 20 feet (6), then cut left into a depression that runs up the middle of the slab. Climb this for a ways, then go left and belay beneath a small tree (140 feet). 3. Climb up and left across the expansive slab and belay along the south margin (2, 155 feet). 4. Move right, then climb to the south summit (2, 120 feet).

## 10.  EAST FACE 4

This route generally follows the north margin of the east face. Begin at the northeast corner of the east face, just left of a small overhang, up a slab, and out right to the edge of the face. Follow a narrow slab up the north edge of the face all the way to the summit. The gully to the left is easier but less aesthetic.

## Goose Eggs

There are several satellite rocks below the east face of the Goose referred to as the Goose Eggs. The Southern Goose Egg is the largest and the most spectacular of these, and of course is the most southerly. The Fern Canyon Trail passes very near the south side of the Southern Goose Egg and provides the quickest approach to the south and east sides of the rock. The three "eggs" farther to the north (Broken Egg, Smallest Egg and Northern Egg) are smaller and perhaps less elegant, but together form the Fern Canyon Amphitheater, which is used as a training area by various climbing schools. There are at least two eye bolts above the steep west side of the amphitheater. Only the Southern Egg is described here in detail. The other three each have easy east slab routes.

## SOUTHERN GOOSE EGG

The Southern Goose Egg, which does not resemble an egg, is a tall, slender flatiron with a vertical south face split by a ramp. Approach via the Fern Canyon Trail. Just before reaching the Slab Overlook, a footpath leads up the forested slope to the southeast corner of the rock. To descend from the north summit, move south and downclimb a short, steep wall (class 4).

## 1.  RUDE WELCOME 11B/C

This route is located just beyond the Slab Overlook and 20 yards north of the Fern Canyon Trail. Climb an overhanging wall with four bolts.

## 2.  SOUTH RAMP CLASS 4

Begin toward the right side of the south face and follow a thirty-foot-wide ramp to the south and higher summit of the Southern Goose Egg.

## 3.  POWER BACON 10A ★

FA: RICK LEITNER, BRIAN HANSON, MIKE SPAUR.

Locate a steep wall a short way right from the South Ramp. Start up and right along some cracks, then branch left and follow four bolts to a two-bolt anchor (80 feet).

**NEBEL HORN, from the northeast**

Devil's Thumb

The Slab

FERN CANYON

The Goose

Seal Rock

Harmon Cave

Bear Peak

Nebel Horn

Gnome Wall

South Pinnacle

Poot Ridge

Bear Creek Spire

Overhang Rock

Dinosaur Mountain

Harmon Cave Trail

Fern Canyon Trail

Bear Canyon Trail

Mesa Trail

Service Road

NEBEL HORN, from the east

Bear Peak

Nebel Horn

The Goose

FERN CANYON

Seal Rock

Southern Goose Egg

The Penguin

Pup

The Goose Eggs

### 4. FRUITY PEBBLES 9 ★

FA: RICK LEITNER, BRIAN HANSON, MIKE SPAUR.

Begin as for the preceding route, but continue up and right, then climb past three bolts and lower off from the same anchor. A large stopper may be placed on the initial traverse.

### 5. THE SEA AND THE MIRROR 10c

FA: DAVE CRAWFORD AND JULIE IRWIN.

Begin a short way right of the preceding routes, near the southeast corner of the Southern Goose Egg. Ascend a wall with huecos. Four bolts to a two-bolt anchor.

### 6. EAST FACE CLASS 4

Begin from the bottom of the east face and scramble 450 feet to the north summit of the Southern Goose Egg. No problem.

## THE PENGUIN

This small flatiron is located just south from bottom of Seal Rock. Approach as for the south face of Seal Rock, but continue hiking south through the trees. To escape from the summit, scramble down the east face for 50 feet, then descend grooves to the southeast.

### EAST FACE 4

Begin at the low point of the rock. Climb up and left, passing the south side of a small overhang, then stay toward the left side of the face and continue to the summit. 250 feet in all.

## SEAL ROCK

Seal Rock towers high above the trees and dominates the landscape on the northeast shoulder of the Nebel Horn. Its great east and north faces are visible from almost anywhere in Boulder and are host to some very dramatic climbing.

**Approach**—The easiest approach to any aspect of Seal Rock is via the Harmon Cave Trail; the trick is in knowing where to cut off to the south. To reach the bottom of the east face, hike past Harmon Cave and head south once in line with a huge boulder in the trees on the left (south). This approach is also useful in reaching the south face by continuing around past the bottom of the east face. To reach the north face, continue up the Harmon Cave Trail to where a steep slab rises up on the left, then hike left (south) along the base of the slab until it fades into giant talus. From this point, the north face looms above the trees and leaves little need for map and compass. Hike west a bit, then up along a faint path to the bottom of the face.

**Descent**—The easiest descent from the summit is to rappel from the bolt anchors on the route Sea of Joy. This may be done in one 60-meter plunge from the edge of the north face, about 50 feet east of the summit. One may also downclimb Shortcut: Descend the north side of the east face for 150 feet to a sloping ramp on the north face that leads to the ground. As a final option, rappel or downclimb 40 feet to the notch west of the summit, descend a big ramp to the southeast and rappel 135 feet south from an eyebolt.

## 1.   EAST FACE LEFT 4

Climb a clean slab to the left of the little flatiron (the Pup) that leans up against the main east face, work left to the south edge of the face, and continue to the summit.

## 2.   AN ARM AND A LEG 9 +

FA: JIM ERICKSON, SOLO, 1976.

This climbs an off-width crack through a roof on the north side of the Pup, the small flatiron that leans up against the lower east face.

## 3.   EAST FACE RIGHT 4 ★

A Flatiron classic that combines solid rock with exhilarating exposure. Begin at the low point of the east face and follow its far right (north) edge all the way to the summit. About two-thirds of the way up, Shortcut leads off north into the trees – a convenient escape if needed. The angle steepens above this point and the best climbing on the route is encountered. Stay hard to the right edge, or work left about 30 feet and climb a beautiful, 100-foot long finger crack (2) to the final slabs.

## 4.   SHORTCUT 4 ★

FA: (?) R. ROSSITER, SOLO, 1988.

This is the easiest way to reach the summit. Approach as for the north face of Seal Rock. Walk left (east) beneath the high, vertical aspect of the north face until it is possible to scramble up and left onto the north edge of the east face.

## 5.   SEA OF JOY 13A A0 ★

FA: RICHARD AND JOYCE ROSSITER, 1988. REDPOINT: ANDY DONSON, 1999

Follow eight bolts up the massive grey slab in the middle of the north face and belay on a narrow ledge (11b, 90 feet). 2. Turn a large, diagonal roof and gain a sling belay from two bolts (5 bolts, 11b, 40 feet). 3. Follow eight bolts up the daunting head wall to a two-bolt anchor at the top of the face (13a, 60 feet).

## 6.   ARCHEOPTERYX 11D VS ★

FA: JEFF ACHEY AND ROGER BRIGGS, 1982.

Archeopteryx ascends the right side of the hanging headwall about 30 feet to the right of Sea of Joy. Begin at the bottom of the north face at the same spot as Sea of Joy. 1. Work up and right along a lichen-covered ramp (6) to where it fades out by a small tree and belay. 2. Make unprotected moves (9s) up and left to broken strata (10b/c), then up and right (8) to a belay stance with a bolt or pin, 120 feet overall. 3. Climb up and left to the apex of a massive roof (strenuous 11b/c). Turn the roof (11a), then go up and left to a good stance with two drilled baby angles at the base of the hanging headwall (40 feet). 4. Start up and left (10d), then work up and right along a wide, shallow groove (11d vs, 20 feet above pro), and finally, straight up (10d s) to the summit (80 feet). Supposedly, some protection is possible along the upper part of the lead.

## 7. SOUTH FACE 4

FA: CORWIN SIMMONS AND DAVE HUSBANDS, 1959.

Begin beneath some junipers that are 20 feet above the ground. Climb up and right for 50 feet and belay. Continue up and right to a wide trough or ramp. Follow the ramp up and left to the summit.

## OVERHANG ROCK

Overhang Rock is located just above the Bear Canyon Trail on the north slope of the Nebel Horn. This narrow, serrated crag has a very impressive west face with several excellent sport climbs. The steep and narrow north face has a single and rather fierce route. The south end of the rock culminates in a lower summit called the South Spire.

**Approach**—Hike the Bear Canyon Trail until across from Stonehenge (see Dinosaur Mountain), then break off to the south and follow a steep path that leads to the talus field beneath the west face. To reach the South Spire, hike to the top of the Harmon Cave Trail, then hike downhill to the north.

**Descent**—To escape from the main summit, make a 135-foot rappel southeast to the ground. Or rappel 60 feet into the notch below the South Summit, and again from a tree to the ground.

**SEAL ROCK**
3. East Face Right 4 ★
4. Shortcut 4 ★
5. Sea of Joy 13a ★
6. Archeopteryx 11d vs ★

Roger Briggs and Pat Adams on *Sea of Joy* (5.13a), Seal Rock. Photo by Richard Rossiter.

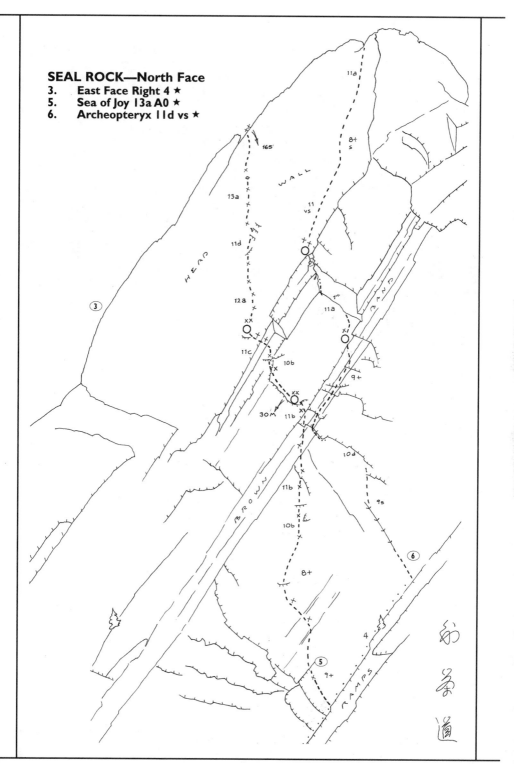

## SEAL ROCK—North Face
3.  East Face Right 4 ★
5.  Sea of Joy 13a A0 ★
6.  Archeopteryx 11d vs ★

**NEBEL HORN,
from the north**

The Goose

Seal Rock

Harmon Cave

Nebel Horn Summit

Gnome Wall

Poot Ridge

South Pinnacle

Overhang Rock

## 1. ROGUE'S ARÊTE 10A s ★

FA: LAYTON KOR AND PAT AMENT, 1963.

This route ascends the narrow north face in two pitches and would likely be popular but for a general lack of protection. Begin from broken ledges at the bottom of the face. 1. Lieback up a strenuous dihedral to a stance on the right side of the face. Step left, then diagonal up to the right and climb the arête to a narrow stance with a bolt. 2. Traverse six feet left, then diagonal up and right on slightly loose rock, lie back up a flake, then diagonal about 35 feet up and right to the top of the face

## 2. SNAKE WATCHING 13A ★

FA: JIM SURETTE.

Begin beneath an overhang at far left side of the west face. 150 feet, 15 bolts. This route has a two-bolt anchor at 80 feet and can be done in two pitches.

## 3. TITS OUT FOR THE LADS 12B ★

FA: JIM SURETTE AND GREG MCCAUSLAND, 1988.

This is the left of three bolt routes in the middle of the west face. Proceed from a ledge 30 feet above the talus that is formed by a huge flake. Seven bolts, 80 feet.

## 4. THE BIG PICTURE 12A ★

FA: DAN MICHAEL AND PAUL PIANA, 1987

This is the middle of three routes that begin atop a huge flake midway along the base of the west face. Eight bolts, 80 feet.

## 5. MISSING LINK 12B/C ★

FA: CHRISTIAN BAROODY, BC HANEY, 1989.

Begin up on the big flake, 20 feet right of The Big Picture. Follow six bolts to a two-bolt anchor.

Jimmy Surrette on his route *Snake Watching* (5.13a), Overhang Rock. Photo by Dan Hare.

### 6. SHORT ATTENTION SPAN 11D ★

FA: KEN TROUT, STEVE STUBBLEFIELD.

Begin a short way right of the big block at the bottom of the wall, about 20 feet right of Missing Link. Six bolts to a two-bolt anchor, 55 feet.

### 7. JUNIOR ACHIEVEMENT 8

FA: BOB CORMACK AND DAN VASICEK, 1972.

Begin 200 feet up and right from The Big Picture, at the farthest left of a series of broken right-facing dihedrals. Scramble up to the right of a small buttress and rig a belay in funky rock. Move up and left through a bulge (6) and belay at the base of an overhanging, right-facing dihedral. Climb straight up the dihedral (crux), then angle up and right to a belay on the scenic summit ridge. To avoid the overhanging dihedral, climb a clean slab to the right and follow the next dihedral system (A Chorus Line) to the summit.

### 8. A CHORUS LINE 9

FA: MIKE BROOKS AND ASSOCIATES, 1984.

Begin in a dihedral system 50 feet right of Junior Achievement. Look for a bolt at an overhang about 60 feet up. The upper part of this route is loose and poorly protected.

### 9. SHIBBOLETH 8

FA: MIKE BROOKS AND ASSOCIATES, c. 1984.

Climb the second dihedral to the right from Junior Achievement.

### 10. WEST SIDE (STORY) 6

Begin about 30 feet to the right of Shibboleth. Climb past a tree to an indistinct right-facing corner system. Reach the summit ridge in two pitches.

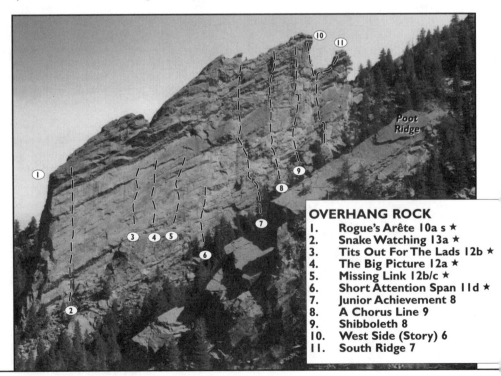

**OVERHANG ROCK**

1. Rogue's Arête 10a s ★
2. Snake Watching 13a ★
3. Tits Out For The Lads 12b ★
4. The Big Picture 12a ★
5. Missing Link 12b/c ★
6. Short Attention Span 11d ★
7. Junior Achievement 8
8. A Chorus Line 9
9. Shibboleth 8
10. West Side (Story) 6
11. South Ridge 7

**OVERHANG ROCK—West Face**
1. Rogue's Arête 10a s ★
2. Snake Watching 13a ★
3. Tits Out For The Lads 12b ★
4. The Big Picture 12a ★
5. Missing Link 12b/c ★
6. Short Attention Span 11d ★
7. Junior Achievement 8
8. A Chorus Line 9
9. Shibboleth 8
10. West Side (Story) 6
11. South Ridge 7

## 11. SOUTH RIDGE 7
FA: JIM ERICKSON, SOLO, 1976.
This route ascends the south ridge of the south summit and was first done as a descent!

## 12. EAST SIDE 6
Begin on the east side of the crag, beneath the notch between the two summits. Climb a crack system on the right (easy) or lieback up a flake (7) to the notch. From here, climb the steep south wall of the main peak past two pitons, traverse right after about 30 feet and finish with an easy groove.

## 13. SOUTH SPIRE 4
Reach the notch between the two summits as described above, then climb an easy pitch to the top of the pinnacle.

# POOT RIDGE

Poot Ridge is the long, narrow spine of rock west of Overhang Rock and across Bear Creek from Stonehenge. The low (north) end of the ridge forms a steep buttress that is ascended by a single route, Shoot to Thrill. The east side is low-angle and brushy, but the west side is steep and has a few routes. The upper part of the ridge fades into the trees, then rises up again, even higher, with a steep and smooth west face called Gnome Wall.

## 1. SHOOT TO THRILL 12A ★
FA: PAUL GLOVER AND HANK CAYLOR, 1987.
To reach this route, hike the Bear Canyon Trail until across the stream from Stonehenge. Then, head up to the south through trees and talus to the base of the buttress. The route is easily identified by a line of bolts. Crux is at the sixth bolt. Six bolts to a two-bolt anchor.

## 2. ROCKABYE 12A
FA: PAT ADAMS, TODD BIBLER, GREG DAVIS.
This route is located around to the left from Stoned Operation and on the same big block. Three bolts to a two-bolt anchor.

## 3. STONED OPERATION 12A ★
FA: MIKE DOWNING AND PAUL GLOVER, 1987.
This steep route is on the west face of a large, freestanding block about 100 yards up along the west face of Poot Ridge. Four bolts with the crux at the second. Lower off from two bolts.

# Gnome Wall

This is the highest section of Poot Ridge, though it is completely separated from the lower section by a wide gap. All known routes ascend the super-clean west face.

**Approach**— To reach Gnome Wall, hike to the top of Harmon Cave Trail and angle southwest over talus toward an indistinct break in Poot Ridge. When the main summit of Overhang Rock is directly in line with NCAR, you are at the right point along the ridge. Scramble up through the notch, then up to the south along the west side of the ridge for about 200 feet. This area may also be approached from Bear Canyon via the broad talus gully between Overhang Rock and Poot Ridge. Gnome Wall is about a 15 minute hike from The Big Picture.

## 4. DARK FOREST 11B
FA: TRIPP COLLINS, MARK HANNA, NANCEY DOUGLAS, 1989.
Begin from a narrow ledge along the left side of a very smooth wall. Climb a left-angling seam with a fixed pin and descend from two bolts near the top.

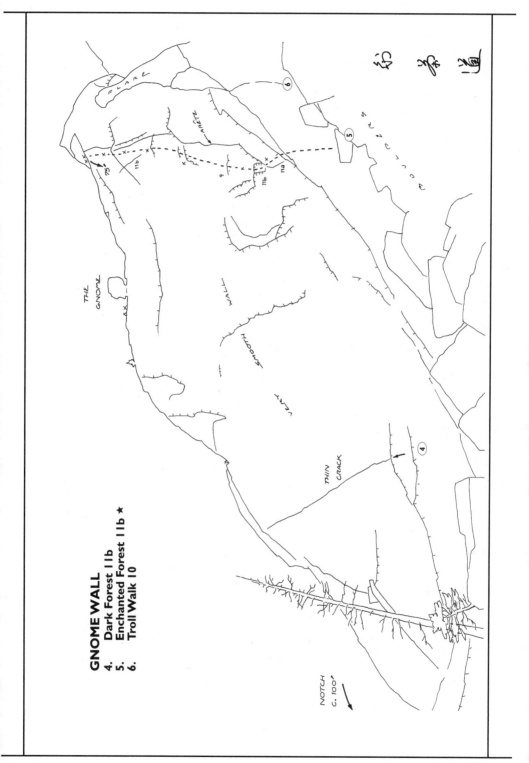

**GNOME WALL**
4. Dark Forest 11b
5. Enchanted Forest 11b ★
6. Troll Walk 10

NOTCH
C. 100'

### 5. ENCHANTED FOREST 11B ★

FA: RICHARD AND JOYCE ROSSITER AND ROB WOOLF, 1988.

Begin just left of a blunt arête, toward the right side of the flat west face. The crux is in turning the initial bulge and getting stood up on a pedestal, but other challenging moves are encountered near the top. Stick clip the first bolt. Six bolts to a two-bolt anchor (75 feet).

### 6. TROLL WALK 10

Begin up and right from Enchanted Forest. Climb a big detached flake and continue to the crest of the ridge.

## GIANT BOULDERS

The talus field west of Poot Ridge is peppered with gigantic boulders. The following routes have been climbed on a 30-foot-high block some 200 feet west from Stoned Operation. A single ring bolt was placed to toprope each route. FA: Paul Piana, Bret Ruckman, 1988.

### 1. BIG IF YER NOT 12c TR

This is the left of two routes. Climb a steep right-facing dihedral on the north side of the block.

### 2. JAP EL CAP 12a TR

Climb a diagonal crack/seam right of the preceding route.

## THE SANCTUARY

The Sanctuary is the next rock rib west of Poot Ridge. The bottom of the rib forms a steep, north-facing buttress with several toprope problems developed by Christian Griffith during 1986. Approach via the Bear Canyon Trail. Once below the bottom of the farthest west ridge of Dinosaur Mountain, break off to the south and hike about 20 yards up to the objective. Long runners around trees serve as anchors above the overhanging wall.

### 1. LOVE 12B ★

Start at the easiest point along the left side of the wall. Climb up to an arête, step right and continue to the to of the wall.

### 2. FIRE 12D ★

Climb the face just right of the Love arête. Make a long reach between two holes and finish with desperate thin edges. One may also reach the arête of Love from Fire by moving left at the first finger hole (12c).

### 3. SANCTUARY 12B/C ★

Climb the black streak to the right of Fire via pebbles and holes

## SOUTH PINNACLE

Some 300 feet straight west from Gnome Wall a curious finger of rock protrudes into space at an unlikely angle. A short scramble along its upper side brings one to the very airy summit. Once on top, its hard to believe that the whole thing isn't going to tip over with you, but the view of Bear Canyon and Dinosaur Mountain is grand.

Joyce Rossiter on *Enchanted Forest* (5.11b), Gnome Wall.
Photo by Richard Rossiter.

GREEN MOUNTAIN
from Chautauqua
Meadows

# PART II. GREEN MOUNTAIN

The boundary of Boulder Mountain Park encloses four large forested peaks. They are, from south to north: Boulder Mountain (8549 feet), Green Mountain (8144 feet), Flagstaff Mountain (6950 feet) and Mount Sanitas (6879 feet). From Downtown and the University area, Green Mountain is the most prominent of these and presents the Flatiron backdrop for which the city of Boulder is famous. The broad east face of Green Mountain features a vast array of slabs and towers that may be described in several terrain groups: Dinosaur Mountain at the southeast corner, the primitive Skunk Canyon, the Central Flatirons or Royal Arch area, the Bluebell Canyon/Third Flatiron area, and the First and Second Flatirons on the northeast shoulder. The Gregory Canyon Amphitheater area is located at the northeast corner of Green Mountain, and the west-facing Sacred Cliffs are located along the high-flying south ridge.

**Mesa Trail**—This important trail runs north and south for 6.9 miles between Chautauqua Park and Eldorado Springs and provides a link in the approach to many of the crags on Green Mountain. See Mesa Trail under Boulder Mountain.

**Bear Canyon Trail**— Bear Canyon climbs west between the north slope of Bear Peak and the south slope of Green Mountain. There are several ways to reach the Bear Canyon Trail: Hike the NCAR Trail to the Mesa Trail, then continue south to a gravel service road in lower Bear Canyon. This point may be reached from a different trailhead: From Broadway, go west on Table Mesa Drive, left on Lehigh Street, right on Bear Mountain Drive, right again on Stoney Hill Road, and park at a cul de sac. Walk northwest through a wooden gate, cross Bear Creek, and gain the gravel service road on the opposite bank. This service road may also be reached from a trailhead along Bear Mountain Drive or from Wildwood Road (off Bear Mountain Drive).

The unpaved service road crosses Bear Creek just below the deep upper section of the canyon. At this point a poor trail breaks off along the north side of the creek and may be followed past Bear Creek Spire and Stonehenge until it intersects the main Bear Canyon Trail after a half mile or so. To reach the regular beginning to the Bear Canyon Trail, continue walking south along the service road (which, in this section, is also the Mesa Trail) past two broad switchbacks, to a junction on the right beneath some power lines. The Bear Canyon Trail proceeds west from here. After about a half mile the trail enters the bottom of the canyon and crosses to the north side of the stream. From this section of the trail, one may reach any of the gullies that climb northwest between the prominent rock ribs (strata) on Dinosaur Mountain.

**Mallory Cave Trail**—A useful approach to east side crags of Dinosaur Mountain is the Mallory Cave Trail, which climbs southwest from the Mesa Trail at its south junction with the NCAR Trail. The trail passes Square Rock , then climbs beneath the north face of Dinosaur Rock followed by Der Zerkle, Der Freischutz and The Hand. The trail ends beneath the Finger Flatiron, whence a short scramble leads up a groove to Mallory Cave.

**The Hand Corridor**— This rugged trail leads to the small cirque or cove between Der Freischutz and The Hand on Dinosaur Mountain. The Hand Corridor breaks left from the Mallory Cave Trail at the southeast corner of The Hand, just past a ten-foot-tall pillar of red rock (on the right) and ascends the wooded gully (corridor) between the north face of Der Freischutz and The Hand.

**The Box Trail**— This signed and manufactured trail breaks right from the Mallory Cave Trail just before its end beneath the Finger Flatiron. The Box Trail enters the gully between the Finger Flatiron and the Red Devil (Box Alley) and climbs past the south side of The Box. Near the saddle west of The Box, the trail climbs southwest into Second Gully (the long talus gully between the Second and Third Strata on Dinosaur Mountain).

**Porch Alley**— This trail ascends the forested gully between the Front Porch and the Veranda on Dinosaur Mountain and continues without significant interruption to the notch between Fum and Dum (Fum-Dum Col). It may be used to reach the Front Porch, the Lost Porch, the Back Porch, the Dreadnaught Flatiron and Dum. Hike the Mallory Cave Trail for 300 feet (150 feet past a brushy draw), then break right and follow a narrow trail (Porch Alley) northwest back into the draw. The trail passes beneath the south side of the Front Porch and the Lost Porch, then continues to the bottom of the Back Porch and up along its south side. Veer left and follow the path uphill (south) to the saddle above The Box, then go west around the north side of Fum and gain the Fum-Dum Col.

**Skunk Canyon Trail**—This primitive but wonderful trail climbs westward into the lost world of Skunk Canyon and leads to the summit of Green Mountain. The trail begins from a westward switchback in the Mesa Trail about 200 yards from the north junction of the NCAR Trail and several switchbacks north from the crossing of Skunk Creek. This is not yet an "official" trail and should not be confused with the lower Skunk Canyon Trail that begins from Deer Valley Road and climbs west to the Mesa Trail. This upper Skunk Canyon Trail is the only way to reach crags on the north side of Dinosaur Mountain as well as the big ridges on the north side of Skunk Canyon. The trail follows Skunk Creek past Ridge Four, then climbs along the west side of the ridge to a saddle and continues to the summit of Green Mountain...a splendid hike.

**Royal Arch Trail**— This popular trail begins just south of Bluebell Shelter. It winds up Bluebell canyon beneath the Third Flatiron, then climbs to Sentinel Pass, and continues south to reach a natural bridge called the Royal Arch in 0.9 mile.

**Bluebell Canyon Trail**—This trail is used to reach Approach III for the Third Flatiron, the Ironing Boards and the Eyes of the Canyon. Hike the Royal Arch Trail to the point where it begins to climb southward out of Bluebell Canyon. At the first switchback to the left is a large boulder with a painted sign that reads, "Royal Arch" with an arrow pointing left. Break right and follow a secondary trail until it fades beneath the West Ironing Board.

**Tangen Tunnel Route**— Hike the Royal Arch Trail to Tangen Spring, then break west and hike directly upslope to the gap between Lower Tangen Tower and the Fourth Flatiron. Huge chockstones appear to block the way, but the route continues around and beneath them to the wooded gully above. Hike southwest staying left of Schmoe's Nose and gain the crest of the southeast ridge of Green Mountain just north of the Hippo Head. Hike along the crest of the ridge over a false summit and pick up the Greenman Trail on the far side. Turn left on the trail and reach the summit of Green Mountain within a quarter mile.

**Woods Quarry Trail**— This trail breaks off to the right (north) from the Mesa Trail at the junction with the Enchanted Mesa Trail (about 0.5 mile from Bluebell Shelter area) and leads to Woods Quarry within 0.5 mile. An old spur of this trail heads back to the north about 100 feet north of the quarry and leads around to the Mesa Trail. This old spur is unsigned, but well established.

**South Woods Quarry Trail**— This trail begins from the south side of Woods Quarry and leads up the Tangen Spring drainage to intersect the Royal Arch Trail 150 feet south of Sentinel Pass.

**Sentinel Crest Trail**— This footpath runs between Woods Quarry and Sentinel Pass (on the Royal Arch Trail) and passes beneath the north side of the Sentinel Boulders. The path breaks west from Tomato Rock Trail about 200 feet south of Woods Quarry.

**Tomato Rock Trail**— Use this trail to reach a huge, rounded boulder called Tomato Rock, Woods Quarry and the Sentinel Crest Trail. The trail (an old road) begins a short way southeast of the Mesa Trail-McClintock Trail junction and goes west to Tomato Rock, then bends around to the south and joins the Woods Quarry Trail just north of Woods Quarry.

**Enchanted Mesa Trail**— This trail follows an old dirt road from Chautauqua Park (behind the auditorium) and intersects the Mesa Trail at the beginning of the Woods Quarry Trail. One may also begin from a trail head at the top of Mariposa Street. Mariposa runs east and west, two blocks south of Baseline Road.

**McClintock Nature Trail**— This trail begins as for Enchanted Mesa, but branches right and follows the south rim of Bluebell Canyon to the Mesa Trail in 0.7 mile.

**Kinnikinnic Road**— This paved service road (closed to cars) leads from Chautauqua Park to Bluebell Shelter and provides access to several important trails including the Mesa Trail.

**Bluebell Mesa**— This trial runs between Kinnikinic Road and the Bluebell-Baird Trail. It is parallel to and a short way south of the Chautauqua Trail.

**Chautauqua Trail**— This important trail begins just west of the ranger station in Chautauqua Park and leads southwest toward the First Flatiron where it joins the Bluebell-Baird Trail after 0.6 mile. To reach the First Flatiron Trail or Bluebell Shelter, go left on the Bluebell-Baird Trail.

**Bluebell-Baird Trail**— This trail runs between the Bluebell Shelter area and Gregory Canyon. It is used as a link to reach the First and Second Flatirons Trail.

**Third Flatiron Trail**— This official climber's trail begins from the service road just southwest of Bluebell Shelter. It heads west, then curves around to the south. After about 150 yards, it crosses a shallow draw. About 15 yards east of the draw, make a sharp right turn onto the new Third Flatiron Trail. About 30 yards after the trail crosses a talus field, the Second Flatiron Trail branches off to the right. About 50 yards beyond that junction, a left branch in the trail cuts across a second talus field and leads to the East Bench of the Third Flatiron. The main trail continues steeply beneath the north face of the Third Flatiron and leads to the West Bench.

**First and Second Flatirons Trail**—This official climber's trail leads to the very base of the First Flatiron, then works up along the south edge of the face to the col between the First and Second Flatirons. A left branch after about the first 100 yards leads to the low point of the Second Flatiron and on around to the north to join the Third Flatiron Trail. The First Flatiron Trail cuts off to the west from the Bluebell-Baird Trail about midway between Bluebell Shelter and the junction with the Chautauqua Trail, which is to say, about 50 yards from either one.

**Spy Express**— This short trail goes north from the bottom of the First Flatiron, beneath the First Flatironette and ends at the foot of a small pinnacle called The Spy in 0.1 mile.

**Amphitheater Trail**— This trail begins from a small parking area in the bottom of Gregory Canyon, just off Baseline Road where it begins to climb up Flagstaff Mountain. The trail crosses a bridge and intersects the Bluebell Baird Trail, then climbs around behind the Amphitheater (climbing area) and ends at the Saddle Rock Trail.

Green Mountain Summit

The Thing

Third Flatiron

Second Flatiron

First Flatiron

Woods Quarry

BLUEBELL CANYON

Spy

Willy B

**Amphitheater Express**—This trail branches right from the Amphitheater Trail, passes beneath the north face of the Amphitheater, then continues past the west side to rejoin the Amphitheater Trail.

**Gregory Canyon Trail**—This trail runs west from the parking area in lower Gregory Canyon, past a junction with the Saddle Rock Trail, to a service road that connects with Flagstaff Road and the Ranger Trail.

**Saddle Rock Trail**—This trail branches left from the Gregory Canyon Trail after about 0.25 mile and climbs past a junction with the Amphitheater Trail to an overlook at Saddle Rock. It then continues to a junction with the Greenman Trail high on the north slope of Green Mountain.

**E.M. Greenman**—This trail branches left (east) from the Ranger Trail 0.3 mile above Greenman Lodge and continues to the summit of Green Mountain.

**Ranger Trail**—Park at Realization Point, 3.0 miles up Flagstaff Road. Find the trail down a dirt service road on the south side of Flagstaff Road. The trail follows the dirt road south to Greenman Lodge, then climbs to the summit of Green Mountain.

**Green Mountain West Ridge**—Park at a marked trailhead where Flagstaff Road leaves the western boundary of Boulder Mountain Park. The trail goes east along a wooded ridge and intersects the Ranger Trail a short way from the summit of Green Mountain. This trail provides access to the south ridge of Green Mountain and the Sacred Cliffs area.

# THE FLATIRONS OF GREEN MOUNTAIN

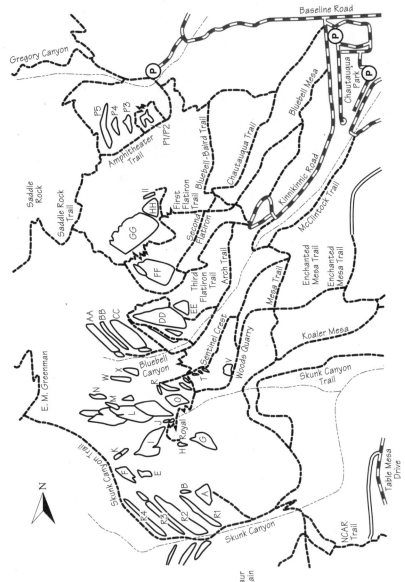

# THE FLATIRONS OF GREEN MOUNTAIN

## Skunk Canyon Ridges

R1 Ridge One
R2 Ridge Two
R3 Ridge Three
R4 Ridge Four

## Central Flatirons

A Hillbilly
B Hobo
E Hourglass
F Hippo Head
G The Regency
H Royal Arch
I Fifth Flatiron
J Tangen Towers
K Schmoe's Nose
L Fourth Flatiron
M Green Mountain Pinnacle
N The Spaceship
O Fourth Flatironette
R Hammerhead
S Tow Move Rock
T Sentinel Boulders
U Lost Sentinels
V Woods Quarry

W Willy B
X The Thing
Y Eyes Of The Canyon

## Third Flatiron Area

AA West Ironing Board
BB The Fin
CC East Ironing Board
DD Third Flatiron
EE Third Flatironette
FF Second Flatiron
GG First Flatiron
HH First Flatironette
II The Spy

## Gregory Canyon Crags

P1 First Pinnacle
P2 Second Pinnacle
P3 Third Pinnacle
P4 Fourth Pinnacle
P5 Fifth Pinnacle
P Parking

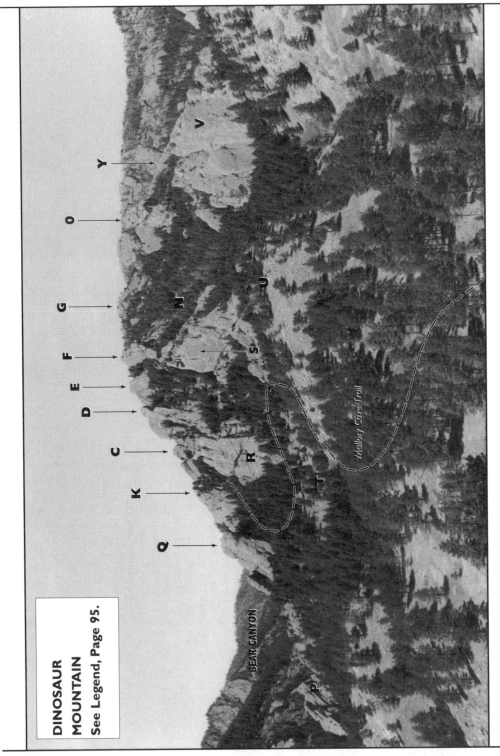

DINOSAUR
MOUNTAIN
See Legend, Page 95.

BEAR CANYON

Mallory Cave Trail

92

# DINOSAUR MOUNTAIN

Dinosaur Mountain (7360 feet) rises majestically between Bear Canyon and Skunk Canyon and forms one of the most beautiful and complex aspects of the Boulder Range. Viewed from the east, the topography presents such a perplexing array of towers, fins, and gullies as to defy familiarization. But from vantages to the south, the crags of Dinosaur Mountain are seen to conform with four tilted strata of rock that run in orderly fashion, north and south across the mountain. The four great ridges on the north slope of Skunk Canyon are formed by these same four strata or ribs. There is another less distinct stratum just east of the main four that gives rise to the Front Porch on Dinosaur Mountain, and further north, to Hillbilly Rock. The west side of Dinosaur Mountain is connected to the south ridge of Green Mountain by a broad saddle that is open to the south and heavily forested on the Skunk Canyon Side.

The most popular feature on Dinosaur Mountain is Mallory Cave, which lies near the middle of the east face between The Hand and the Finger Flatiron and is approached by a good trail. As for climbing, the mountain offers fine slab routes on the east faces of most features and excellent sport climbs on the steeper planes. It is a pleasure just wandering through the maze of towers and small flatirons, going from one route to another.

## Trails

To reach the east side of Dinosaur Mountain, take Table Mesa Drive to NCAR and hike the NCAR Trail west to its junction with the Mesa Trail. The Mesa Trail runs north and south along the east side of the mountain and provides a link in the approach to many of the crags. See Mallory Cave Trail and Porch Alley. The south side of Dinosaur Mountain is most easily reached from Bear Canyon. See Bear Canyon Trail.

## Dinosaur Mountain Route

This interesting route is a combination of several trails and is used to reach the summit of Dinosaur Mountain. Hike the NCAR Trail to the Mesa Trail and continue west on the Mallory Cave Trail. From the top of the Mallory Cave Trail, branch right on The Box Trail and gain the saddle above The Box. Follow a footpath west, passing around the north side of Fum, and gain the Fum-Dum Col. Scramble west into the Bowling Alley and hike north to the saddle just east of the summit of Dinosaur Mountain. A short scramble leads to the very top. The Balanced Rock of Dum lies 150 feet to the east. The Dinosaur Mountain Route can be combined with the following route to create a loop.

## Southwest Slope Route

This route leads to the summit of Dinosaur Mountain from Bear Canyon. Hike the NCAR Trail to the Mesa Trail, then go south to the service road in Bear Canyon. Continue south on the service road (Mesa Trail) and gain the Bear Canyon Trail, then follow it west, 100 yards past the crossing of Bear Creek. Leave the trail and hike up the broad grassy slope west of the South Ridge to within 100 yards of the saddle at its top. Scramble east through a break in the South Ridge and enter the Bowling Alley, then hike to a zenned-out saddle just east of the highest point and climb easily to the top of Dinosaur Mountain (Class 3). It is also possible, though less pleasant, to hike the entire Bowling Alley from Bear Creek.

Note: Crags are listed from south to north along each of the five strata, beginning with the westernmost in Bear Canyon and working east. Crags accessed from Skunk Canyon are listed from left to right across the north slope of Dinosaur Mountain. Routes on each crag are listed from left to right.

# DINOSAUR MOUNTAIN AND SKUNK CANYON

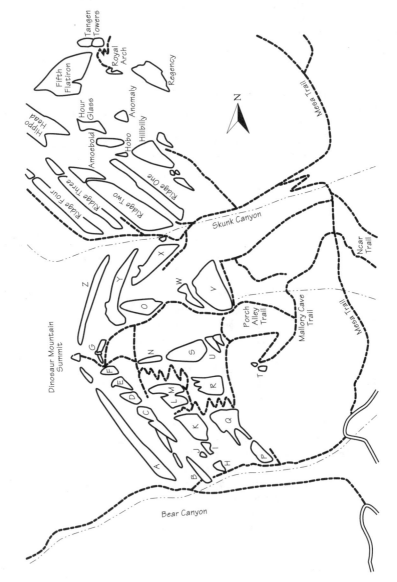

## LEGEND

A   South Ridge
B   Stonehenge
C   Fee
D   Fi
E   Fo
F   Fum
G   Dum
H   Southern Dinosaur Egg
I   Northern Dinosaur Egg
J   The Bubble
K   Der Freischutz
L   The Hand
M   Finger Flatiron
N   The Box
O   Back Porch
P   Bear Creek Spire
Q   Dinosaur Rock
R   Der Zerkle
S   Red Devil
T   Square Rock
U   Veranda
V   Front Porch
W   Lost Porch
X   Achean Pronouncement
Y   Dreadnaught
Z   North Ridge

## Skunk Canyon Ridges

R1   Ridge One
R2   Ridge Two
R3   Ridge Three
R4   Ridge Four

DINOSAUR
MOUNTAIN,
from the south
See Legend, Page 95.

Summit

South Ridge

96

DINOSAUR
MOUNTAIN,
from the south
See Legend, Page 95.

97

DINOSAUR MOUNTAIN, from the southeast
See Legend, Page 95.

Green Mountain Summit

BEAR CANYON

## FOURTH STRATUM

The fourth stratum of rock is the farthest west and runs without significant interruption from Bear Creek to Skunk Creek and includes the summit of Dinosaur Mountain. The Bear Canyon side of the stratum is called the South Ridge and the Skunk Canyon side is called the North Ridge. The long talus gully east of the South Ridge is called the Bowling Alley or Third Gully.

### South Ridge

Several routes have been climbed low on the west side of the Fourth Stratum. From the point where the Bear Canyon Trail crosses to the north side of the creek, continue about 100 yards west. Leave the trail and hike 150 yards up the slope below the southwest face of the rib. Look for two bolt routes in the vicinity of a large juniper tree.

### 1.   MEGASAURUS 10D ★
FA: Dan Hare and Mike Downing, 1987.

Locate a line of four bolts on a "bubbled wall" near a large juniper and 20 feet left of Liquid Crystal. Lower off from a two-bolt anchor above and between this and the following route.

### 2.   LIQUID CRYSTAL 11C ★
FA: Downing and Hare, 1988.

Climb past five bolts about 20 feet right of Megasaurus. Crux is at second bolt.

### 3.   JUST ANOTHER PITCH 8
FA: Ron and Cathy Lenz, 1988.

Climb a crack about 30 feet to the right of Liquid Crystal.

### 4.   BARELY THERE 9
FA: Jim Erickson, solo, 1976.

The exact location of this route is not known. Begin 200 feet above the stream. Climb a tight, overhanging chimney and a right-facing dihedral.

## THIRD STRATUM

The following crags lie along the third rock stratum on Dinosaur Mountain, including Stonehenge in Bear Canyon and the small flatirons called Fee, Fi, Fo, and Fum. The Dreadnaught in Skunk Canyon is part of the same stratum.

### FUMBLEDEEDUM CLASS 4 ★

An offset in the west side of the Third Stratum creates a long ramp that begins in Bear Canyon as a separate rib and merges along the west side of Fee. The ramp continues northwest past various caves and cruxes and eventually tops out at the Fum-Dum Col. From the col, descend west into the Bowling Alley and hike to the saddle just east of the summit of Dinosaur Mountain. A short scramble leads to the very top.

## STONEHENGE

The Third Stratum begins from Bear Creek as an extremely clean, narrow buttress that climbs to the north for about 200 feet, then ends abruptly in a stand of trees. The huge boulder called The Bubble is nearby to the northeast, and the south ridge of Fee lies a stones throw to the northwest. Several fine routes have been established on this formation. Approach via the Bear Canyon Trail. The clean south face is visible through the trees to the north just before the trail crosses the creek. One may drop down to the bottom at this point or walk back to the east from the crossing.

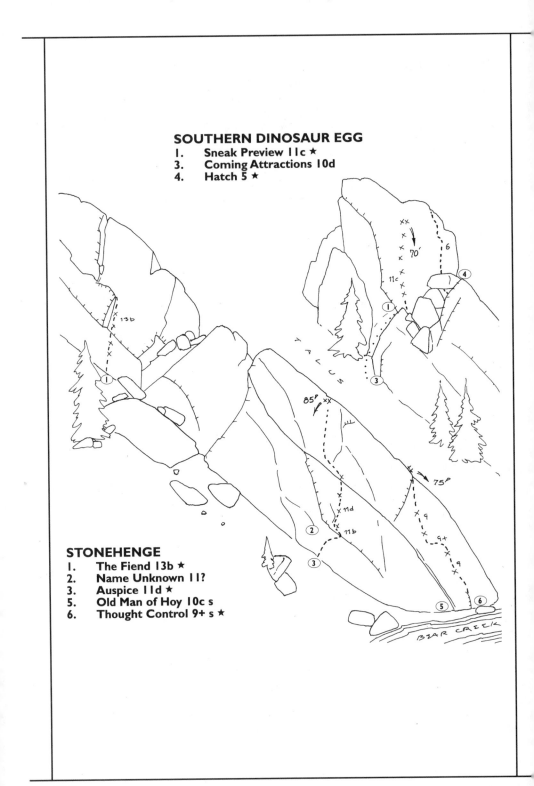

**SOUTHERN DINOSAUR EGG**
1.     **Sneak Preview 11c ★**
3.     **Coming Attractions 10d**
4.     **Hatch 5 ★**

**STONEHENGE**
1.     **The Fiend 13b ★**
2.     **Name Unknown 11?**
3.     **Auspice 11d ★**
5.     **Old Man of Hoy 10c s**
6.     **Thought Control 9+ s ★**

## 1.   THE FIEND 13B ★
FA: DAN MICHAEL, 1987.
Find this route on the west face, 150 feet above the creek. Climb a yellow, right-facing, right-leaning dihedral above an overhang. Four bolts and a pin. Bring a #1/2 Friend or equivalent TCU.

## 2.   NAME UNKNOWN 11?
Begin as for Auspice, then break left and follow three bolts up a left-facing dihedral.

## 3.   AUSPICE 11D ★
FA: DAN MICHAEL, 1987.
Begin along the southwest face, 30 or 40 feet above the creek. Turn a clean roof and follow four bolts up the left side of a smooth wall, then move left and continue up easier rock (no pro) to a bolt anchor on the crest of the rib (85 feet).

## 4.   NAME UNKNOWN 12?
The face has been climbed about 12 feet right of Auspice. Look for an old ring bolt.

## 5.   OLD MAN OF HOY 10C S
FA: PAT AMENT AND RICK ACCOMAZZO, 1981 (FIRST PITCH). FA: RICK ACCOMAZZO AND DAN HARE, 1981 (SECOND PITCH).
Begin at the left (west) edge of the south face, 10 feet to the left of Thought Control. Follow a crack/groove up onto the southwest face, cross Auspice and belay at a flake with a 1.5-inch crack (10). Angle up and left in a wide open book that leads to the top of the rib (10).

## 6.   THOUGHT CONTROL 9+ S ★
FA: DAN MICHAEL, 1987.
Begin at the bottom the south face, along the bank of Bear Creek. Work up and left into the middle of the face, make a hairy traverse left, then climb straight up and around the right side of a roof. Four bolts to a two-bolt anchor (70 feet). During the early 1980s Charlie Fowler climbed a route called Measure For Measure that may be the same line as Thought Control.

## 7.   MOUNTAINEER'S ROUTE 4
Begin just above the stream at the lowest point of the east face. Climb the east face just right of the south face and gain the crest of the rib. Follow the narrow arête to the bolt anchor above Auspice and belay (140 feet). Continue up the arête to the summit of Stonehenge. A short downclimb leads back to the gully between Stonehenge and the Southern Dinosaur Egg.

# FEE

Fee is the lowest and farthest south of the four tooth-like flatirons along the Third Stratum. Fee lies due west of Der Freischutz and is approached in the same manner as Fi (below). To descend from the summit, downclimb the short north ridge.

## 1.   SOUTH RIDGE 4
FA: GERRY ROACH, 1982.
This long route is best approached from Bear Canyon. Hike the Bear Canyon Trail to where it first crosses the Bear Creek, then head up the gully between the Second and Third Ribs and find the toe of the south ridge just above an enormous boulder called The Bubble. Climb without difficulty for several hundred feet to a rounded false summit. Drop into a chimney and work out onto the east face, then head for the top. The summit offers unique views of the Finger Flatiron, The Hand, and Der Freischutz.

## 2.   EAST FACE 5 S ★
FA: ROSSITER, SOLO, 1988.
Begin across the gully from Der Freischutz and find a break in the low overhang that runs across the bottom of the face. Climb a clean red slab to the false summit. Cross the notch and continue to the top.

## FI

Fi is the next flatiron north of Fee and is straight west of the Sharks Fin. Fi has a dramatic profile from the summits of Der Freischutz or the Finger Flatiron and its steep, smooth east face beckons the climber.

**Approach**—Hike the Mallory Cave Trail past the bottom of Der Freischutz, then take The Hand Corridor trail to the alcove between Der Freischutz and The Hand. Scramble west over some boulders into the long gully between the Second and Third Strata. Fee lies due west. The next rock to the right is Fi. Some hueco-type bouldering is available on the steep south face, just around from the low point of the east face.

**Descent**—To descend from the summit, make a short rappel into the huge chimney between Fi and Fo and downclimb the remainder of this feature (2) to the long gully just west of the Finger Flatiron. The climb Monodoigt is due east of this spot. One may also go west from the this gap and follow the Fumbledeedum ramp to the Fum-Dum Col, thence east and back to wherever.

### 1.   FI FUN 0 ★
FA: GERRY ROACH, SOLO, 1987.
This route follows the left side of the face all the way to the summit, and is a lot easier than it looks from the east. Begin at the low point of the east face and climb to the summit in three pitches.

### 2.   HI FI 8 ★
FA: ROSSITER, SOLO, 1988.
An excellent variation begins around to the left on the south face and climbs 60 feet of vertical rock via huecos and a thin crack before swinging around onto the east face.

### 3.   EXTRATERRESTRIAL 6 S ★
FA: ROSSITER, SOLO, 1988.
Climb the middle of the east face to the summit.

## FO

Fo is the next rock north of Fi. It is just across a wooded gully to the northwest of the Finger Flatiron. Approach via the Mallory Cave Trail and The Box Trail. To escape from the summit, downclimb 40 feet to the west, turn north and descend a ramp east into the notch between Fo and Fum. The gully to the east is steep and difficult to downclimb. Instead, go north along the west side of Fum and walk through a large hole. Scramble north beneath the west face of Fum (see Fumbledeedum) to the Fum-Dum Col, then back to the east into Second Gully (the long gully between the Second and Third Strata).

### 1.   QUADRATIC EQUATION 6 ★
FA: GERRY ROACH, 1987.
Begin this climb at the lower left side of the east face. Climb two pitches straight up to the ridge crest, and follow it to the southeast side of the summit block. Drop down into a crevice, move out onto the east face, and continue to the top.

### 2.   BINARY SURD 6 ★
FA: ROSSITER, SOLO, 1988.
Begin toward the right side of the east face and climb directly to the summit.

## FUM

Fum is the highest of the four flatirons along the Third Stratum. It sits southeast of Dum and west of The Box. Approach via the Mallory Cave Trail and The Box Trail and gain the saddle just west of the Box. Fum lies a short way to the west. To descend from the summit, downclimb a crack system on the northwest side 50 feet to the Fum-Dum Col.

### 1. EAST FACE LEFT 6 s ★

FA: (?) ROSSITER, 1988.

Begin at the low point of the face and climb a clean, unprotected slab for 200 feet toward the southeast side of the summit. Cross a ledge/gully and finish on easier rock.

### 2. EAST FACE RIGHT 4

Begin at the right side of the face. Climb directly to a ledge/gully that diagonals across the face, cross to the right and continue to the top.

## DUM

The highest point of the Third Stratum is a small, rounded crag that serves as a pedestal for an enormous, flat boulder that reigns over all the surrounding terrain but for the summit of Dinosaur Mountain (which is a few feet higher and about 150 feet to the west). Approach via Porch Alley or The Box Trail and gain the saddle above The Box, then hike northwest along a footpath to the Fum-Dum Col (see Dinosaur Mountain Route). There are at least four ways to reach the Balanced Rock of Dum.

### 1. WEST SIDE CLASS 3

Pass through the Fum-Dum Col into the Bowling Alley (the sandy gully between the Third and Fourth Strata). Head north until the balanced rock is just above to the right. Scramble to the ridge crest and up onto the zendo of Dinosaur Mountain. One may also mantle onto the boulder from the west side.

### 2. SOUTH RIDGE 5

Begin from the Fum-Dum Col. Climb north along a spine of naked rock to a false summit. Climb straight up onto the next section and gain a second false summit. Descend a short way along the north edge of the east face, then traverse down and right to a notch. Scramble up the ridge to the south and onto the balanced summit rock.

### 3. EAST SIDE 4

The 450-foot east face of Dum may be reached by hiking northwest from the south end of the Dreadnaught or by hiking downhill to the northeast from the Fum-Dum Col. Begin from the low point of the east face. Climb straight up the face for 300 feet. The line of least resistance here is to scramble up a gully on the left, which leads to the west side of the crest. Scramble 50 feet south to the balanced rock summit.

## SECOND STRATUM

The following crags are located along the south side of the second rock stratum on Dinosaur Mountain. The highest point along this broken rib is the summit of The Box. The long talus gully to the west of the rib is called the Second Gully. The Second Stratum includes the Achaean Pronouncement and Ridge Two in Skunk Canyon and Poot Ridge on the Nebel Horn.

Dinosaur Rock

South Ramps
5.5

Dinosaur Tracks
5.3

East Bone
Class 3

West Bone
Class 3

④

Southern
Dinosaur Egg

①

③

**SOUTHERN DINOSAUR EGG**
1. Sneak Preview 11c ★
3. Coming Attractions 10d
4. Hatch 5 ★

## SOUTHERN DINOSAUR EGG (See topo p. 100.)

This crag climbs right out of Bear Creek at the south end of the second stratum on Dinosaur Mountain. Approach as for Bear Creek Spire, but continue past its south face for several hundred feet to the Southern Dinosaur Egg. The Egg may also be reached by a short walk east from Stonehenge. To descend from the summit, rappel 50 feet down the south face to a huge flat-topped chockstone, then scramble off to the west.

### 1.    SNEAK PREVIEW 11c ★
FA: MIKE DOWNING, 1987.
This route ascends the southwest face of the summit tower. Begin from a broken ledge down and left (northwest) from the chockstone on Hatch. Six bolts to a two-bolt anchor.

### 2.    LEFT SIDE 10 TR
Climb the slab just left of an arête down and right (southwest) from Sneak Preview.

### 3.    COMING ATTRACTIONS 10D
FA: PETE ZOLLER AND ED MCKIGNEY.
Begin just around to the right from the preceding route. Four bolts to sling around a horn.

### 4.    HATCH 5 ★
Begin on the east side of the crag. Climb a crack and chimney 150 feet to the top of a large, flat-topped chockstone, then work straight up the south face to the summit (crux).

## NORTHERN DINOSAUR EGG

This interesting pinnacle is located just south of Der Freischutz. The large, rounded boulder known as The Bubble lies in the gully just below and to the west. The Southern Dinosaur Egg sits a short way to the southeast and rises directly out of Bear Creek. Approach from Bear Canyon or by hiking down the gully beneath the west side of Der Freischutz. To escape from the summit, scramble out along a ridge to the west and rappel down the short north face. Then scramble west through a notch and down a chimney to the ground.

### 1.    CLOUD WALKER 10c ★
FA: MIKE ENGLE AND DAN HARE, 1989.
This route ascends the steep southwest face in the manner of Sneak Preview on the Southern Dinosaur Egg. Five bolts to a two-bolt anchor.

### 2.    REHATCH 5 ★
This is a good two-pitch climb. Begin below the east face and climb a chimney to a platform just south of the summit tower. From the upper of two chockstones climb the imposing south face (crux).

## THE BUBBLE

The Bubble is a huge boulder in the gully below the west face of the Northern Dinosaur Egg. It is easily reached from the Bear Creek Trail by hiking up the gully between the Southern Dinosaur Egg and Stonehenge.

### 1.    COLD SWEAT 11B
Climb past three bolts on the west side of the rock.

### 2.    HOT SPIT 11c ★
FA: PAUL PIANA AND ERIC JOHNSON, 1987.
Climb overhanging huecos on the southwest face. Three bolts to a two-bolt anchor.

**NORTHERN DINOSAUR EGG**
1. Cloud Walker 10c ★
2. Rehatch 5 ★

Mike Downing on first ascent of *Liquid Crystal* (5.11c), Bear Canyon. Photo by Dan Hare.

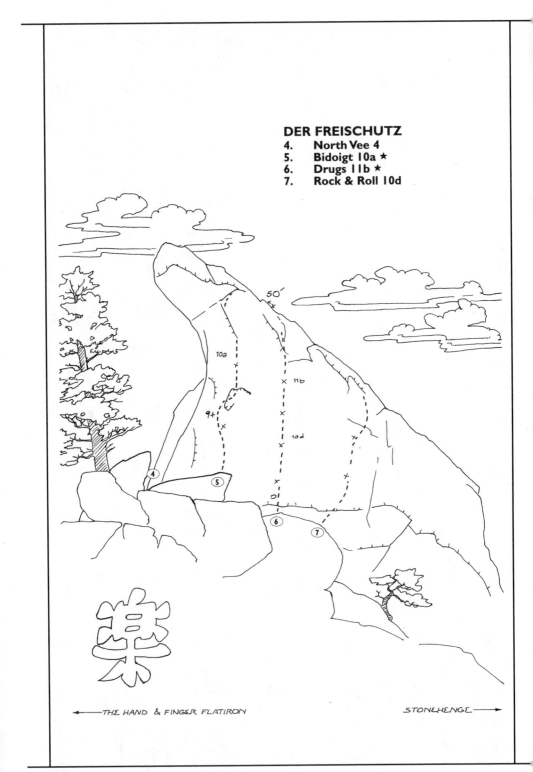

**DER FREISCHUTZ**
4. North Vee 4
5. Bidoigt 10a ★
6. Drugs 11b ★
7. Rock & Roll 10d

THE HAND & FINGER FLATIRON

STONEHENGE

# DER FREISCHUTZ

This excellent crag is located immediately west of Dinosaur Rock and 100 feet south of The Hand. It is distinguished by good scrambling routes on its south and east sides and by several bolt-protected face climbs on its west face. The little flatiron sitting up against the bottom of the east face is called The Overture. To reach Der Freischutz, follow the Mallory Cave Trail, past Dinosaur Rock, to the northeast corner of the crag. Hike south, then west to reach the south ridge. To reach the steep west face, hike The Hand Corridor trail, past the Dwarf and Frankensteins Castle, into the little cirque below the south face of The Hand. From here the northwest arête of Der Freischutz is seen in profile to the south and is about 100 feet away. Scramble out onto an idyllic, flat boulder below Bidoigt and enjoy the rugged beauty. The rock to the west across Second Gully is Fee. To escape from the summit, rappel 80 feet west from two bolts or downclimb North Vee.

### 1.   SOUTH RIDGE CLASS 4 ★

This 600-foot route is characterized by scenic grandeur and good rock. From the saddle between Dinosaur Rock and the Overture, scramble down to the south, then west, and gain the south ridge. Climb the ridge past an arch and pass three bulges before reaching the summit. The line of least resistance stays to the west.

### 2.   FREE SHOT CLASS 3 ★

Begin on either side of the Overture and climb up into a crack and ledge system that traverses south across the east face. Join the South Ridge and continue 200 feet north to the summit.

### 3.   EAST FACE CLASS 4 ★

Begin at the little alcove to the north of the Overture and climb directly up the east face to the summit.

### 4.   NORTH VEE 4

FA: ROSSITER, SOLO, 1988.

This is the most hassle-free downclimb and may also serve as a quick scramble to the summit. Wind up through some giant boulders along the upper north face and climb a right-leaning V-shaped dihedral to the notch just east of the summit, then scramble to the top. A crack to the right of the "Vee" may also be climbed (7).

### 5.   BIDOIGT 10A ★

FA: RICHARD AND JOYCE ROSSITER, 1988.

Also known as Sex. Begin on a big boulder beneath the northwest arête. Climb the steep wall past two bolts and a short thin crack. Bring a small TCU and a couple of mid-range RPs.

### 6.   DRUGS 11B ★

FA: HANK CAYLOR AND PAUL GLOVER, 1987.

Begin just below and south of the flat boulder beneath Bidoigt. Climb past four bolts about 15 feet right of Bidoigt.

### 7.   ROCK & ROLL 10D

Climb past two bolts a short way right of Drugs.

### 8.   SIDEWALK STROLL 10?

This route is located on the lower west face of Der Freischutz some 200 feet down and right from Drugs. Three bolts.

### 9.   Lucy And Devi 11a
FA: Scott Resnick and David Light, 1989.

Begin just right of the preceding route. Climb the steep slab past some underclings. Four bolts to a two-bolt anchor, 65 feet.

## THE DWARF

This is the large boulder on the left as one hikes up into the cirque between Der Freischutz (left) and The Hand (right).

### 1.   Hiss and Spray 12a
FA: Paul Glover, 1987.

Climb through two roofs on the east face (11c and 12a). One pin and two bolts.

### 2.   Eat Cat Too 11b/c ★
FA: Paul Glover, 1987.

Climb the left side of the north face. Go left after third bolt. Three Bolts.

### 3.   Cat-O-Nine Tails 12 TR

Shallow groove with pebbles to right of Eat Cat Too.

## FRANKENSTEINS CASTLE

This is a huge black block west of The Dwarf, along the north side of Der Freischutz. It is hidden by trees until you are very close.

### 1.   Street Hassle 12c ★
FA: Hank Caylor and Paul Glover, 1987.

Follow a line of four bolts on the north face. Bring a clip stick.

### 2.   Frankenstein B1
FA: Hank Caylor, 1987.

Climb the steep slab next to the northwest corner.

### 3.   Gash Burn 11d
FA: Paul Glover, 1987.

Ring bolt followed by an overhanging crack, around to the right. SR.

## THE HAND

The Hand is located west of Der Zerkle, south of the Sharks Fin, and north of Der Freischutz. From the east it bears a vague resemblance to a mitten with the thumb on the north side.

**Approach**—The Mallory Cave Trail passes the bottom of the east face before reaching the Finger Flatiron. To reach the south and west faces, break left on The Hand Corridor trail which climbs the wooded gully between The Hand and Der Freischutz.

**Descent**—All bolted routes on The Hand have anchors at their tops from which one may lower off. To descend from the summit, scramble north to the notch between The Hand and the Sharks Fin, then make a short rappel from a tree to Mallory Cave. To descend from the notch without a rope, climb through a hole to the west, then scramble north up a gully for 100 feet to the south side of the Finger Flatiron. Climb west through a small notch into Second Gully. From the summit, it may also be possible to rappel 120 feet from the two-bolt anchor atop Rock Atrocity.

The Hand & Finger Flatiron
See Legend, Page 95.

## THE HAND
8.    Power Bulge 12c ★
9.    Back in Slacks 11c ★
10.   East Face 4 ★
## SHARKS FIN
2.    South Side 6
## FINGER FLATIRON
1.    East Face 4
2.    East Face Right 7 ★
10.   Mere Wall 8 ★

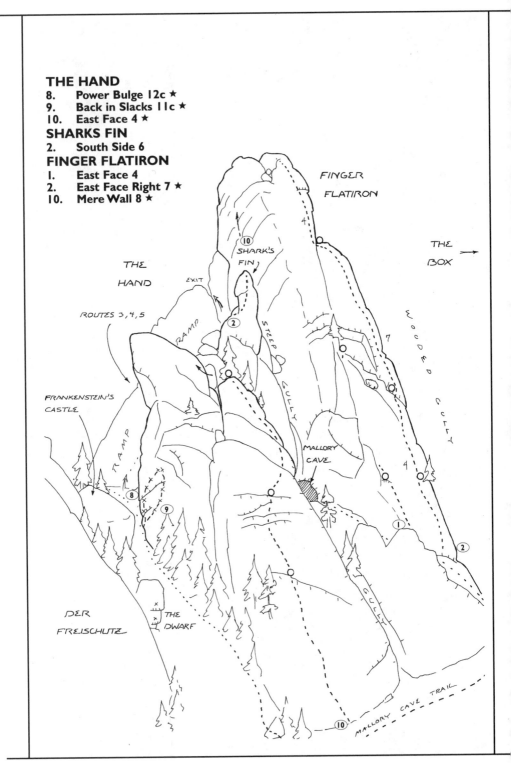

## West Face

The following routes are on the steep west face of The Hand above a smooth V-shaped ramp/gully.

### 1.   I MET SCOTT NEAR HIS HOME 7
FA: PAUL GLOVER, 1987.
Begin about 150 feet down and right from the Sharks Fin. Climb a left-facing dihedral and crack just left of New Saigon.

### 2.   NEW SAIGON 11A ★
FA: HANK CAYLOR, ERIC JOHNSON, PAUL GLOVER, 1987.
This is the farthest north of the bolt routes on the west face. Three bolts to a two-bolt anchor, 45 feet.

### 3.   NAME UNKNOWN 11
This route is just right of New Saigon.

### 4.   FATHER ON FIRE 10D
FA: PAUL GLOVER, 1987.
Climb a crack with three bolts to right of New Saigon. Two-bolt anchor, 45 feet.

### 5.   THE PERFECT KISS 11D ★
FA: COLIN LANTZ AND GREG ROBINSON, 1987.
Follow a line bolts at the southwest corner of The Hand, 60 feet left of Power Bulge. Six bolts to a two-bolt anchor.

### 6.   ROCK ATROCITY 13D ★
FA: COLIN LANTZ.
Climb the big roof above The Perfect Kiss. Nine bolts to a two-bolt anchor.

## South Face

The following routes are located on the bulging south face, across from Der Freischutz.

### 7.   MEALS OF TRUMAN 11C
FA: PAUL GLOVER AND HANK CAYLOR, 1987. NEED FIVE QD.
Begin at a decomposed recess to the right of the Perfect Kiss, where the wall bends around to face south. Climb up into a right-angling crack. Look for a ring bolt low on the route.

### 8.   POWER BULGE 12C ★
FA: HANK CAYLOR, 1987.
This route takes the best line on the south face of The Hand and climbs the imposing bulge between Meals of Truman and Back in Slacks. Five bolts to a two-bolt anchor.

### 9.   BACK IN SLACKS 11C ★
FA: PAUL GLOVER, 1987.
Climb the overhanging, pocketed wall to the right of Power Bulge. Four bolts to a two-bolt anchor.

### 10.   EAST FACE 4 ★
Begin from the Mallory Cave Trail. Climb two long easy pitches to some ledges below a steep headwall. Master the bulge via sharp holds and continue up into an area of ramps and ledges that angle up to left. Climb a deep chimney on the left, or move to the right (north) edge of the face and pass another steep bulge (crux). The last pitch goes left across the top of the deep chimney (or from it, if you went that way), then up and left to the summit.

## SHARKS FIN

This small pinnacle resides above Mallory Cave, between The Hand and the Finger Flatiron. It does not much resemble the fin of a shark. It may be approached from the gully to the west, from the alcove immediately east of Mallory Cave, or from the V-shaped gully below the west face of The Hand, all of which are fairly obvious on location. To descend from the summit, downclimb the east face (3) and scramble west between the Sharks Fin and the Finger Flatiron.

### 1.   WEST FACE 10D
There is a bolt on the short west face and apparently a short route to go with it.

### 2.   SOUTH SIDE 6
Begin from the entrance to Mallory Cave. Climb an 80-foot chimney (6) to the south and gain the notch between the Sharks Fin and the Finger Flatiron. Work around to the south side of the tower and climb the final 30 feet on the east side.

### 3.   NORTH SIDE 3
Begin 80 feet east from the opening to Mallory Cave. Gain a ramp on the north side of the Finger Flatiron and follow it up to the left until above the cave, then traverse left into the gully between the Sharks Fin and the Finger Flatiron. Climb the gully for 80 feet to where it steepens, then move right and finish with a ramp that leads to the notch along the north side of the Sharks Fin. Hike around the west and south sides of the pinnacle and climb the east side.

## FINGER FLATIRON

This long, narrow pinnacle is located immediately right of The Hand and Mallory Cave and 150 feet west of Der Zerkle. It has a number of interesting routes including a fine slab climb up its 600-foot east face and several face climbs on the upper north and west faces. To reach the bottom of the east face (and Mallory Cave) hike to the top of the Mallory Cave Trail. To reach the upper north and west sides, continue up The Box Trail, which climbs the wooded gully beneath the north face (Box Alley) and exits into the Second Gully. To escape from the summit, rappel 60 feet northwest from slings.

### 1.   EAST FACE 4
FA: GERRY ROACH, 1982.

This is the easiest route to the summit of the Finger Flatiron. Begin at the bottom of the east face, just right of the diagonal groove that leads up to Mallory Cave. Move up past some trees and follow the left (south) edge of the face for two pitches. Angle in toward the center of the face, climb a groove/crack system through a bulge and belay at the top of the crack. Move left and run the rope out to the summit. One may also begin this route 20 feet below the entrance to Mallory Cave: Climb the pocketed right wall of the gully passing left of a small tree (6) and join East Face (Richard Rossiter, solo, 1988).

### 2.   EAST FACE RIGHT 7 ★
FA: RICHARD ROSSITER, SOLO, 1988.

This is one of the better east face routes on Dinosaur Mountain. Begin near the groove that angles up and left to Mallory Cave. Climb onto the wall and head for the right side of the face. After about 350 feet, encounter the crux which is a narrow rib directly above the north face. Once committed to the rib there is no protection for about 50 feet, but the rock is solid and the exposure is exhilarating. There is a good belay at the top of this section. Move left and continue to the summit.

### 3.   FLAKE 8
Begin from some blocks and flakes near the middle of the north face. Climb a right-facing flake with an off-width crack and join East Face Right.

### 4. PATIENCE 12B
FA: CHRISTIAN BAROODY, B.C. HANEY, 1989.

This route ascends the lichen-streaked north face 100 feet left from Nude Figures. Four bolts to a two-bolt anchor. Crux is at the last bolt.

### 5. ARCHER 11A/B
FA: CHUCK REYNOLDS AND RUSTY HOLCOMB.

Locate a protruding block between two cracks, near the middle of the north face. This route takes the left crack. Step onto the wall from a sloping ledge, then traverse down and left to a left-facing dihedral with a finger crack. Climb the dihedral past a roof, and finish with a V-shaped dihedral that leads to the top of the wall. This may be the same route as Lost Enchantment.

### 6. LOST ENCHANTMENT 11 ★
FA: BOB HORAN, 1981.

Begin near Northwest Corner and undercling left to a dihedral.

### 7. NORTHWEST CORNER 9
FA: JIM ERICKSON AND ROGER BRIGGS, 1980.

Begin at some flakes and blocks, 50 feet from the west edge of the north face. Climb up to a roof, pull left, then follow a thin crack in a left-facing dihedral.

### 8. RIGHT CRACK 8
FA: ROGER BRIGGS AND JIM ERICKSON, 1980.

Begin as for Northwest Corner, but follow a two-inch crack up and right, turn a roof, and finish with a thin crack in the head wall.

### 9. NUDE FIGURES IN A HOLLOW FRUIT 11A ★
FA: PAUL GLOVER AND ERIC JOHNSON, 1987.

Start behind a 30-foot tree at the farthest west aspect of the north face. Climb through two short roofs and continue up the smooth face. The first roof is 10b and the second is the crux, which can be avoided by moving right and up a short diagonal ramp (10b). Three bolts. Lower off 50 feet from slings.

### 10. MERE WALL 8 ★
FA: JOE O'LAUGHLIN AND BOB JENSEN, 1969.

This route ascends the south face from the notch north of the Sharks Fin. Begin west of a large chockstone. Climb a crack that angles up and right and gain a rounded ramp. Follow the ramp up to the west (left) for 100 feet (5), and belay where another crack angles up to the right. Continue up the ramp a short way, master a bulge (8), and finish along the ramp (7).

### 11. MONODOIGT 11C ★
FA: RICHARD AND JOYCE ROSSITER, ROB WOOLF, KAREN KUDDES, 1988.

Directly below the western arête of the summit tower is a concave face. Begin with a mantle, then follow three bolts to the top of the face. Just before the crux is a perfect one-finger hole.

### 12. THINNER 11A ★
FA: JOYCE AND RICHARD ROSSITER, 1988.

Begin beneath a roof around to the right from Monodoigt. Turn the roof and follow a very thin crack to the top of the face.

### QUEST FOR BALANCE 11B
FA: DAVE CRAWFORD AND JIM LESUER.

Begin behind a tree about 100 feet down and right from Monodoigt. Five bolts to a two-bolt anchor.

**THE BOX
from the Southwest**

## THE BOX

The Box is the steep and narrow crag west of the Red Devil and about 200 feet north of the Finger Flatiron. The Box is easily recognized by its summit tower, which resembles the dorsal fin of a shark. The small pinnacle above Mallory Cave is actually named the Sharks Fin, but is a weaker resemblance. The upper south face of The Box forms a remarkable concave wall of distinct beauty that is host to the routes Cornucopia and Discipline. The wooded gully between the Finger Flatiron and The Box, and farther east between Der Zerkle and the Red Devil, is called Box Alley. Approach via The Box Trail or Porch Alley. To escape from the summit, downclimb 50 feet to the notch just east of the summit, then down a ramp to the northwest (Class 4). Lower off or rappel from all sport routes.

### 1.   DOWNCLIMB CLASS 4

This is the shortest route to the summit and the easiest downclimb. Walk around to the north side of the crag, past the bolt routes, and begin from a stone platform where the ground drops away to the east. Scramble up a crest, then drop down to the east and gain a notch in the summit ridge. Scramble 50 feet west to the summit.

### 2.   HAND CRACK 9

Begin up on a block and climb a hand crack up to a right-angling roof, then climb out along the roof and gain the summit ridge.

### 3.   AUNT JENNIFER'S TIGERS 10D

FA: ERIK FEDOR AND FRED KNAPP.

Begin up on a block, just right of an obvious hand crack. Climb up and right past two bolts and finish with a crack.

**THE BOX**
1. Downclimb Class 4
6. Prow 11d TR
7. Stone Love 10c ★

**Concave Wall**
8. Cornucopia 13a ★
9. Discipline 12b ★
11. Side Line 7
12. South Ramp 6 ★

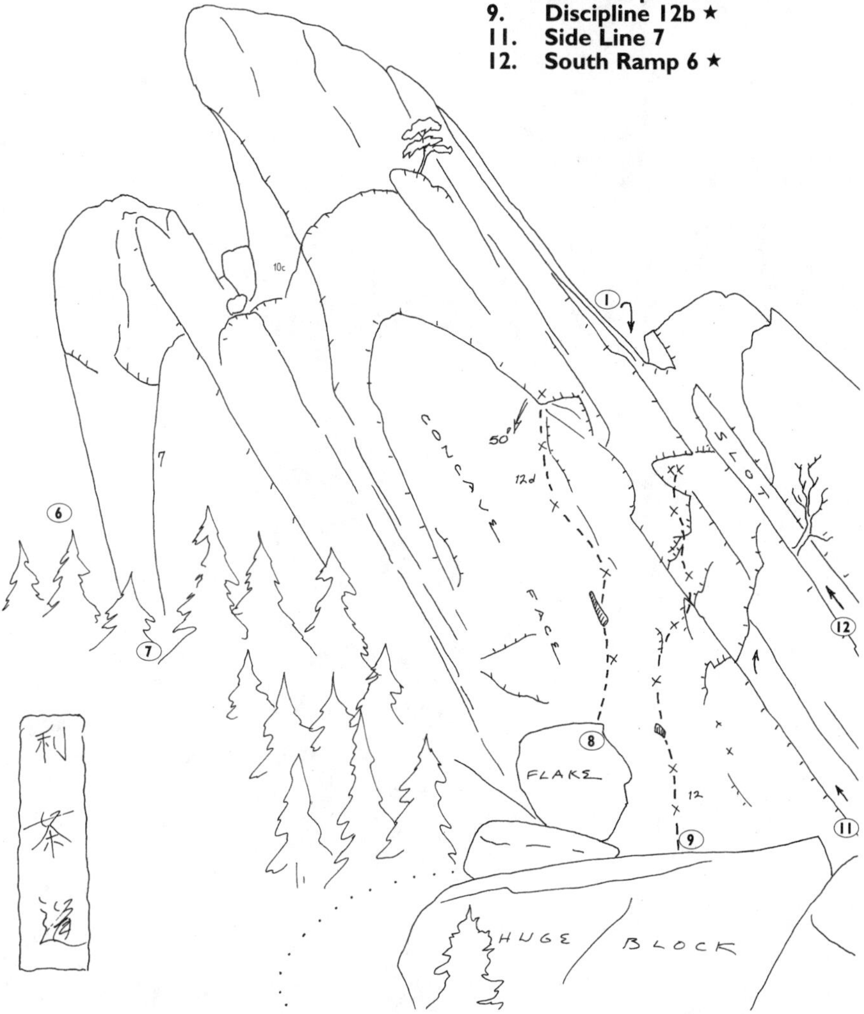

Dale Goddard on *Cornucopia* (5.13a), The Box.
Photo by Dan Hare.

### 4. FACT OF A DOOR FRAME 11b/c

FA: FEDOR AND KNAPP.

Begin along the right side of the north face. Clip a pin and turn a roof, then follow bolts up a steep wall covered with bright yellow lichen. Four bolts and two pins to a two-bolt anchor. Both pitons are missing.

### 5. SAMPLE THE DOG 12b

FA: CURT FRY.

This route ascends the north face of a huge block that forms the west end of The Box. Four bolts to a two-bolt anchor.

### 6. PROW 11d TR

Climb the prow of the big block at the north end of The Box. Anchors in place.

### 7. STONE LOVE 10c ★

FA: RANDY LEAVITT AND BOB HORAN, 1981.

Begin at the southwest corner of The Box. Climb a hand and fist crack (7) to broad ramp and belay. Climb a diagonal finger crack in the overhanging summit tower.

## Concave Wall

The following routes begin from some enormous cleaved blocks along the upper south face of The Box.

### 8. CORNUCOPIA 13a ★

FA: DALE GODDARD, 1986.

This route ascends the exquisite concave wall at the upper south face of The Box. Begin from the top of a large flake and follow five bolts to the top of the face.

### 9. DISCIPLINE 12b ★

FA: HANK CAYLOR AND PAUL GLOVER, 1987.

Begin at the nadir of the concave wall, 15 feet right of Cornucopia. Follow six bolts to the top of the wall and belay from a two-bolt anchor on a ramp. Bring a clip stick for the first bolt.

### 10. OLD BOLT ROUTE ?

There are two old bolts with Leeper hangers to the right of Discipline.

### 11. SIDE LINE 7

FA: ROSSITER, SOLO.

Begin from the east end of the big blocks beneath Discipline and a few feet left of the third pitch of South Ramp. Follow a narrow ramp for 40 feet, move up and right, and climb a right-facing dihedral to join South Ramp.

### 12. SOUTH RAMP 6 ★

Begin at the low point of the crag, above a switchback in the Box Trail. 1. Follow a faint ramp in excellent rock past some dwarfed pines. Step left and turn a roof, then climb 40 feet up the main ramp and belay from a pine (6, 140 feet). 2. Climb past a Douglas fir and stem up the V-shaped ramp to a surprising off-width and fist crack that leads to a ledge with another tree (6, 90 feet). 3. Continue up the ramp for about 100 feet and climb a wide crack or squeeze chimney to the notch between the top of the east ridge and the true summit. The downclimb goes north and west from this notch. Jam an easy crack 50 feet west to reach the top (2, 150 feet). Note: This route may be started with pitch three from the big blocks beneath Discipline.

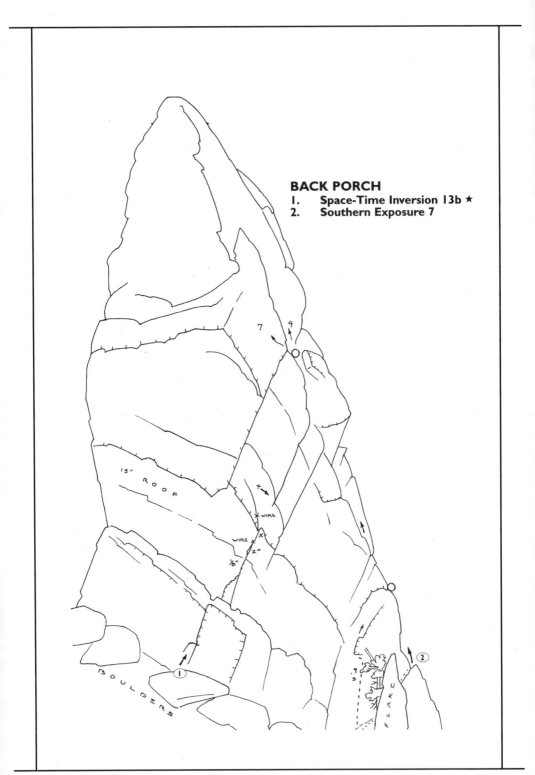

**BACK PORCH**
1. Space-Time Inversion 13b ★
2. Southern Exposure 7

## BACK PORCH

This massive free-standing tower lies north across a forested gully from The Box and uphill to the west of the Front Porch. It is characterized by a large, V-shaped overhang on its east face and an immense, flat overhang on its west face, 50 feet off the ground. The Back Porch is most easily reached from Porch Alley (see under Green Mountain). To escape the summit, rappel 150 feet west from two bolts. It may be possible to do two 75-foot rappels down the west face. One may also rappel from trees down the east face.

### 1.   SPACE-TIME INVERSION 13B ★
FA: ROGER AND BILL BRIGGS, 1971 (5.8 A4). FFA: DALE GODDARD, 1985.

Free ascent known as the Five Year Plan. This awesome route looks a lot more like a space-time inversion than a five-year plan, though you may decide not to climb it for at least the next five years. Hike around to the west side of the tower and behold one of the most impressive overhangs in all of Boulder. It has a crack running through its right side; this is the route.

### 2.   SOUTHERN EXPOSURE 7
FA: JOE O'LAUGHLIN AND ROBIN RICH, 1965.

Begin behind a large, free-standing flake along the highest part of the south face. Traverse east to a tree on the south edge of the east face and belay. Climb up a ramp system that diagonals toward the west and belay near a big, square flake. Head west, then back up to the summit (Joe O'Laughlin and George Hurley, 1968), or climb up above the square flake and continue along a diagonal ramp to the summit. A direct start (9+ s) climbs the steep and poorly protected face just across from the free-standing flake and eventually joins the ramp system below the square flake (Corwin Bell and Todd Gilbreath, 1986).

### 3.   SOUTHEAST CORNER 11?
Follow several bolts up a very steep face just right of the southeast corner of the rock. The first bolt is a long way up. No details of this route are known.

### 4.   EAST FACE 6 ★
FA: BOB BEATTY AND BOB JICKLING, 1956.

Begin below a small arch, 200 feet up along the north side of the east face. Traverse out left onto the east face and climb up to the north side of the V-shaped overhang. Go up a steep slab (6), left through the overhang (6), and up to a belay at the larger of two trees (150 feet). Angle out into the middle of the face and jam a fist crack through a five-foot roof (6). A final clean slab leads to the summit. There are a number of variations. The original second pitch stays near the north edge of the face. One may also begin at the low point of the face: Turn a roof (7) and join the regular line beneath the V-shaped overhang.

### 5.   NORTH FACE ?
A route has supposedly been climbed on the north face, but no details are available.

## FIRST STRATUM

The following crags lie along the farthest east of the four major strata on Dinosaur Mountain. The gully to the west of this stratum is called First Gully. The lower south section of this gully provides access to the east sides of the Dinosaur Eggs and to the southwest side of Dinosaur Rock. The last 100 yards of the Mallory Cave Trail follows First Gully to the Finger Flatiron.

## Bear Creek Spire

Bear Creek Spire is the first large crag encountered on the north side of Bear Canyon when hiking in from the east. Except for the shorter north side, its faces are rotten, precipitous, and barred by tremendous overhangs. There is a large eyebolt about 70 feet south of the summit, the origin and intended use of which are not known. To reach the summit, walk the dirt service road into Bear Canyon, head up the rough trail along the north bank of the stream, and stumble up a steep scree gully along the east side of the crag. Climb the northeast corner of the crag beginning with an east-facing ramp (Class 4, 200 feet) or start with a short north-facing wall with a small tree (6). Note: This crag and the area 100 yards around it is closed to the public.

# DINOSAUR ROCK

Dinosaur Rock looms up dramatically on the skyline to the southwest of Square Rock. The new Mallory Cave Trail goes directly to the northeast corner of Dinosaur Rock, then climbs beneath the north face affording easy access to the east and west face routes. To escape from the summit, scramble down the West Face. Routes on the lower southwest side are most easily reached from Bear Canyon.

### 1.   SOUTH RAMPS 5
(See photo p. 102.) From the south side of the east face, scramble around to the south face of the crag. Climb a long pitch up either of two ramps.

### 2.   RUG MUNCHERS 4
Begin to the left (south) of an extra stratum at the bottom of the east face. Climb the left side of the east face to the summit. 300 feet.

### 3.   EAST FACE RIGHT 3
Begin to the right of the extra stratum and climb solid rock directly to the summit. 300 feet.

### 4.   WEST FACE CLASS 4
Follow the Mallery Cave Trail until level with the west end of Dinosaur Rock and gain a notch between the west face and a large rock outcrop. Turn east and climb a short chimney, a short face and a final, aesthetic 20-foot wall to the summit ridge.

Three spurs connect to the south side of Dinosaur Rock and provide interesting approaches to the main feature. This entire area is closed to the public from February to August.

### 5.   DINOSAUR TRACKS 3 ★
(See photo p. 104.) This route ascends the more westerly of the three spurs. Hike up First Gully past the west side of Bear Creek Spire and begin around to the east from a short wall at the foot of the rib. Scramble up the wide rib for several hundred feet to a small arch where one may escape to the west or continue with the West Face route.

### 6.   WEST BONE CLASS 3 ★
(See photo p. 104.) This route ascends the middle of the three ribs and leads into the middle of the south face. Approach via First Gully. The rib begins about 50 feet west from the saddle at the north side of Bear Creek Spire. Climb the rib, then connect with South Ramp (5). The narrow gully between West Bone and East Bone can be hiked and leads to the bottom of the east face of Dinosaur Rock.

### 7.   EAST BONE CLASS 3
(See photo p. 104.) This route ascends the more easterly of the ribs between Bear Creek Spire and Dinosaur Rock. Begin along the east side of a talus gully, at the east side of Bear Creek Spire. Scramble up the rib to the wooded area at the bottom of the east face of Dinosaur Rock.

Dale Goddard on *The Five Year Plan* (5.13),
Back Porch. Photo by Dan Hare.

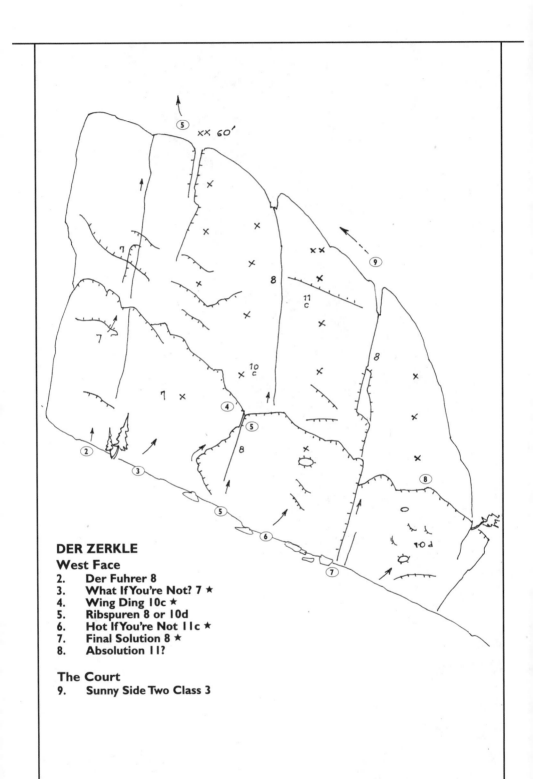

## DER ZERKLE

### West Face

2. **Der Fuhrer 8**
3. **What If You're Not? 7 ★**
4. **Wing Ding 10c ★**
5. **Ribspuren 8 or 10d**
6. **Hot If You're Not 11c ★**
7. **Final Solution 8 ★**
8. **Absolution 11?**

### The Court

9. **Sunny Side Two Class 3**

## DER ZERKLE

Der Zerkle is located 150 yards southwest of Square Rock. It is easily identified by its summit, formed of three parallel rock fingers. Several quality slab climbs, sport climbs, and Hueco-style bouldering can be had here. Approach via the Mallory Cave Trail. Hike past the area called The Court, which can be accessed from a switchback in the trail before reaching The Hand. The west face can be reached by hiking around to the left from The Court or from farther up the trail. To descend from the summit, downclimb the Northwest Corner, or rappel 100 feet west from an old bolt (not recommended).

### 1.  NORTHWEST CORNER CLASS 4

Also known as West Face. From the saddle northwest of the summit, scramble up a short way and climb a shallow dihedral with a large tree to a notch north of the summit. Finish by climbing a ramp up to the right.

## West Face

The following routes are located on the steep and pocketed west face of Der Zerkle, beneath the ramp of Sunnyside Two. Some of the anchors and protection bolts have been removed from this popular wall and should be replaced.

### 2.  DER FUHRER 8

This is the farthest left route on the steep west face. Face climb up to a break, turn a roof, then veer right and finish in a crack.

### 3.  WHAT IF YOU'RE NOT? 7 ★

FA: FRED KNAPP AND SHARON SADLEIR.

Begin 25 feet right from the north end of the wall. Climb the steep, pocketed wall to the big ramp of Sunnyside Two. Two old bolts are set in the ledge, three feet back from the edge of the face. Bring a long runner for toproping.

### 4.  WING DING 10c ★

FA: SANDY COX, STEVE ZICLA, JOHN SAGE, 1989.

Climb the steep, pocketed wall just left of Ribspuren. Four bolts to a two-bolt anchor. Note: All bolts have (for no apparent reason) been removed from this excellent pitch.

### 5.  RIBSPUREN 8 OR 10D

FA: HANS WENINGER, BILL BELL, 1989.

Begin just right from the left end of a flake. Climb a short, thin crack, then step right and continue in another thin crack to the big ledge (8). A second pitch called Happy Ending climbs the summit tower taking the left of two cracks at the top (10d).

### 6.  HOT IF YOU'RE NOT 11c ★

FA: ERIK FEDOR AND FRED KNAPP.

Climb in from the left along a flake, then tackle the overhanging wall just right of Ribspuren. Three bolts to a two-bolt anchor. This route at one time had a difficult direct start, but the single bolt protecting it has been removed.

### 7.  FINAL SOLUTION 8 ★

FA: JIM ERICKSON, SOLO, 1976.

Begin at a steep crack along the lower right side of the west face. Climb this crack system and finish on the big ramp of Sunnyside Two. The upper part is the crux.

### 8. ABSOLUTION 11?

Climb the first ten feet of Final Solution, then move right and follow three bolts up the overhanging wall. It is also possible to boulder up to the first bolt six feet right of Final Solution (no pro). I do not know the real name of this route.

## The Court

The following routes are located in (or begin at) a large alcove at the southwest corner of Der Zerkle. Look for a broad ramp on the left and an overhanging pocketed wall on the right.

### 9. SUNNY SIDE TWO CLASS 3

Begin at the southwest corner of Der Zerkle, at the left side of "The Court." Scramble up a broad ramp to the north, go around either side of a large block, and finish with the Northwest Corner.

### 10. APRIL FOOLS! 11A ★

FA: WILL NICCOLLS AND IKE NICOLL.

Start up the ramp of Sunnyside Two, then follow four bolts up the overhanging wall on the right to a two-bolt anchor. Bring small stoppers.

### 11. TOUCH MONKEY 11B ★

FA: ERIC JOHNSON, HANK CAYLOR, PAUL GLOVER, 1987.

Begin near the start to Sunnyside Two. Climb an overhanging wall with huecos (50 feet). Three bolts and a fixed nut to a two-bolt anchor.

### 12. KNOT CARROT 11A

FA: PAUL GLOVER, 1987.

Climb a small dihedral with a roof just right of Touch Monkey. Three bolts to the anchor on Touch Monkey.

### 13. PASSOVER 10D S OR 9 S

FA: PAUL GLOVER, 1987.

Begin to the right of Knot Carrot and climb either of two starts 20 feet to a ledge. Move left and finish as for Knot Carrot.

### 14. SUNNYSIDE ONE 6

Begin at a ramp about 100 feet left from the southeast corner of the rock. Climb the ramp for 140 feet passing a small arch, then traverse right to a ledge beneath the big overhang that runs across the east face. Climb through a hole (6) and continue with East Face Left . It is also possible to continue down and north across the ledge and join East Face Right.

### 15. EAST FACE LEFT 6 ★

Begin at the low point of the face. Climb straight up the east-facing slab to the base of a major roof band that runs across the face. Pass this overhang by climbing through a hole with a bolt (6), then follow easier rock to a gully south of the summit. From the top of the gully angle right and climb the middle finger to the top.

### 16. EAST FACE RIGHT 7 ★

FA: LARRY DALKE AND PAT AMENT, 1962.

Begin at the north side of the east face. Climb a long pitch and belay on a ledge beneath the north end of the long overhang that cuts across the face. Lieback off a flake (7) to pass the overhang or climb the face to the left (7), then climb straight up slabs into a gully that is followed to a notch on the right side of the summit tower. A ramp leads up and left to the top.

## RED DEVIL

This flatiron lies west-northwest of Square Rock and across the gully to the north from Der Zerkle. The narrow crag directly above it (to the west) is The Box. Due north across a broad, forested gully lies the Lost Porch. The Red Devil may be recognized by its very flat, reddish east face. A wedge-shaped slab known as the Unicorn leans up against the east face and offers a short moderate route of its own. Approach via the Mallory Cave Trail and The Box Trail. To escape from the summit, scramble off to the northwest.

### 1. SOUTH FACE 4

This route is north, across the gully from the bottom of the Finger Flatiron. Approach via the Mallory Cave Trail and The Box Trail. Climb a zigzag crack system with a tree to a ledge with a large tree (100 feet), then scoot around onto the east face and climb 50 feet to the summit.

### 2. EAST FACE 5

Scramble up the gully between the Unicorn and the Red Devil and climb around the north end of a low overhang, then continue up a red slab to the summit.

### 3. BERSERKER 6 s ★

FA: GERRY ROACH AND ALAN McCARTNEY, 1982.

This four-pitch route masters the low overhang near a small tree, traverses left, and proceeds up the south side of the east face.

## Front Stratum

The following crags are located along a less-distinct rock stratum, east of the main four, that gives rise to the Front Porch on Dinosaur Mountain, and to Hillbilly Rock north of Skunk Canyon.

## SQUARE ROCK

The Mallory Cave Trail leads directly to the north side of Square Rock, about 0.25 mile from its junction with the Mesa Trail. The massive block is 20 feet high on the west and 40 feet high on the east, and there are a number of bolts on its flat summit for toproping. Routes are listed counter-clockwise beginning with the shortest and easiest at the northwest corner.

### 1. NORTHWEST CORNER 8 ★

Turn your back to the tree and make several interesting moves to reach the summit. Rappel or reverse the route.

### 2. MEREST EXCRESCENCES B1+ ★

FA: JOHN ALLEN, 1981.

Climb the rounded arête in the middle of the west face.

### 3. SOUTH FACE LEFT 11 (?)

Begin at the left edge of the south face, Make a long reach or lunge for a small, left-facing flake, then move up to the right.

### 4. CENTER ROUTE 11 ★

Begin on a low, flat boulder below the center of the south face, and proceed upwards.

### 5. FLAKE 10

Climb a right-facing flake along the southeast corner of Square Rock.

### 6. CRACK 11c

Climb the steep, challenging crack a couple of feet right of the southeast corner.

**SQUARE ROCK AND DINOSAUR ROCK, from the Mallory cave trail**

## SQUARE ROCK—east side

1. **Northwest Corner 8 ★**
6. **Crack 11c**
7. **Android Powerpack 12c/d ★ TR**
8. **Yellow Christ 12b s ★**
9. **Blue Angel 12d TR**
10. **Stoic Buttress 11c ★ TR**
11. **No Sign of Life 12 TR**

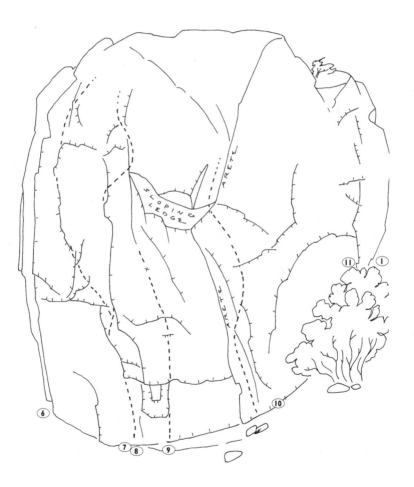

### 7.   ANDROID POWERPACK 12c/d ★ TR
FA: HARRISON DEKKER AND CHRISTIAN GRIFFITH, 1981.

Begin in the center of the east face. Swing up to a left-facing flake on Yellow Christ, move left (crux) and follow a shallow, right-facing system to the top.

### 8.   YELLOW CHRIST 12b s ★
FA: CHRISTIAN GRIFFITH, 1980; LEAD, 1984.

A well-known painting by Paul Gauguin...its relationship to this route is unknown. Make a dynamic move to a left-facing flake, then climb a left-facing corner for 25 feet, break right to a conspicuous face hold, and back up to the left to finish.

### 9.   BLUE ANGEL 12d TR
FA: CHRISTIAN GRIFFITH, 1987.

Locate an odd bolt halfway up the wall, on the right side of the east face, and begin just right of a U-shaped thing. Climb up to the bolt, then up and left to join Yellow Christ at a sloping shelf.

### 10.   STOIC BUTTRESS 11c ★ TR
FA: HARRISON DEKKER, 1981.

Begin just right of the northeast corner. Climb a crack to a mantle, then move left and up a thin face to the top.

### 11.   NO SIGN OF LIFE 12 TR
FA: CHRISTIAN GRIFFITH, 1981.

Begin about ten feet left of the northwest corner of Square Rock. Climb straight up past a white, left-facing flake.

## BABYHORN

The Babyhorn is small but cool. You could bump into it while backing up to look at the west face of Square Rock. A bolt has been placed on the summit. The east side is the easiest (Class 4). The south face is more interesting (7). The west is best (9).

## VERANDA

This little flatiron, also known as the Gazebo, is located a short way northwest of Square Rock and immediately east of the Red Devil. There is a bolt on the western of its two summits. A bit of scrambling, toproping and bouldering are possible here. The west face provides two short but exciting routes: a wide crack on the left (7) and a hand traverse on the right (8 s). The Mallory Cave Trail passes directly beneath the south end of the east rib, about 100 yards beyond Square Rock. Porch Alley passes beneath the north face.

## FRONT PORCH

The Front Porch is the broad flatiron low on the northeast shoulder of Dinosaur Mountain, about 300 yards north of Square Rock. Hike the NCAR Trail and take the north branch to the Mesa Trail. From here a footpath leads west up a rocky shoulder to the upper right side of the east face. The best approach is via Porch Alley, which leads directly to the bottom of the east face. To escape from the summit, scramble down the northeast ridge, then back along the base of the east face. One may also rappel from a tree west of the summit. Various routes will be evident on location, two of which are described below.

### 1.   EAST FACE SOUTH CLASS 4
Begin at the low point of the east face. Climb straight up past a bulge to the summit ridge, then follow the ridge crest to the top. Four pitches.

DINOSAUR MOUNTAIN, north side
See Legend, Page 95.

GREEN MOUNTAIN SOUTH SUMMIT

G

O

Y

X

SKUNK CANYON

R2

R1

Satan's Slab

W

V

PORCH ALLEY

Summit

G

N

O

Y

Z

W

V

X

**DINOSAUR MTN**
from the north
See Legend, Page 95.

## 2.    TIPTOE SLAB 3 ★

Begin to the right of the central rib and climb a smooth slab (with two bolts) directly to the summit. 400 feet.

# LOST PORCH

This small flatiron is located a short way west of the Front Porch and is easily reached via Porch Alley. The east face offers a 400-foot scramble to the summit. Porch Alley passes beneath the lower west face, which provides excellent hueco bouldering. To escape from the summit, downclimb the northeast ridge.

## Dinosaur Mountain, Skunk Canyon Crags

The following crags are located along the north slope of Dinosaur Mountain in Skunk Canyon. All features are approached from the Skunk Canyon Trail. The entire area is closed to hiking and climbing from February to August.

# ACHEAN PRONOUNCEMENT

The Achean Pronouncement is the first significant feature on the left, when entering the narrows of Skunk Canyon from the east. It sits directly across from Satans Slab and is the same stratum of rock. Approach via Skunk Canyon Trail. Descend from the summit tower via 50-foot rappel to the south. Once in the trees, hike back down beneath the east face. For routes on the northwest face, scramble south along the crest until it is possible to downclimb northwest among cliffbands and gullies into the jungle.

## 1.    DARK OBSESSION 9 s ★

FA: RICHARD ROSSITER, SOLO.

Begin 175 feet up along the east face, ten feet left of a steep thin crack.. Lieback an overhanging flake to gain a horizontal hold, climb another ten feet , then pull right onto the steep slabs of the east face. Climb straight up to the crest of the ridge, then traverse south to the summit. Finish as for the following route or downclimb the short south ridge.

## 2.    EAST FACE 7 ★

This route follows a wide crack in a big right-facing dihedral, at the far right side of the east face. Begin at a platform, 75 feet above the stream, beneath a break in the long overhang that runs along the bottom of the east face. 1. Angle right across a slab to a ledge with two large trees, at the base of a long crack (7, 50 feet). 2. Jam the fist crack to another tree and belay (4, 160 feet). 3. Climb 90 feet to a spectacular belay at some fixed pins on the summit ridge (4). 4. Step left onto the east face and climb to the exposed ridge crest Follow the crest for 120 feet and belay (4). 5. Continue up the now easy crest for 120 feet to the northeast corner of the summit tower. 6. Traverse left beneath an east-facing overhang and climb the steep south face of the summit tower (7).

## 3.    NORTHEAST ARÊTE 7 ★

FA: ROSSITER, SOLO.

Gain the ledge with two trees as for the preceding route (7). Move right and climb the very north edge of the east face for two pitches. Join East Face on the ridge crest.

## 4.    THIRD EYE 9 + ★

FA: ROGER BRIGGS, STEVE NELSON, 1971. FFA: BRIGGS, ROPE SOLO, 1972.

This route follows an obvious open-book dihedral in the lower northwest face. Scramble up a ramp to a point beneath the dihedral. Climb in from the right and pass through a chimney, then lieback the open-book dihedral. Finish with a six-inch slot.

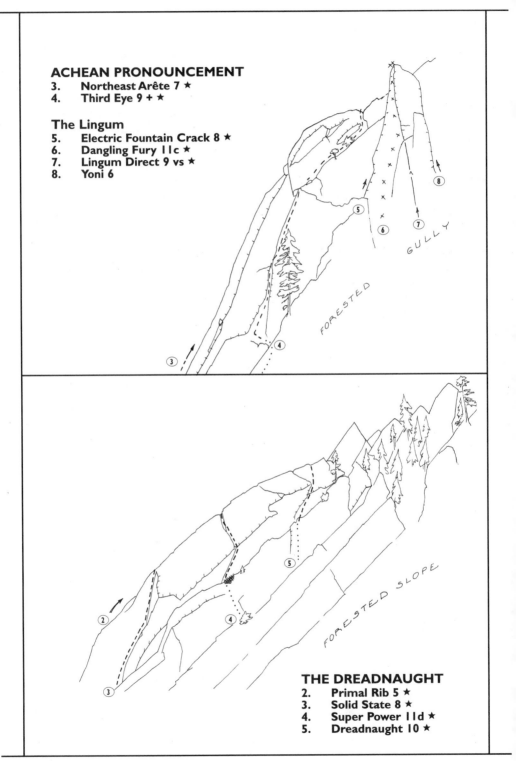

## ACHEAN PRONOUNCEMENT
3. Northeast Arête 7 ★
4. Third Eye 9 + ★

The Lingum
5. Electric Fountain Crack 8 ★
6. Dangling Fury 11c ★
7. Lingum Direct 9 vs ★
8. Yoni 6

## THE DREADNAUGHT
2. Primal Rib 5 ★
3. Solid State 8 ★
4. Super Power 11d ★
5. Dreadnaught 10 ★

## The Lingum

The following four routes ascend the dramatic pinnacle known as The Lingum, which stands erect in the center of the northwest face.

### 5.   ELECTRIC FOUNTAIN CRACK 8 ★
FA: ROGER BRIGGS AND KRISTINA SOLHEIM, 1970.
Scramble up a steep ramp and climb the wide crack along the left side of The Lingum.

### 6.   DANGLING FURY 11c ★
FA: PETE ZOLLER AND MIKE SCHLAUCH, 1989.
Follow eight bolts up the stunning north face of The Lingum. Three-bolt anchor on the summit.

### 7.   LINGUM DIRECT 9 vs ★
FA: ERIC GUOKAS, SOLO, 1984.
Climb the northwest arête of The Lingum.

### 8.   YONI 6
Jam the wide crack at the right side of the Lingum.

## THE ARGONAUT

The Argonaut is a gigantic block in the bottom of Skunk Canyon, below the west face of the Achean Pronouncement. The flat top of the block may be accessed from the west for purposes of toproping. There is a single-bolt anchor above the west arête and above the southwest face. The hangers and nuts are missing from both. The routes are high quality.

### 1.   SOUTHWEST FACE 10?
Climb a steepening face past three bolts, 45 feet.

### 2.   WEST ARÊTE 11?
Begin just right of the preceding route. Climb the curving arête past a single bolt with an old Leeper hanger.

### 3.   RIGHT SIDE 12?
Begin at or near the low point of the rock. Climb a blunt arête that merges with the west arête near the top. Five (?) bolts, 60 feet

## THE DREADNAUGHT

The Dreadnaught begins a short way to the west of the Achean Pronouncement and climbs a thousand feet from the deeps of Skunk Canyon to its summit just west of the Back Porch. A small flatiron leans up against the south end of the Dreadnaught. Approach the low point or the northwest face by hiking up from the narrows of Skunk Canyon. Approach the flatiron at the top of the ridge as for the Back Porch. To descend from the high point, downclimb to the west and south.

### 1.   EAST FACE LEFT 3
The flatiron at the south end of the Dreadnaught provides easy access to the summit and affords a dramatic view of the Back Porch. Begin in the trees, 200 feet south from the notch west of the Back Porch. Ascend the south side of the east face for 300 feet to a ledge with big trees. Continue up the south side of the final blocks. The middle of the east face also provides a pleasant climb.

## 2. PRIMAL RIB 5 ★

This route follows the east side of the arête from its origin in Skunk Canyon to the summit behind the Back Porch. Hike up the gully to the east of the ridge until the rock becomes well-formed. Work out across the east slab toward the arête. Ascend an east-facing dihedral via a three-inch crack, past a bush (crux), and continue up easier terrain. A long easy pitch leads to a big ledge, above which the ridge lifts up and becomes more dramatic. Climb along the stunning arête for 400 feet, cross a notch and scramble another 250 feet to the summit. 1000 feet in all.

## 3. SOLID STATE 8 ★

FA: ROGER BRIGGS AND MARK HESSE, 1973.

Climb a clean dihedral and hand crack in the lower third of the northwest face. Continue with Primal Rib or scramble off on the east side of the rib.

## 4. SUPER POWER 11D ★

FA: JIM ERICKSON AND ROGER BRIGGS, 1980.

Begin 100 feet up along the northwest face from Solid State where a crack pierces the dramatic overhang. Climb a moderate pitch to get up under the roof and belay. Jam the upside-down crack past a wide spot and power up onto the wall above.

## 5. DREADNAUGHT 10 ★

FA: SCOTT WOODRUFF AND DAN HARE, 1975.

The upper end of the long, west-facing roof is interrupted by a right-facing dihedral. Climb a pitch of rotten rock up to the roof and belay. Climb the dihedral past two overhanging sections.

## 6. GRANDPA'S GARDEN 9+

FA: KEVIN HEAP AND LEE BABOUR, 1971.

The location of this route is not known. [If anyone finds this route, please call and let me know which crag it is on: 303-443-2439] Begin beneath a long roof. Climb up and left to an alcove beneath the roof. Chimney up where the roof fades. Jam out to the right or turn the roof at a hidden crack (8). Climb the right of two cracks and belay on a two-foot ledge. Continue up the crack for ten feet, then traverse left into a difficult dihedral. Pull up through some bushes and gain a good ledge.

## NORTH RIDGE

A long, serrated ridge climbs out of the jungle to the west of the Dreadnaught and continues southward in steps and blocks all the way to the summit of Dinosaur Mountain. The rock is heavily lichened and in places decomposed, but may nevertheless be climbed. Approach via the narrows of Skunk Canyon, pass the Achean Pronouncement and the Dreadnaught, stay to the left, and work up onto the foot of the ridge. The first tower is clean and tidy (4), but higher, the quality will vary according to choice of difficulty. A good deal of the terrain is fourth class, but short steep sections keep things interesting.

Skip Guerin on *Anthem to the Sun* (5.11), Ridge Four, Skunk Canyon. Photo by Jim Sanders.

**SKUNK CANYON, northside and central Flatirons**

Fourth Flatiron

Fifth Flatiron

Anomaly

Hippo Schmoe's Head Nose

Hour Glass

Amoeboid

Hobo Hillbilly

Ridge One

Ridge Two

SKUNK CANYON

# SKUNK CANYON
. . . . . . . . . . . . . . . . . . . . . . . . .

## (SEE MAP P. 94.)

Skunk Canyon is a wild place occupying the void between the south and southeast ridges of Green Mountain. The bottom of the canyon is a deep, narrow gorge pinched between the Achean Pronouncement and Satan's Slab. Gigantic free-standing boulders like the wrecks of old warships are wedged into this shadowy gap. A stream of crystal clear water gurgles out from beneath the towering blocks. Wild flowers and plants such as devil's club (related to ginseng), not normally found along the Front Range, flourish in these arcane depths.

Above the gorge, the walls draw back to form a vast clandestine cirque, barely visible from the plains to the east. The high, western rim of this cirque is the back side of the Sacred Cliffs. The south side is walled in by Dinosaur Mountain. On the north side of the canyon, four great rock ribs climb northward for 1500 feet to terminate along the crest of the southeast ridge of Green Mountain. These features correspond to the same strata on Dinosaur Mountain and are numbered from east to west as Ridge One (Stairway To Heaven), Ridge Two (Satan's Slab), Ridge Three (Angel's Way), and Ridge Four (Mohling Arête). Approach all features via the Skunk Canyon Trail.

**Note:** This trail (and the entire canyon, including the Sacred Cliffs) is closed to the public from February to August due to eagle nests on Super Power on the Dreadnaught and The Inferno on Ridge Two. Ridge One is open (1999).

**Another Note:** Routes are numbered beginning with "1" on each ridge. Hence, on photos and topos with more than one ridge pictured, there may be more than one route numbered "1", etc. Refer to the route descriptions under each individual ridge to determine which route is which.

## RIDGE FOUR

This long, slender rib is also known as Mohling Arête. The bottom of the rib is distinguished by a smooth slab, capped by a roof. Ridge Four has three notches or gaps, the upper of which being the easiest to navigate. All recorded routes lie along the west (southwest) face except for Mohling Arête which ascends the 1,500-foot ridge crest from bottom to top. The gullies on either side of the ridge may be hiked.

### 1.    UNDER THE INFLUENCE 11
FA: BOB HORAN AND JOHN BALDWIN, 1982.
Begin a short way down and right from the highest gap in the ridge. Climb a face and right-facing corner to a ledge and belay. A huge roof looms overhead, pierced by an off-width crack. Climb through the roof using hand jams hidden up in the off-width, then continue to the ridge crest. Traverse north and downclimb into the upper gap.

### 2.    ANTHEM TO THE SUN 11
FA: BOB HORAN AND JOHN BALDWIN, 1982.
About 30 feet to the right from Under the Influence, climb a cave to a severely overhanging crack. Rappel 60 feet.

### 3. CARROT FLAKE 10c

FA: BOB HORAN AND STEVE SANGDAHL, 1984.

Begin at Dialing for Dollars, but angle up to the left along a flake.

### 4. DIALING FOR DOLLARS 9 + ★

FFA: JIM ERICKSON AND BOB GODFREY, 1976.

One hundred feet down and right from the upper gap and 75 feet left from a massive overhang, is a green face with a shallow right-facing corner and a scoop about 50 feet up. This is about a thousand feet from the south end of the ridge. Climb the corner up the middle of the green face (9) and belay on a ledge. Angle up and left across a red wall near a left-facing corner (9 +).

### 5. HAMMER CASE 10 A2

FA: JOHN BALDWIN, BOB HORAN, STEVE SANGDAHL, BARRY RUGO, 1984.

This route ascends a massive overhanging wall 100 feet right of Dialing For Dollars. Climb a line of fixed pins, bashies, and bolts through a bulge, then follow a crack in the upper wall.

### 6. CLUB SALUTE 11D

FA: BALDWIN, HORAN, SANGDAHL, RUGO, 1984.

At the right end of the bulging overhang is another gap, left of midway along the west face. Begin right of the gap, near a small pine tree. Climb the face on the right, then move left into a left-facing, left-leaning dihedral.

### 7. GRAND PARADE 11D ★

FA: BOB HORAN AND RANDY LEAVITT, 1981.

Begin 300 feet up from the south end of the ridge and to the left of a pinnacle. Scramble 50 feet up to a ledge and belay. Climb a steep crack through a roof.

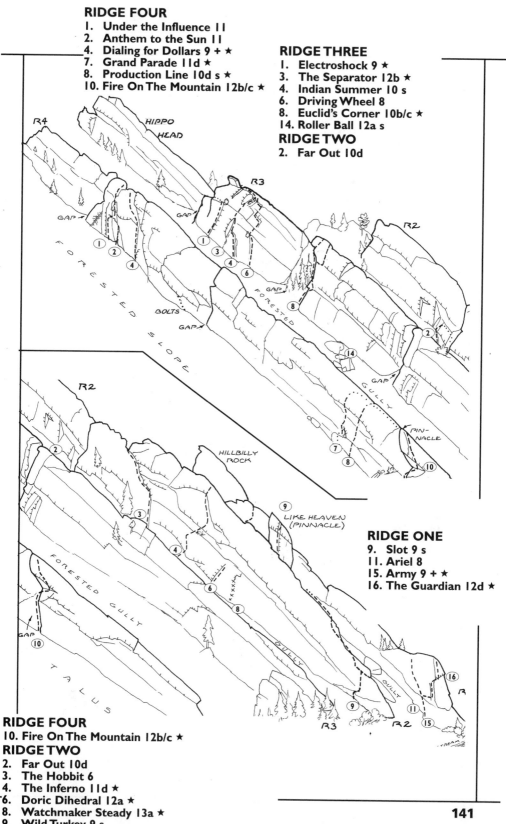

**RIDGE FOUR**
1. Under the Influence 11
2. Anthem to the Sun 11
4. Dialing for Dollars 9 + ★
7. Grand Parade 11d ★
8. Production Line 10d s ★
10. Fire On The Mountain 12b/c ★

**RIDGE THREE**
1. Electroshock 9 ★
3. The Separator 12b ★
4. Indian Summer 10 s
6. Driving Wheel 8
8. Euclid's Corner 10b/c ★
14. Roller Ball 12a s

**RIDGE TWO**
2. Far Out 10d

**RIDGE ONE**
9. Slot 9 s
11. Ariel 8
15. Army 9 + ★
16. The Guardian 12d ★

**RIDGE FOUR**
10. Fire On The Mountain 12b/c ★

**RIDGE TWO**
2. Far Out 10d
3. The Hobbit 6
4. The Inferno 11d ★
6. Doric Dihedral 12a ★
8. Watchmaker Steady 13a ★
9. Wild Turkey 9 s

141

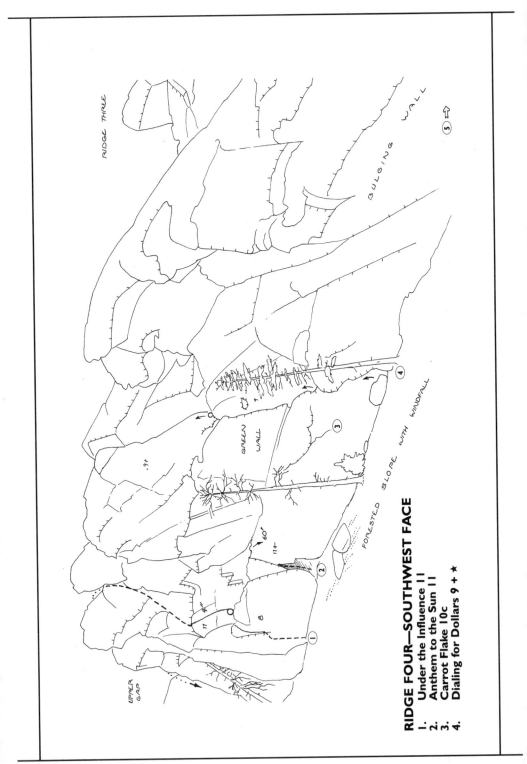

## RIDGE FOUR—SOUTHWEST FACE

1. **Under the Influence** 11
2. **Anthem to the Sun** 11
3. **Carrot Flake** 10c
4. **Dialing for Dollars** 9 + ★

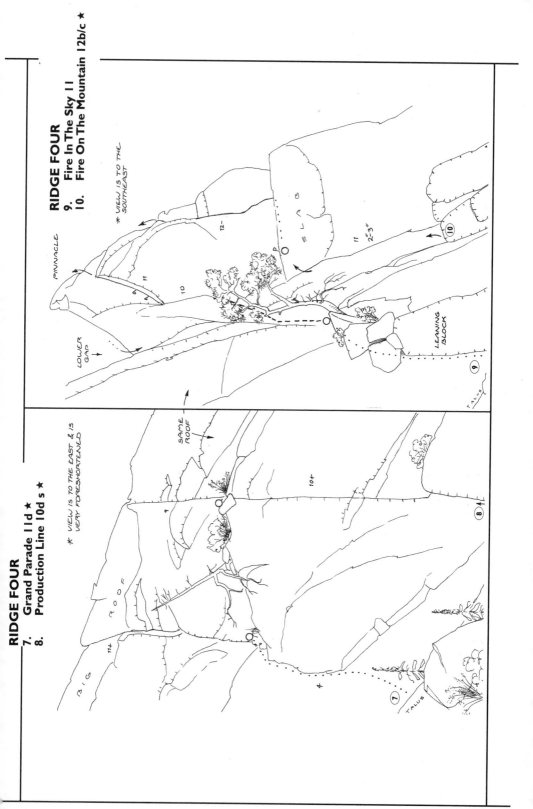

RIDGE FOUR
7.  Grand Parade 11d ★
8.  Production Line 10d s ★

* VIEW IS TO THE EAST & IS
  VERY FORESHORTENED

RIDGE FOUR
9.  Fire In The Sky 11
10. Fire On The Mountain 12b/c ★

* VIEW IS TO THE
  SOUTHEAST

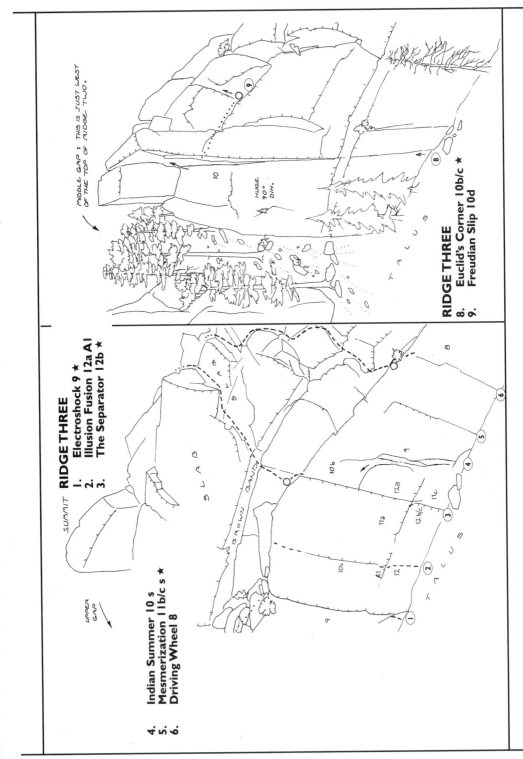

SUMMIT **RIDGE THREE**

1. Electroshock 9 ★
2. Illusion Fusion 12a A1
3. The Separator 12b ★

4. Indian Summer 10 s
5. Mesmerization 11 b/c s ★
6. Driving Wheel 8

**RIDGE THREE**

8. Euclid's Corner 10b/c ★
9. Freudian Slip 10d

## 8. PRODUCTION LINE 10D S ★

FA: BOB HORAN AND RANDY LEAVITT, 1981.

Climb a thin crack in a shallow right-facing corner (crux) and belay on the ledge to the right of Grand Parade. Continue up through a roof and gain the ridge crest (9).

## 9. FIRE IN THE SKY 11

FA: BOB HORAN AND JOHN BALDIN, 1982.

Begin beneath a large left-facing dihedral formed by a pinnacle. Scramble onto a leaning block and belay behind a pine. Climb into the main corner, then out right into a hanging dihedral (crux).

## 10. FIRE ON THE MOUNTAIN 12B/C ★

FA: BOB HORAN AND JOHN BALDWIN, 1982.

Begin at some blocks just right from Fire In The Sky. Climb a hand and fist crack to a hanging slab and belay. Move right and climb a wide crack through a big roof. Rack up to 4 inches.

## 11. MOHLING ARÊTE 5 ★

This route climbs the entire crest of Ridge Four. Begin from the very bottom of the ridge. Climb a pretty slab up and around the right end of the overhang and run the rope out to a belay near the crest. The next pitch passes the east side of a pinnacle and the first gap. If the entire ascent is belayed, expect ten or twelve pitches. The route is named for Franz Mohling, a climber who died in 1982.

# RIDGE THREE

Ridge Three begins just west of Satan's Slab and a little farther above the stream. It is not visible from the approach until you are very near. There are three gaps along the upper half of this ridge. The lowest is the most difficult to navigate; the middle gap is just west from the top of Ridge Two; the upper gap separates the ridge from the Hippo Head, which is of the same rock stratum and could be considered the actual summit of the ridge. Note, however, that the Hippo Head is not described with Ridge Three. All routes are on the west face except for Angel's Way which treks the entire ridge crest to the upper gap.

## 1. ELECTROSHOCK 9 ★

FA: DAN HARE AND SCOTT WOODRUFF, 1977.

Begin 50 feet right of the upper gap, directly below the summit block which sticks out like a diving board. Climb a rounded, left-facing dihedral to a small tree.

## 2. ILLUSION FUSION 12A A1

FA: BOB HORAN, 1988.

Begin midway between Electroshock and The Separator. Climb through a bulge (12a) and continue up a steep face (A1), then climb a left-facing corner to a ledge (10c).

## 3. THE SEPARATOR 12B ★

FA: BOB HORAN AND JOHN BALDWIN, 1985.

Begin a few feet left of Indian Summer. Climb up through a bulge (crux), then continue more easily up the right-facing dihedral. A scary variation climbs the clean face left of the dihedral.

## 4. INDIAN SUMMER 10 S

FA: ROGER BRIGGS AND CHRIS ROBERTS, 1971. FFA: SCOTT WOODRUFF, DAN HARE, PAT SMITH, 1975.

Follow a crack system up and left into the same right-facing dihedral as The Separator, move up to a ledge and belay. Follow a right- facing system to the top of the ridge. The original aid route probably climbed the whole dihedral of The Separator.

### 5.  MESMERIZATION 11B/C S ★
FA: Bob Horan and Randy Leavitt, 1981.
Just right from Indian Summer is an obtuse dihedral with a couple small roofs. Climb the dihedral and the smooth, unprotected face above, into a slot, and walk off to the north.

### 6.  DRIVING WHEEL 8
FA: Scott Woodruff and Dan Hare, 1975.
Begin 50 feet left of the middle gap and 30 feet right of The Separator. Climb the right of two finger cracks to a ledge that slopes down to the right. Traverse left and belay. Zig zag through short corners to the top of the ridge.

### 7.  WALKING SHOES 9 S
FA: Dave Rice and Eric Johnson.
Begin on a south-facing wall just across the gap from Euclid's Corner. Climb parallel cracks, up through a bulge, then continue up pocketed wall.

### 8.  EUCLID'S CORNER 10B/C ★
FA: Roger Briggs, Steve Nelson, 1971.      FFA: Scott Woodruff, Dan Hare, 1975.
Identify a dramatic buttress with a huge 90-degree dihedral capped by a roof, just right of a 30-foot gap with large trees growing in it.. Climb the dihedral and the roof.

### 9.  FREUDIAN SLIP 10D
FA: Jim Erickson, Dave Erickson, Al Czecholinski, 1979.
Climb the first 50 or 60 feet of Euclid's Corner, traverse around the arête on the right, and belay on a ledge beneath a roof. Climb a hand crack through the roof.

### 10.  GUOKAS ROUTE 10D VS
Begin a short way right of Euclid's Corner. Climb a right-facing dihedral to a ledge beneath a large roof.

### 11.  THIN CRACK 11 TR
Climb a thin crack a few feet right of Guokas Route. A two-bolt anchor is located directly above this route, 65 feet above the ground.

### 12.  SWITCHBLADE 10B/C S
FA: Scott Woodruff and Dan Hare, 1977.
A large roof develops to the right of Euclid's Corner and continues 60 feet above the ground to the lowest gap in the ridge. This route climbs a thin crack up to the roof in the middle of the wall.

### 13.  SHORT CORNERS 12 TR
Begin several yards right of Switchblade. Climb a short left-facing corner to a short right-facing dihedral to a huge roof.

### 14.  ROLLER BALL 12A S
Begin from a large block, 150 feet right of Euclid's Corner. Climb a thin crack with two pins (crux) through a roof and continue to a horizontal crack. Move left and climb a crack with another pin to a ledge beneath a big roof. A two bolt anchor is located up to the left. Rappel 65 feet to the ground.

### 15.  ANGEL'S WAY 0
Counting the Hippo Head, Ridge Three consists of four distinct sections, separated by gaps. Begin at the bottom of the lowest section, gain the crest, and scramble all the way to the top of the ridge. The Hippo Head is optional.

Bob Horan on the first ascent of *Beware the Future* (14a), Satan's Slab. Photo: Bob Horan collection.

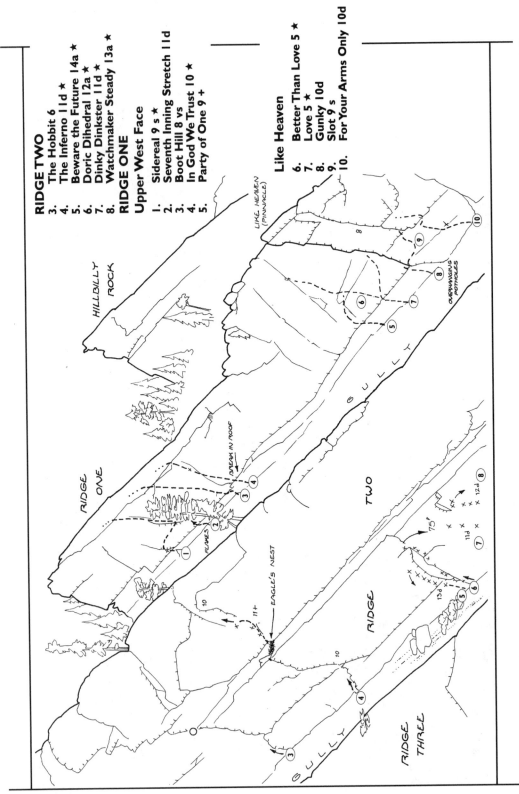

**RIDGE TWO**
3. The Hobbit 6
4. The Inferno 11d ★
5. Beware the Future 14a ★
6. Doric Dihedral 12a ★
7. Dinky Dinkster 11d ★
8. Watchmaker Steady 13a ★

**RIDGE ONE**

**Upper West Face**
1. Sidereal 9 s ★
2. Seventh Inning Stretch 11d
3. Boot Hill 8 vs
4. In God We Trust 10 ★
5. Party of One 9 +

**Like Heaven**
6. Better Than Love 5 ★
7. Love 5 ★
8. Gunky 10d
9. Slot 9 s
10. For Your Arms Only 10d

# RIDGE TWO

The megalith of Satan's Slab rises out of the deeps and dominates the mind with its overbearing presence. It is the most impressive crag in Skunk Canyon, and unlike the other ridges, it has routes on all sides. The long Satan's Slab route is a Flatiron classic not to be missed. The gullies on either side of the ridge can be hiked. To escape from the summit, scramble down into a large chimney that spits the summit area. Bridge west through the 20-inch slot, then follow a ledge 40 feet north to hiking terrain. To return to the east side of Ridge Two, scramble down steep but pleasant terrain beneath the north edge of the east face.

### 1.　SLAUGHTERHOUSE 12A S
FA: SKIP GUERIN AND CHIP RUCKGABER, 1982.
Begin along the upper west face of the ridge, 150 yards north of The Inferno. Climb a small overhang to a rotten band, followed by a tiny left-facing dihedral that becomes a right-facing dihedral.

### 2.　FAR OUT 10D
FA: JIM ERICKSON AND RON MATOUS, 1979.
Begin about 200 feet uphill from The Inferno. Climb a severely overhanging, flared crack.

### 3.　THE HOBBIT 6
FA: ROGER BRIGGS AND KRISTINA SOLHEIM, 1970.
Begin 50 feet left of The Inferno. Climb a left-facing dihedral system up and left through some large roofs. Two pitches. Downclimb west from the top of the ridge.

### 4.　THE INFERNO 11D ★
FA: ROGER BRIGGS, BILL BRIGGS, 1971. FFA: JEFF ACHEY, ROGER BRIGGS, 1981.
Begin about 600 feet up from the bottom of the ridge. Look for a long, shallow left-leaning corner above the lip of a large overhang. There is an eagle's nest on a ledge at the top of the first pitch. The second pitch has a couple of bolts near the bottom and ascends a bulging wall to the crest of the ridge.

### 5.　BEWARE THE FUTURE 14A ★
FA: BOB HORAN, 1988.
Climb the overhang just left of Doric Dihedral. Six bolts to a two-bolt anchor.

### 6.　DORIC DIHEDRAL 12A ★
FA: ROGER BRIGGS AND STEVE NELSON, 1971. FFA: CHIP RUCKGABER, 1983.
Begin along the west face, 400 feet from the bottom of the ridge. Climb a prominent right-leaning, right-facing dihedral.

### 7.　DINKY DINKSTER 11D ★
FA: BOB HORAN, 1988.
Follow a line of four bolts up the wall and merge with the top of Doric Dihedral.

### 8.　WATCHMAKER STEADY 13A ★
FA: BOB HORAN, 1988.
Begin just right of Dinky Dinkster. Follow bolts up to the right , then straight up the fall line. Six bolts to a two-bolt anchor, 70 feet.

### 9.　WILD TURKEY 9 S
FA: DAN HARE AND SCOTT WOODRUFF, 1976.
Begin along the west face, 150 feet from the bottom of the ridge. Step off a boulder and pull through an overhang with no pro, then climb to a hole with good pro and belay. Move up and right along a flake and pass a bulge, then continue up a pebbly wall to the ridge crest. Join Satan's Slab.

## RIDGE TWO
10.　Satan's Slab 8 s ★
11.　The Omen 7 s ★
12.　East Face 6 s ★
## RIDGE ONE
16.　The Guardian 12d ★
17.　Stairway to Heaven 4 ★

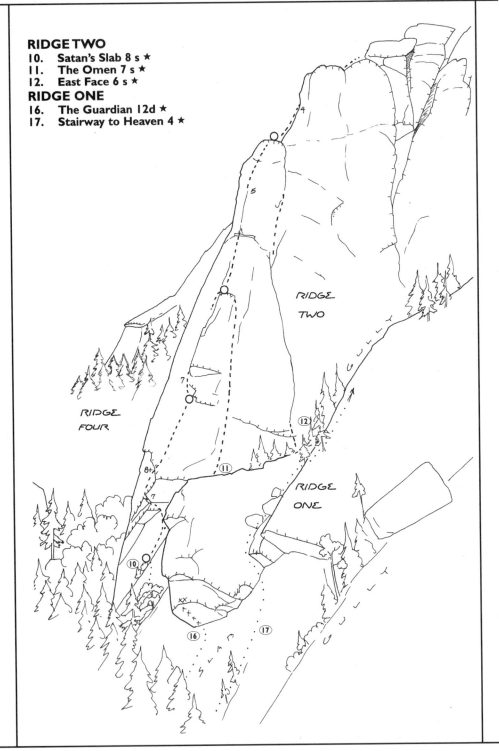

## 10. SATAN'S SLAB 8 s ★

FA: Layton Kor and Pat Ament, 1963.

A Flatiron classic. From the very bottom of the gorge, scramble up a slab toward a big roof and belay on a sloping ramp. 1. Angle left (west) just beneath the roof and pass a slot at its left end. Climb straight up over a bulge (crux) and up a steep slab to belay beneath a small overhang. 2. Climb around the left side of another roof (7), then continue up the steep slab for 100 feet and belay atop a pedestal. 3. Climb a long pitch to a ledge (5). 4. Climb to the top of the next section (4). From here one may downclimb a gully/chimney to the east and reach the forested gully between Ridges One and Two. 5. Climb one last pitch to the summit of Satan's Slab (4).

## 11. THE OMEN 7 s ★

Begin this excellent route right of Satan's Slab. Climb the rounded arête that forms the junction of the south and east faces and pass the two roofs on the right. Join the regular line atop the pedestal.

## 12. EAST FACE 6 s ★

FA: Gerry and Barbara Roach and Dave Palke, 1974.

This classic route ascends the shallow trough 60 feet right of The Omen. Three long unprotected pitches to the ridge crest. Finish as for Satan's Slab.

## 13. ENCHANTED DEVIL 5 ★

FA: Gerry Roach, 1977.

The east face of Satan's Slab is divided by chimneys or cracks into four sections. The previous three routes are on the lowest and largest section; this one climbs the east face of the third section. Climb up and left to a pocket in the solution gully between the second and third sections. Continue up along the south edge of the third section for three more pitches. Join the final pitch of Satan's Slab.

## 14. 666 6 ★

FA: Richard Rossiter, solo, 1996.

Begin 900 feet up the gully beneath the east face, at the lowest point of the highest section of Satan's Slab. 1. Climb the arête and belay at a tree on the right (4, 90 feet). One may also begin up to the right and climb straight left the tree. 2. Move up and left and follow the arête to a good ledge with a crack (4, 140 feet). 3. Continue up the arête and belay at a horizontal crack (4, 100 feet). 4. Climb through a beautiful smooth section, then continue past two diagonal cracks and belay at a ledge along the arête (6, 150 feet). 5. Climb another smooth section just right of two small trees and run the rope out to the top (6, 160 feet).

## RIDGE ONE

First thing on the right, steep slab to a huge overhang...you can't miss it. This elegant rib is 1000 feet long and has three summits. As with the other three ridges, most of the climbing is on the steep west side (which actually faces southwest). Halfway up the ridge is an impressive pinnacle called Like Heaven (the lowest summit). To escape the true summit at the north end of the ridge, downclimb a knife-edged ridge to the north, then go down another 40 feet east to a large tree. Rappel 60 feet from the tree or downclimb to the ground. One may also climb off to the east from two places below the Like Heaven pinnacle.

## Upper West Face

The following routes are located on the upper west face, to the north of the pinnacle called Like Heaven.

### 1. SIDEREAL 9 s ★

FA: BRAD GILBERT, SCOTT WOODRUFF, DAN HARE, 1975.

Begin about 100 feet down along the west face from the upper end of the ridge, on a pedestal of shattered rock. Clip an old piton and turn a roof. Traverse right to a right-facing dihedral and climb to the crest of the ridge.

### 2. SEVENTH INNING STRETCH 11D

FA: RICK ACCOMAZZO AND CHRISTIAN GRIFFITH, 1981.

Climb the large overhang about 45 feet right of Sidereal.

### 3. BOOT HILL 8 vs

FA: DAN HARE, SCOTT WOODRUFF, JIM MICHAEL, 1975.

Begin down to the right past the low overhang and 40 feet left of a gully. Climb mostly straight up and belay in a dihedral below the right end of a rotten roof. Climb the steep wall above.

### 4. IN GOD WE TRUST 10 ★

FA: ERIC GUOKAS AND ROB HERING, 1980.

Climb the wall to the right of Boot Hill. Look for a bolt about two-thirds of the way up.

### 5. PARTY OF ONE 9 +

FA: JIM ERICKSON, SOLO, 1978.

Climb an overhanging crack system about 30 feet uphill from Love.

## Like Heaven

The following routes are located on or near a dramatic pinnacle in the center of the long west face.

### 6. BETTER THAN LOVE 5 ★

FA: GERRY AND BARBARA ROACH, 1972.

Climb the initial overhang of Love, then angle up to the north (left) and climb a rib to the middle summit of Ridge One.

### 7. LOVE 5 ★

FA: PAT AMENT AND MIKE VANLOON, 1967.

Begin from a large block, 60 feet north of Like Heaven. Stretch up to place a stopper, then pull across the void and climb up on good holds. Traverse right into a huge dihedral, then climb straight up to a notch along the ridge crest. Follow an arête southwest to the summit of Like Heaven.

### 8. GUNKY 10D

FA: SCOTT WOODRUFF, TIM BEAMAN, BRAD GILBERT, 1975.

Begin below the left (northwest) side of Like Heaven. Climb an overhang with some potholes to a ledge, then climb an easy gully, blast out right over a roof and belay. Continue up and right on steep but moderate terrain.

### 9. SLOT 9 s

This route takes the big slot through the west overhang near the top of Like Heaven. Begin just right of Gunky. Climb a rotten overhang and go to the right end of a ledge. Work up and right along an edge and follow a left-facing dihedral to the base of the slot. Belay here or continue up through the slot (8) and exit at the very top. It is also possible to begin this route from directly beneath the slot, which may be the original line.

## 10. FOR YOUR ARMS ONLY 10D

FA: ED WEBSTER AND CHESTER DIEMAN, 1983.

Begin about 40 feet right of Love (the dihedral on the left side of the tower). Climb an overhang with a fixed pin (9), then up to a ledge and belay. Hand traverse right to the crest and work your way up over strenuous terrain.

# Lower West Face

The following routes are located at the bottom of the west face, just left of the huge south face overhang. There are two ways to access these routes: Climb in from the left and reach a bush on a long sloping ledge, or farther right, climb pockets through a roof (10a) beneath Arms Reduction.

## 11. ARIEL 8

FA: SCOTT WOODRUFF AND SUE KENT, 1975.

Scramble up to a bush and move a short way right, then climb into a left-facing corner, go left below a roof, and up a thin crack.

## 12. ARIEL DIRECT 10A

FA: DAN HARE AND SCOTT WOODRUFF, 1986.

Continue straight up the left-facing corner.

## 13. ARMS REDUCTION 11B

FA: DAN HARE AND SCOTT WOODRUFF, 1986.

Traverse in from Ariel or climb directly up via overhanging pockets requiring Tricams (10a). Move up, sling a flake, pass a small left-facing corner (crux), and continue to the crest. Tricky pro.

## 14. ARMED FORCES 11B ★

FA: DAN HARE AND MIKE O'DONNEL, 1986.

Climb to the ledge as for Arms Reduction and traverse a few feet right. Climb straight up past several bolts to a two-bolt anchor.

## 15. ARMY 9 + ★

FA: DAN HARE AND SCOTT WOODRUFF, 1975.

Begin as for Ariel or climb through the roof as for Arms Reduction and gain a crack the angles right and leads to the south edge of the west face. Belay at the top of the crack. Move right and climb two grooves along the west edge of the south-facing overhang.

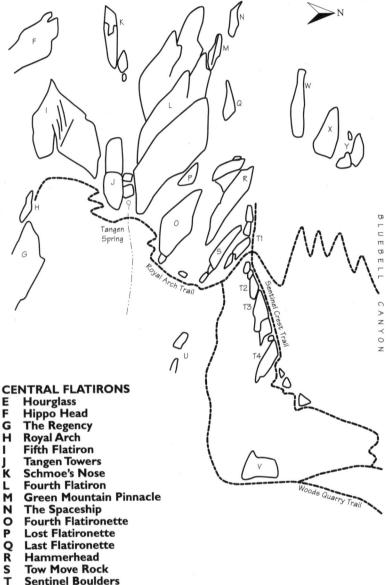

## CENTRAL FLATIRONS

E   Hourglass
F   Hippo Head
G   The Regency
H   Royal Arch
I   Fifth Flatiron
J   Tangen Towers
K   Schmoe's Nose
L   Fourth Flatiron
M   Green Mountain Pinnacle
N   The Spaceship
O   Fourth Flatironette
P   Lost Flatironette
Q   Last Flatironette
R   Hammerhead
S   Tow Move Rock
T   Sentinel Boulders
    T1   West Sentinel Boulder
    T2   East Sentinel Boulder
    T3   Easy Street
    T4   Downclimb
U   Lost Sentinels
V   Woods Quarry
W   Willy B
X   The Thing
Y   Eyes Of The Canyon

# CENTRAL FLATIRONS

This chapter covers the crags between Skunk Canyon and Bluebell Canyon. With the exception of the immensely popular Royal Arch, these are among the least visited of the Flatirons on Green Mountain. Most features are approached from the Mesa Trail or the Royal Arch Trail.

## HILLBILLY ROCK

This small flatiron is situated below and directly east of the summit of Ridge One. The consistent nature of the east face offers excellent route-finding opportunities, since the only real error of consequence would be to climb off the edge of the rock. Approach via NCAR and the Mesa Trail. Once directly east of the rock, hike cross-country to its base. An easier approach is to hike the Skunk Canyon trail until 350 feet from the bottom of Ridge One, then follow a steep path northwest up an open slope to the bottom of the east face. To descend from the summit, downclimb the North Face route (Class 4) or rappel 60 feet to the north. Huge blocks just south of Hillbilly Rock offer some short scrambles and interesting bouldering.

**1. EAST FACE LEFT 0**
Begin at the low point on the south side of the east face and head for the top.

**2. EAST FACE 0**
Begin near the right side of the face. Three pitches.

**3. NORTH FACE CLASS 4**
Begin beneath the north side of the summit. Climb one short pitch with a bulge in the middle.

**4. WEST FACE 12?**
Begin 100 feet down and right from the highest part of the west face. Climb past a bashie, then continue up the steep wall. Three bolts to a two-bolt anchor.

**5. WEST FACE RIGHT 12?**
Begin at a left-facing corner with a good crack, 50 feet right of the preceding route. Climb the crack, then follow three or four bolts around onto the west face and finish at the same anchor as above.

## THE HOBO

This small crag is located 50 yards west of Hillbilly Rock. Climb 120 feet up the east face to the exposed summit, then reverse the route. Class 3

## AMOEBOID

This small flatiron is located southeast of the Hourglass and southwest of the Royal Arch. Hike around the west side of the Royal Arch and continue south to the foot of the crag. There is a single route recorded on the east face called Buckets, which climbs potholes along a solution groove. Class 4, 300 feet.

## ANOMALY

This is an even more obscure flatiron below and northeast of the Amoeboid and 200 yards west of the Royal Arch. A single route goes up the east face. Class 4, 200 feet.

CENTAL
FLATIRONS
See legend, p. 154.

*Green Mountain Summit*

## THE HOURGLASS

This unusual crag lies south of the Fifth Flatiron and east of the Hippo Head. Approach via the Royal Arch Trail. From the Royal Arch, hike west through the trees to the base of the rock. The east face is Class 4 and is dotted with little trees. From the summit, scramble off to the south.

## HIPPO HEAD

The Hippo Head, also known as The Fist, sits high on the southeast ridge of Green mountain above the Hourglass and the Fifth Flatiron. It is immediately north of Ridge Three (Skunk Canyon) and is part of the same rock stratum. It has routes on all sides but the west, which is guarded by a very impressive overhang. Approach routes on the north and east sides by hiking straight up from the Royal Arch. Approach the south ridge by hiking up from the Hillbilly and staying south of the Hourglass. To descend from the summit, downclimb 30 feet to the east (4) or rappel to the same point, then rappel 50 feet north to the ground. One may also rappel 80 feet west to the ground. Or rappel down the east face.

**I.   SOUTH RAMP 6**

The route is 600 feet long, though somewhat discontinuous. Climb the first ramp and gully system west of the south ridge and mount the summit block by a crack on the east side.

**2.   SOUTH RIDGE 6**

This route ascends the long south ridge from the low point of the rock. Climb a crack around on the right side of the ridge and eventually gain the ridge crest. Where a buttress impedes progress, follow a ledge system across the east face and finish with the East Face route.

**3.   EAST FACE 6**

The east face can be climbed in three pitches. The important feature to find is a hand crack that leads to the broad ledge south of the summit block. Master the final 30 feet via a crack on the east side.

**4.   NORTH FACE 7**

The north face is only 50 feet high and is overcome by climbing a crack that diagonals up to the right.

## THE REGENCY

This seldom-visited flatiron is below and immediately east of the Royal Arch. It features one of the best Class 3 routes in the Flatirons and may be combined with an ascent of the Royal Arch. To escape the summit, downclimb the east face for 100 feet to a broken area and walk off to the north. One may also downclimb 20 feet to the east and go around to the west side. Downclimb 30 feet to the west and cross a gap, then head back east along a ramp. Climb down to the west through a deep crack and arrive beneath the east side of the Royal Arch.

**I.   EL CAMINO ROYALE CLASS 3 ★**

Leave the Mesa Trail about 100 yards south of Woods Quarry and follow a smaller trail up into the draw southeast of the objective. Begin at the low point of the rock and follow the southeast ridge for 500 feet to the summit.

## ROYAL ARCH

This curious rock draws a lot of attention from hikers, but has not caught on with climbers. The arch may be climbed from the east or from the west , or one could do the "grand traverse," up the west side and down the east side. Approach via the Royal Arch Trail.

### 1. EAST RIDGE CLASS 3 ★

Begin just above the Regency, at the lowest point of the rock. Climb 200 feet to the summit. One may also begin near the inside of the arch on the south side.

### 2. WEST FACE 6

Climb the steep west side of the arch. 40 feet.

## FIFTH FLATIRON

"The Fifth" is the elegantly pointed flatiron south of the Fourth Flatiron and west of the Royal Arch. It is characterized by a series of grooves in the middle of the east face called the Cat Scratches, a very clean southeast buttress, and of course, by its narrow, pointed summit. Approach via the Royal Arch Trail and cut up to the west shortly after passing Tangen Spring. One may also contour northwest from the Royal Arch. To escape the summit, rappel 75 feet west from an eyebolt. To return to the bottom of the rock, hike down around the south side. One may also hike down around the north side of the Fifth Flatiron and around the north side of Tangen Towers, but it is steeper and brushier. See Tangen Tunnel Route.

### 1. EAST FACE LEFT 5 ★

Begin at an alcove below the south side of the east face and climb directly up excellent rock staying left of the Cat Scratches. 550 feet.

### 2. CAT SCRATCHES 4 TO 6

The Scratches, on close observation, are not clean cracks, but deep chimneys and are not as fun as one might imagine. Hike up to the center of the face below the Scratches, passing a large chockstone in the approach gully. Begin some 30 feet south of the chockstone. Climb a rib for 300 feet into the center of the face. Climb another 100 feet to a broken area below the Cat Scratches. Climb one of four chimneys: the channel to the right is perhaps the least objectionable, and the scratch in the center is the most difficult (6). Or work up and right to the ridge crest where one last pitch leads up the crest to the summit.

### 3. REGULAR ROUTE 4 ★

Begin just left of a huge crack that runs up the north side of the east face, and maintain that relationship until the crack fades out and it is possible to angle right (north) to a prominent niche on the north ridge (four pitches). Two more long pitches up the aesthetic ridge crest bring one to the summit.

### 4. NORTHEAST BUTTRESS 6 s ★

This is the best line on the Fifth Flatiron. It is also the longest (900 feet), the steepest, the most committing, and has the poorest protection. Ascend the north edge of the east face all the way to the top.

## LOWER TANGEN TOWER

This steep-sided tower stands just above and south of Tangen Spring immediately west of the Royal Arch Trail. To escape the summit, rappel 40 feet west into the notch between Lower and Upper Tangen Towers. Scramble down beneath giant boulders on the north side.

### 1. UPPER SOUTH FACE 5

FA: GERRY ROACH AND BARB INYAN, 1984.

Hike around to the upper south face. Climb the left of two cracks, follow a ramp up to the west, and finish with a short southwest-facing wall.

### 2. SOUTH FACE RIGHT 9

Begin from a block about 50 feet above the Royal Arch Trail. Climb a short crack in a wall of holes, pass a ramp that angles up to the west and climb past a flake to gain the east face. Scramble to the top.

## UPPER TANGEN TOWER

This is the higher of the two towers and lies directly west of the lower one. To escape the summit, hike off to the west and north.

### 1. EAST FACE 5

GERRY ROACH AND BARB INYAN, 1984.

Begin in the notch between the two towers and pick a ling up the east face.

## SCHMOE'S NOSE

This peculiar rock sits near to the skyline above and between The Fourth and Fifth Flatirons. Hike the Royal Arch Trail over Sentinel Pass to Tangen Spring. Head up between the Tangen Towers and the Fourth Flatiron and weave through some large chockstones (Tangen Tunnel). Once above the Upper Tangen Tower, angle up and left to the south side of Schmoe's Nose.

### 1. SPHERICAL IMPLOSION 8 A3

FA: ROGER AND BILL BRIGGS, 1971.

Find a difficult route up the south face.

### 2. EAST FACE LEFT (RATING UNKNOWN)

FA: TOM HORNBEIN AND PARTNER, 1950s.

Climb the east face and take the dihedral at the left side of the square nose.

### 3. EAST FACE RIGHT (RATING UNKNOWN)

FA: CORWIN SIMMON AND LYNN RYDSDALE, 1950s.

Climb the east face and take the dihedral at the right side of the nose.

### 4. NORTH FACE (RATING UNKNOWN)

FA: CLIFF CHITTIM, JIM AND JOHN VICKERY, KARL GUSTAVSON, 1951.

This was probably the first route on the rock and was managed by lassoing a horn and climbing the rope hand-over-hand to reach the upper east face.

## FOURTH FLATIRON

This sprawling mass of rock lies just southeast of the summit of Green Mountain. From the northeast it appears as a massive slab of vast proportions, but in reality it is three slabs separated by deep gullies that descend diagonally from northwest to southeast. The lowest section lies just above the Royal Arch Trail about 100 yards south of Sentinel Pass. The middle section rises up immediately behind it and reaches its high point as Green Mountain Pinnacle. The upper section appears even larger and reaches nearly to the crest of the southeast ridge of Green Mountain. The whole thing must span a thousand feet or more.

The first three routes are on the upper southwest face of the large middle section of the Fourth Flatiron, about 150 feet down the gully to the southeast from Green Mountain Pinnacle.

### 1. JESTER 10D ★

FA: BOB HORAN AND JOHN BALDWIN, 1988.

Begin about 15 feet right of a pair of Douglas fir trees. Climb up through the left side of a squared off roof (10d), up to a stance with a bolt, and follow a diagonal thin crack to the skyline on the right (10d).

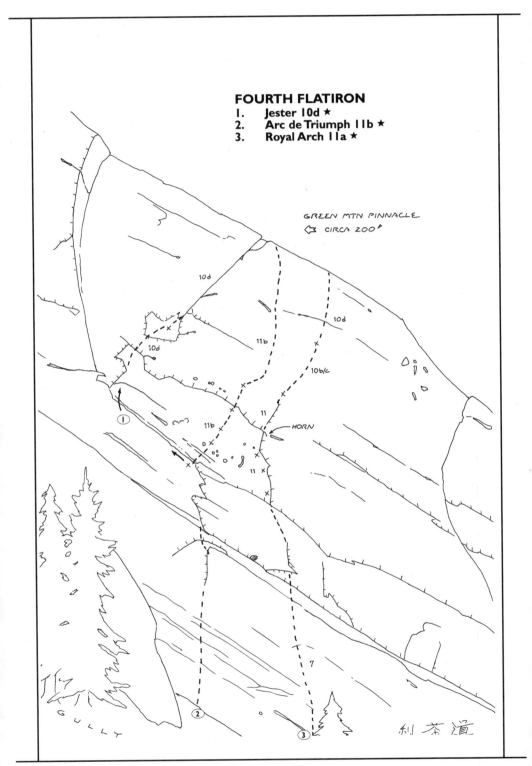

# FOURTH FLATIRON
1. **Jester 10d ★**
2. **Arc de Triumph 11b ★**
3. **Royal Arch 11a ★**

GREEN MTN PINNACLE
CIRCA 200'

10d

10d

10d

11b

10b/c

11b

11

HORN

11

7

1

2

3

GULLY

利茶道

**160**

### 2. ARC DE TRIUMPH 11B ★

FA: BOB HORAN AND DAN MCQUADE, 1988.

Begin this route as for Jester. Follow a line of four bolts up through the roof and the face above. The sections that appear to be runout are on easier ground.

### 3. ROYAL ARCH 11A ★

FA: BOB HORAN AND DAN MCQUADE, 1988.

Begin down to the right from Arc de Triumph. Master the right side of the arching roof at a horn with slings and continue up the steep face past some bolts.

### 4. EAST FACE 4 ★

This long route ascends all three sections of the Fourth Flatiron and requires about twelve pitches. Belays are not described. Begin right off the Royal Arch Trail. Climb to a cave (an incipient arch), then on to the ridge and continue until it is easy to descend into the gully between the lower and middle sections. Move up the gully and get onto the middle section near a large tree. Climb into a large crack in the middle of the face and follow it (or the face to its right) to where it widens and holds a "hanging garden." Continue through the garden into the upper gully, walk west and venture out onto the third and final section. Work out to the left to avoid trees and ledges and gain a crack that runs up the middle of the face. From the top of the crack it is easy to reach the summit. Though it is a short way to hiking terrain on the west side, to get off of the summit you must let yourself down on good holds and drop past an overhang!

## GREEN MOUNTAIN PINNACLE

This small crag has gained wide recognition due to the publication of photographs of the climb Death and Transfiguration. The pinnacle lies northwest and adjacent to the middle section of the Fourth Flatiron and could be seen as the summit of that feature. Approach as for the Spaceship from Sentinel Pass, staying to the right of large blocks and cliffs. To escape the summit, rappel 75 west or downclimb Green Sneak (Class 4).

### 1. FERN ALLEY CLASS 3

This deep gash or moat, separates Green Mountain Pinnacle from the middle section of the Fourth Flatiron and creates an unlikely passage between the east face to the west face. Find the entrance along the north face, 200 feet down and left from the summit. Hike up the gash for 60 feet and scramble past a wedged flake. Near the top of the gash, scramble south to a broken summit area where a block leans against the upper south face of Green Mountain Pinnacle. Scramble west down short steps to the gully between the middle and upper sections of the Fourth Flatiron.

### 2. EAST FACE 6

Hike up into Fern Alley. After 40 feet or so, climb the right wall (6), gain the right (north) side of the east face and scramble to the top (Class 4).

### 3. DEATH AND DISFIGURATION 10

During the 1970s, Jim Erickson became notorious for doing on-sight solos of difficult climbs. What is more remarkable, many of his solos comprised first ascents. As the name may suggest, this particular route attempted in 1973 marked a turning point in Erickson's career as a soloist. Jim, by the way, did not die, but fell from the route breaking both lower legs and crawled 800 feet down the steep rocky slope to the Royal Arch Trail where he was eventually rescued. Up to the right from the entrance to Fern Alley, climb a hand crack in a conspicuous left-facing, out-leaning dihedral.

# GREEN MOUNTAIN PINNACLE
1. **Fern Alley Class 3**
2. **East Face 6**
3. **Death and Disfiguration 10**
5. **Death And Transfiguration 11b ★**
5a. **Transgression 12a ★**
8. **Green Sneak 2**

## THE SPACESHIP
1. **East Face 4 s ★**

### 4. SALSA VERDE 11c

FA: ALAN NELSON, KARL MUELLER, CLAIRE MEARNS, 1989.

Begin downhill and left from Death And Transfiguration. Five bolts to a two-bolt anchor. Bring a #3.5 Friend.

### 5. DEATH AND TRANSFIGURATION 11b ★

FA: ROGER BRIGGS AND LUKE STUDER, 1972.

Climb the obvious right-leaning crack in the middle of the north face and jam out through the roof (crux).

### 5A. TRANSGRESSION 12a *

FA: NEIL CANNON, MARK SONNENFELD, ERIC WINKLEMAN, 1985.

This variation avoids the regular crux and battles out past the west end of the roof (12a).

### 6. PILAF 10

FA: RICK ACCOMAZZO AND ERIK ERIKSSON, 1982.

Hike around to the west side of the crag. Climb a left-leaning ramp, up past a flake, then traverse right over a block and finish with a thin crack (crux).

### 7. TAKING CARE OF BUSINESS 5 ★

Hike around to the west side of the crag, a few feet south of the summit, and find one of the best chimneys in the Boulder area. Scramble up for 30 feet to get started.

### 8. GREEN SNEAK 2

It happens that the west chimney goes all the way through to the east face and divides Green Mountain Pinnacle into two great slices of rock. Enter the chimney from the west and scramble straight east. When you emerge to a commanding view of the Great Plains, make a left and sprint up the east face to the summit.

## THE SPACESHIP

This beautiful little spire, also known as Challenger, is located immediately west of Green Mountain Pinnacle. Hike the Royal Arch Trail to Sentinel Pass, then head west staying north of the rocky crest. Pass the Hammerhead and veer northwest around the Last Flatironette, then work back to the southwest beneath the imposing north face of Green Mountain Pinnacle and gain a small saddle at the bottom of the east face. To escape the summit, downclimb six feet west and cross a gap, then continue west along a fin and cross another gap. Downclimb south to hiking terrain.

### 1. EAST FACE 4 s ★

FA: GERRY AND BARB ROACH, 1969.

Begin in the col between Green Mountain Pinnacle and the Spaceship. Climb to the highest tree on the east face and belay (150 feet). Follow the north edge of the east face to the summit (150 feet).

## FOURTH FLATIRONETTE

This small crag is located east of the Fourth Flatiron. The Royal Arch Trail passed just beneath the foot of the rock about 200 feet south of Sentinel Pass. Climb onto the south edge of the east face and follow it past two large ponderosa pines (4) to the south ridge. Continue up the south ridge past a short headwall and make a 50-foot hand traverse north to the summit. To escape from the summit, scramble south across a 50-foot hand traverse, downclimb past a short headwall, then down a ramp to the west.

## LOST FLATIRONETTE

This small rock is located along the base of the Fourth Flatiron, a short way south of the summit of the Fourth Flatironette. Approach by hiking up along the south side of the Fourth Flatironette or by hiking south from the west face of the Hammerhead. Begin climbing at the bottom of the east face and follow its south edge to the summit (3, 250 feet). Downclimb the short north face.

## LAST FLATIRONETTE

This little flatiron is located about 150 feet north from the top of the first section of the Fourth Flatiron. Approach from Sentinel Pass as for the Hammerhead, but continue another 400 feet west to the bottom of the east face. Climb the middle of the narrow east face (Class 4, 350 feet). Scramble off to the southwest past a horn.

## HAMMERHEAD

The summit of this unusual rock lies 200 feet west of Sentinel Pass. To reach the bottom of the east ridge, hike south from Sentinel Pass along the Royal Arch Trail and find the foot of the 400-foot ridge 75 feet above the trail, hidden in the trees behind Two Move Rock. To reach the impressive summit block without climbing the east ridge, hike straight west from Sentinel Pass, keeping to the right (north) side of the broad, boulder-studded ridge. To escape from the summit, rappel 60 feet west from slings around a horn or downclimb Yodeling Moves.

### 1.   EAST RIDGE CLASS 4 ★

Begin from the low point of the rock. Halfway up, climb right over a surprising 50-foot arch. After 400 feet you will find yourself staring across a notch at the overhanging summit block. Climb down into the notch and skulk around to the west side of the summit. Continue with Yodeling Moves. Or from the notch, climb the steep north face (7) and a short east face to the summit.

### 2.   YODELING MOVES 0 ★

Begin at a large, jammed block. Traverse up and right until it is obvious to pull straight up to the top.

## TWO MOVE ROCK

Two Move Rock is located immediately west of the Royal Arch Trail, about 100 feet south of Sentinel Pass. It may be identified by a large block that leans up against the bottom of the southeast ridge. Climb over the block and up the ridge to a short south-facing wall. Climb the wall and pass a smooth slab (3, the two moves are here), then continue up the ridge to a small summit that overhangs to the west. Escape the ridge here or continue northwest until the ridge fades some 100 feet west of Sentinel Pass.

## Sentinel Boulders

These are a string of small flatirons and boulders along the ridge crest between the Tangen Spring drainage and Bluebell Canyon, and on either side of Sentinel Pass. These features may be reached from the Royal Arch Trail or from the Sentinel Crest Trail above Woods Quarry, which runs just below the north sides of the crags to Sentinel Pass. They provide fun scrambling and interesting views of the Flatirons. Be warned that some of these little crags have difficult routes and no easy escape from their summits. Only the larger features have names and are listed below.

## WEST SENTINEL BOULDER

This large block practically hangs over the path where the Royal Arch Trail begins to descend south from Sentinel Pass. The east face is just west of the trail. There is a single route up the southeast ridge (4). Begin about 60 feet south of Sentinel Pass. Climb to a notch with a tree and gain the ridgecrest. Pass a bulge on the right and finish up along the southeast ridge. Scramble off to the west.

## EAST SENTINEL BOULDER

This steep little crag lies 100 feet east of Sentinel Pass and has two known routes, the easiest being on the north side: Climb up to the notch between Easy Street (the next crag to the east) and the summit block and finish in a squeeze chimney with a chockstone at its top (6). One may also climb in from the south: Cross a gap and get onto the east face, then continue up the steep east side of the summit tower. To escape the summit, sling the chockstone and rappel 40 feet north.

## EASY STREET

This rock is just east across a notch from East Sentinel Boulder. It is a weird sort of flatiron with a low point in the middle that allows easy access to the east face from the north. The east face may also be climbed from its low point on the south side of the crest: Climb 50 feet to a headwall and pass it on the left (2) or climb it directly (6). Scramble another 150 feet to the summit. The north side of the rock features a beautiful overhanging hand crack in a dihedral (11). The short ridge above the notch on the west may also be climbed (4). To escape from the summit, downclimb the west ridge. Or downclimb east 25 feet and go south into the gully between Easy Street and East Sentinel Boulder.

## DOWNCLIMB

This is the farthest east of the Sentinel Boulders and is easily reached from the Sentinel Crest Trail, which crosses from the south to the north side of the ridge crest at the saddle immediately east of this crag. To escape from the summit, downclimb East Face.

### 1.    EAST FACE 3

The east face may be climbed from its low point. Follow the south edge of the face 100 feet to the summit.

### 2.    BIG ROOF 11

The left side of the north face presents a large overhang. Begin from a cave, climb a wide crack to the roof, then finger traverse left to the edge of the east face.

### 3.    NORTH FACE 9

Climb a thin crack with a fixed pin along the right side of the north face. Gain a notch on the west ridge and continue to the summit.

### 4.    WEST RIDGE 7

Begin from a big block beneath the west ridge. Step across to some obvious holds, traverse up and left to a ledge, then climb around to the north. Pass a bulge to a notch beneath the top. Finish as for the preceding route. One may also climb just right of a cave at the step across. Steep with minimal pro (9?).

### 5.    SOUTHWEST CHIMNEY 4

Climb a 40-foot chimney around to the right from West Ridge.

## LOST SENTINELS

Two small rock ribs are hidden in the trees southeast of the Sentinel Boulders. Approach via a vague trail that climbs west from the south side of Woods Quarry. These features will be found 100 feet to the south where this trail steepens. The northern of the two ribs provides a 150-foot scramble up its east ridge. The initial overhang is optional (5). The southern rib provides a 200-foot scramble that includes an elegant arête.

**WOODS QUARRY**
1. Left Arête 5 s
2. Non-Friction 8 s ★
3. The Middle Way 10 TR ★
4. Diatribe 10 TR ★
5. Quarry Wall 8 ★
6. Don't Stop Now 9 s ★

## WOODS QUARRY

Woods Quarry lies west of the Mesa Trail and east of the Sentinel Boulders area. The 90-foot flat face lies back at an angle of about 70 degrees. The wall was exposed by an old quarry operation and is not weathered or lichened. The surface is very smooth and offers several short routes of quality. Approach via the Mesa Trail or the Enchanted Mesa Trail and continue on the Woods Quarry Trail to its end at the wall. One may also approach via the Tomato Rock Trail.

### 1. LEFT ARÊTE 5 s

Begin behind a pine, a short way left from the main wall. Climb a left-facing corner to a ledge with a tree, then step left and climb the left side of an arête to the top of the blunt rib. Belay from a horizontal crack after 120 feet.

### 2. NON-FRICTION 8 s ★

Begin at the left side of the face and follow a line of four bolts. The final section is runout.

### 3. THE MIDDLE WAY 10 TR ★

Climb up to some long scoops about 20 feet off the deck and follow a seam to the top.

### 4. DIATRIBE 10 TR ★

Begin 15 feet to the right of the preceding route. Climb a blank section to the second seam right of The Middle Way.

### 5. QUARRY WALL 8 ★

Follow a line of four bolts and rappel 75 feet from a two-bolt anchor.

### 6. DON'T STOP NOW 9 s ★

Climb a shallow left-facing corner along the right side of the face. There is one bolt about halfway up.

# WILLY B

This fierce, freestanding pinnacle is utterly lacking in the ho-hum slab climbing characteristic of the Flatirons. Where the lower east face is a menagerie of mosses, lichens and twisted trees, a clean, windswept tower rises above and poses a sobering challenge. Approach as for The Thing, but from the vicinity of the Hammerhead, hold more to the west. If you bump into The Thing, rebound toward the southwest; the two crags are not far apart. Begin at the southeast corner of the face, above the rough lower section. To escape the summit, rappel 80 feet west or 100 feet north.

### 1.   EAST FACE 8 s ★
FA: TOM HORNBEIN AND DEXTER BRINKER, 1948.

This is an exciting route that requires some commitment on the part of the leader. Begin at the south side of the east face. Angle up and right toward the north side of the east face, then climb straight up to a good stance above a tree at the bottom of a large, left-facing dihedral (2, 120 feet). Move up to the right and master an exposed bulge that guards access onto a narrow rib (8+ s), or climb ten feet up the right wall of the dihedral and step around onto the rib (8). Continue up the rib and belay from horizontal cracks (6s, 80 feet). A final 100-foot slab (4) leads to the summit.

### 2.   DIHEDRAL 7
Begin as for East Face and belay at the bottom of the large left-facing dihedral. Climb the dihedral for 40 feet, then angle out across the face past the left side of the roof, gain a ramp on the south face and belay at a fixed pin (assuming it is still there). Climb 20 feet up the ramp and mount the wall on the right (crux), pull around onto the upper east face and head for the summit (7, 130 feet) One may also climb out of the ramp at a point much nearer the summit with similar difficulty.

# THE THING

Also known as the Eye Of The Needle for a north-south hole through the summit and as the Morning After for no apparent reason whatever. This beautiful spire has a brilliant slab route up its east face. Approach via the Royal Arch Trail. From Sentinel Pass hike west along the right side of the ridge to near the Hammerhead, then make a rising traverse to the northwest and soon arrive at the objective. The Thing is obscured by trees for nearly the entire approach. To clarify juxtaposition, make a short but delightful ascent of the Hammerhead. To escape the summit, downclimb a ramp to the southeast for 65 feet, then cut back to the southwest along some precarious flakes (4). One may also continue down the ramp and merge into the gully (5). It is, however, a lot easier to rappel 50 feet south from slings near the summit. Note that the gully on the south side of The Thing is not hikeable, but the slope on the north is.

### 1.   EAST FACE 7 ★
FA: JERRY ROACH, JEFF WHEELER, 1956. ROOF: PAT AMENT, LARRY DALKE, 1960.

Begin this classic 450-foot route at the lower north side of the east face. Climb 140 feet to a tree below a roof (4). Climb a crack through the roof (7) and continue to a large belay ledge with trees. Climb a wide crack up to a small tree and continue along the left side of the raised area to a good ledge (2). The last pitch climbs straight up for 60 feet to the summit.

### 2.   RIGHT THING 6 ★
FA: RICHARD AND JOYCE ROSSITER, 1982.

Begin from the lower north side of the east face. Climb around the right end of a roof and up a right-facing dihedral to a ledge with trees (6, 180 feet). Follow cracks up the right side of the face to a ledge at the top of the raised area (6, 150 feet). Climb 60 feet to the summit.

## THE WILLY B
1. **East Face 8 s ★**
2. **Dihedral 7**

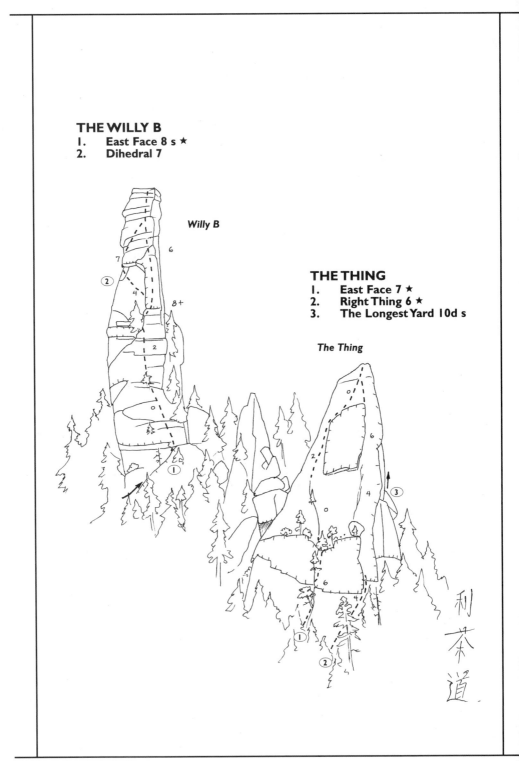

Willy B

## THE THING
1. **East Face 7 ★**
2. **Right Thing 6 ★**
3. **The Longest Yard 10d s**

The Thing

### 3.    THE LONGEST YARD 10d s

FA: DAN STONE AND CHIP CHASE, 1978.

Begin behind a large pine tree. Climb a finger crack, then lieback to a belay in a groove. Climb the overhanging bulge above.

# Eyes Of The Canyon

These small flatirons are located north of The Thing on the wooded south slope of Bluebell Canyon. There are three connected features 150 feet north of The Thing and several other small crags nearer the bottom of the canyon. Three routes have been previously established.

### BLINDED 5

This route ascends the east face of the crag nearest the bottom of The Thing. 200 feet. To descend, leap across a gap from the west side of the summit.

### SIGHT FIGHT CLASS 4

This route ascends the 300-foot east face just right of the previous route, then goes on to the top of a 50-foot free-standing pinnacle to the left. Climb toward the right side of the east face or travel more difficult terrain to the left. After 300 feet gain a broken summit area with a large tree and traverse south to the bottom of the final tower. Climb a crack in the north face, then move around to the east side and surmount the highest point. To escape the summit, reverse the route to the broken ledge and scramble west.

### LICHEN WARS 6

This 400-foot route ascends the narrow east face of a crag in the bottom of Bluebell Canyon. Hike the Royal Arch Trail to the point where it begins to climb southward out of Bluebell Canyon. At the first switchback to the left is a large boulder with a painted sign that reads, "Royal Arch" with an arrow pointing left. Break right and follow a secondary trail west up the draw for 200 feet. The climb begins several feet south of the creek. Climb a smooth lichenous slab for 100 feet (6), then stay near the north edge of the face for another 200 feet and gain a ledge in a broken area. It is possible to walk off to the south at this point or scramble over several summit blocks.

CENTRAL FLATIRONS
AND THIRD FLATIRON
See legend p. 154.

Third
Flatiron

Bluebell
Canyon

West
Ironing Board

East
Ironing Board

Queen Anne's Head

W.C. Field's
Pinnacle

# THIRD FLATIRON AREA

This chapter covers all the crags on the north side of Bluebell Canyon: the Ironing Boards, W.C. Fields Pinnacle, Queen Anne's Head and the Third Flatiron. These crags are closed to the public from February to August as of 1999.

## IRONING BOARDS

Southwest of the Third Flatiron, two magnificent slabs arc northward out of Bluebell Canyon and terminate along the crest of a wooded ridge. The lower slab, nearer to the Third, is the East Ironing Board. The farther west is the West Ironing Board. The west face of the West Ironing Board is irregular and discontinuous, but the same on the East Ironing Board is steep and clean, and presents an immense overhang for two-thirds of its length. A long, graceful rib called The Fin climbs northward between the two Ironing Boards and has a solitary route along its 500-foot arête. This feature or stratum, though broken at its top, continues over the wooded ridge mentioned above and drops into the drainage between the Second and Third Flatirons. On this north-facing slope it forms a jagged ridge known as Jaws, which is also ascended by a single route.

### West Ironing Board

This is the farthest west of the three great ribs and is characterized by a huge right-arching crack in its east face.

**Approach**—To reach the bottom, hike the secondary trail up Bluebell Canyon, pass beneath The Fin, and within another 100 feet arrive at the foot of the rock, 40 feet above the stream. Look for a rhomboid-shaped cave just above you. The upper west face can also be reached from the wooded ridge that runs west from the West Bench of the Third Flatiron.

**Descent**— From any route that reaches the ridgecrest, one may scramble the ridge northwest (Class 3) to hiking terrain. It is also possible to rappel or downclimb to the west, via the chimney that is about ten feet south of Green Crack West (0). At least one of the wide cracks on the upper east face may be downclimbed (Class 4).

**1.   PINE TREE PITCH 9**
FA: JIM ERICKSON, SOLO, 1976.
Near the north end of the west face and 30 feet left of Green Crack West, climb a slightly out-leaning crack to a short slot. Descend via a nearby tree.

**2.   GREEN CRACK WEST 3**
Do not confuse this route with Green Crack (8 +) on the East Ironing Board. Begin 30 feet right of Pine Tree Pitch. Climb a short chimney just right of an easy groove.

**3.   THE DOLMEN 7 s ★**
FA: RICHARD ROSSITER, SOLO, 1988.
At the very foot of the West Ironing Board, not more than 35 feet above the stream in Bluebell Canyon, a blunt tower rises up against the main rock. From points to the east it appears as two thick columns with a massive block set squarely atop. This is not intended as a route in its own right, but as a direct start to Smoother. Begin at the southeast corner of the rock and climb the rounded buttress 100 feet to its flat summit.

THE IRONING BOARDS,
from the southeast

Green
Thumb

West
Ironing Board

The Fin

East
Ironing Board

Third Flatiron

BLUEBELL
CANYON

Approach III

Approach IV

### 4.    SMOOTHER 7 s ★

FA: JIM ERICKSON AND JIM WALSH, 1970.

This exciting route climbs the southeast edge of the West Ironing Board. Begin about 150 feet up from the tiny (seasonal) stream in the bottom of Bluebell Canyon, and left of the huge arching crack of Crescent. Climb the rounded arête all the way to the north end of the rib.

### 5.    CRESCENT 6 ★

FA: RICHARD ROSSITER, SOLO, 1980.

On the lower east face of the West Ironing Board, a huge crack arcs up to the right. Climb the crack which is actually a flared chimney-offwidth, or climb the clean face to the right until it is possible to curve up and left in a smaller crack.

### 6.    VARIATION 6

FA: ROSSITER, SOLO, 1988.

Climb the face to the right of Crescent, but left of a chimney full of ferns and get into a crack that runs beneath and somewhat parallel to Crescent. Climb out to the very end of this crack and merge with Thinsignificance (6).

### 7.    THINSIGNIFICANCE 7 s ★

FA: ROSSITER, SOLO, 1988.

This route takes the center of the east face on a plumb line between Crescent and the obvious wide crack to the right. From the cave at the bottom of the face, scramble up the gully until 30 feet from the wide crack. Climb straight up over little scoops and flakes, staying about 30 feet left of the crack. Three pitches to the ridge crest.

### 8.    MARINE LIFE 6 ★

FA: ROSSITER, SOLO, 1988.

There is a large solution hole (or tank) at the top of the buttress that has little fish swimming around in it (why not?). Forty feet up and right from the wide crack mentioned above, locate two cracks that form a narrow crisscross at mid face. Ascend the cracks for about 200 feet to where they fade out, then run it out for 60 feet to the top. Two long pitches.

## THE FIN

The Fin is the long narrow rib between the West and East Ironing Boards. Approach from the Royal Arch Trail and the secondary trail up Bluebell Canyon.

### I.    INQUISITION 8 vs ★

FA: RICHARD ROSSITER, SOLO, 1988.

This is a beautiful 500-foot route, but there are no cracks for protection or belay anchors. Begin 50 feet above the stream, at the very foot of the arête. Climb 100 feet to a level spot with some trees where one could belay. Above this the route steepens. Pass a bulge (5) and continue skyward along the narrowing arête through a steep section with exhilarating exposure (crux). Another 100 feet (4) lead to scrambling terrain. Continue up the crest until an easy chimney leads off to the east.

## EAST IRONING BOARD

This is the more easterly of the great ribs behind the Third Flatiron. The crag is characterized by an enormous east face with excellent slab climbs and a very steep west face with an array of sport and crack climbs. A steep tower at the north end of the rib called Green Thumb .

**Approach**—To reach the east face, hike the secondary trail up Bluebell Canyon, then break right up the forested gully that climbs beneath the east face. To reach the west face, hike west around the foot of the rock (300 feet or so from the Royal Arch Trail) and continue up the rocky gully to the right of The Fin. A jam of giant boulders part way up the gully may be passed on the left (Class 4), or

*Green Thumb*

*Third Flatiron*

**EAST IRONING BOARD,
upper west face**

by weaving about on the right (easier if you can find the way). Green Thumb and the upper west face may also be reached from the West Bench of the Third Flatiron: Hike west for 300 feet, staying on the north side of the wooded ridge and head south once the Green Thumb pinnacle is apparent on the left.

**Descent**— From the level section of the ridge, north of the crux of Que Rasca and north of The Raven dihedral, rappel 60 feet west from two bolts. One may also downclimb or rappel a crack for 80 feet (east) to a tree, then rappel 150 feet to the gully on the east side of the rib. All of the sport routes on the west face have bolt anchors from which to lower off.

## Green Thumb

The first four routes are on the Green Thumb, a small tower at the north end of the East Ironing board. This is area is 300 feet straight west from the Third Flatiron. There is a third class gully that descends northeast from the top of the ridge. To reach it from Green Thumb, scramble southeast over the crest of the East Ironing Board (just east from the top of Diagonal Finger Crack) and drop down the gully.

### 1.   GREEN CORNER 9 ★
FA: ROGER BRIGGS AND DON PETERSON, 1969.
Climb the obvious crack at the northwest corner of the buttress.

### 2.   FARNIENTE 12A ★
FA: BOBBI BENSMAN, DAN MICHAEL, PAUL PIANA, 1987.
Scramble up to a diagonal slot that cuts across the lower west face. Pull up onto the face and engage the crux. Once above the second bolt the climbing is less severe, but never easy and offers little respite. Six bolts to a two-bolt anchor.

Joyce Rossiter on *Farniente* (5.12a), East Ironing Board.
Photo by Richard Rossiter.

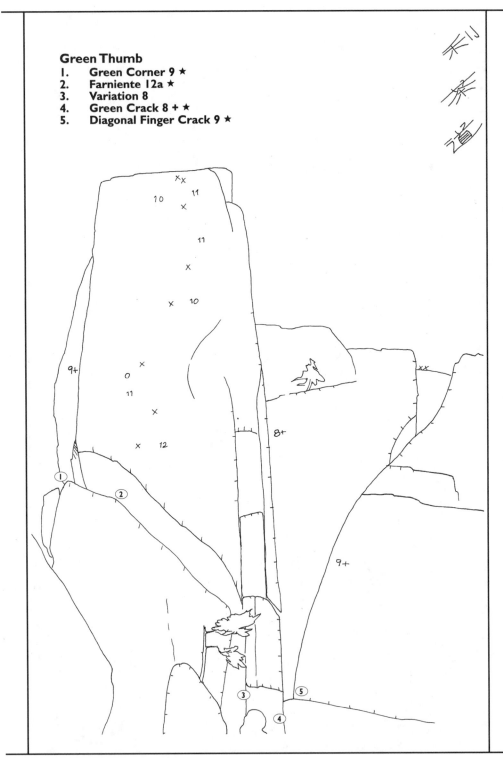

**Green Thumb**
1. **Green Corner 9 ★**
2. **Farniente 12a ★**
3. **Variation 8**
4. **Green Crack 8 + ★**
5. **Diagonal Finger Crack 9 ★**

### 3. VARIATION 8
FA: ROGER BRIGGS, 1968.
Climb the weird corner and flake immediately around to the right from Farniente.

### 4. GREEN CRACK 8 + ★
FA: GERRY ROACH AND STAN SHEPHERD, 1958.
Climb the clean, south-facing dihedral at the right (south) side of Green Thumb.

### 5. DIAGONAL FINGER CRACK 9 ★
Jam the diagonal finger crack to the right of Green Crack. There is an old bolt at the top. Rappel from the smaller of two trees a few yards to the south.

### 6. STAINLESS STEELE 'RETE 10C VS
Climb the arête a short way right of Diagonal Finger Crack. Two bolts.

### 7. L.A.S.T. 8
Begin to the right of Green Crack? The location of this route is not known.

### 8. ZIMBRA 12B ★
FA: STEPHEN HADIK AND CURT FRYE.
Begin about 90 feet right of Farniente and 40 feet left of Hot Toddy. Seven bolts to a two-bolt anchor.

### 9. HOT TODDY
No information on this route.

### 10. GULLWING 10C S ★
FA: SKIP GUERIN, 1981.
Climb to a ledge with a small tree, up a right-facing corner to a flake, and on to a good ledge. Follow a short left-facing dihedral to the top.

### 11. BAZOOKA 8 A4
FA: KYLE COPELAND AND MARK HIRT, 1983.
Begin as for Gullwing. Aid up a very thin crack past a bulge with a bolt and finish with a dihedral to the left.

### 12. SEAM 11D
Begin on a narrow ledge with a "bonsai" tree and face climb along a seam a couple yards right of Bazooka. Three bolts, 45 feet.

### 13. TOMMY GUN 11 ★
FA: TIM ADDISON, CHIP RUCKGABER, AND MATT SLATER, 1981.
Climb a 40-foot flake to a thin dihedral with a bolt, up a short headwall past another bolt to a ledge, then 50 feet left to belay under a roof. Climb the roof and continue up the thin, leaning dihedral.

### 14. FLAKE ON THE RIGHT 10D S
FA: ERIC GUOKAS AND DAN HARE, 1980s.
Begin at the next flake right of Tommy Gun. Climb a right- facing flake up and left to an unprotected headwall of reddish rock. The real name of this route is not known.

### 15. THE RAVEN 11C ★
FA: SKIP GUERIN, 1981.
Locate two dihedrals a short way right of the preceding route. Climb the left of two very steep left-facing dihedrals (thin pro). Rappel 60 feet back to the ground.

GREEN THUMB

60°

FORESTED GULLY

## EAST IRONING BOARD
2.  **Farniente 12a** ★
3.  **Variation 8**
4.  **Green Crack 8 +** ★
5.  **Diagonal Finger Crack 9** ★
6.  **Stainless Steele 'Rete 10c vs**
10. **Gullwing 10c s** ★
11. **Bazooka 8 A4**
12. **Seam 11d**
13. **Tommy Gun 11** ★

大道知者不言

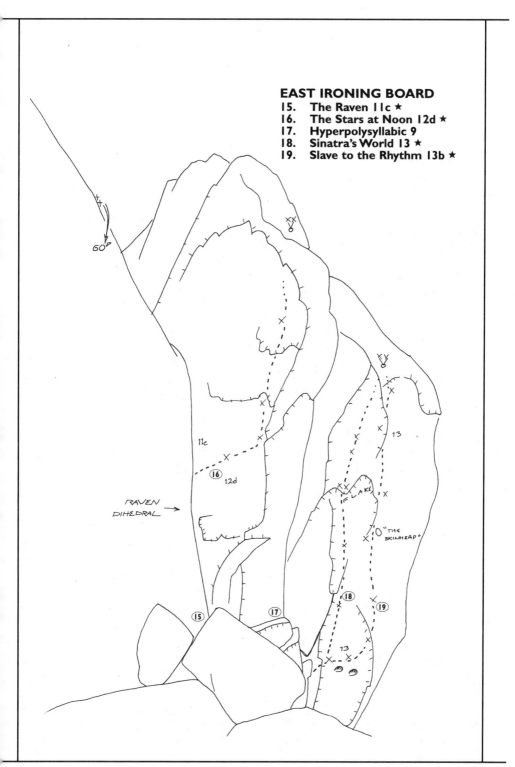

EAST IRONING BOARD
15. The Raven 11c ★
16. The Stars at Noon 12d ★
17. Hyperpolysyllabic 9
18. Sinatra's World 13 ★
19. Slave to the Rhythm 13b ★

GOP

11c

16  12d

RAVEN
DIHEDRAL →

13

FLAKE

"THE SKINHEAD"

15        17        18  19

13

Green Thumb

THE IRONING BOARDS
from the south
2.   Farniente 12a ★
13.  Tommy Gun 11 ★
19.  Slave to the Rhythm 13b ★
20.  Velvet Elvis 11a ★
22.  Sunbreeze 10b
23.  Hunka Hunka Burnin' Love 10b ★

Third Flatiron

East Ironing
Board

West Ironing
Board

The
Fin

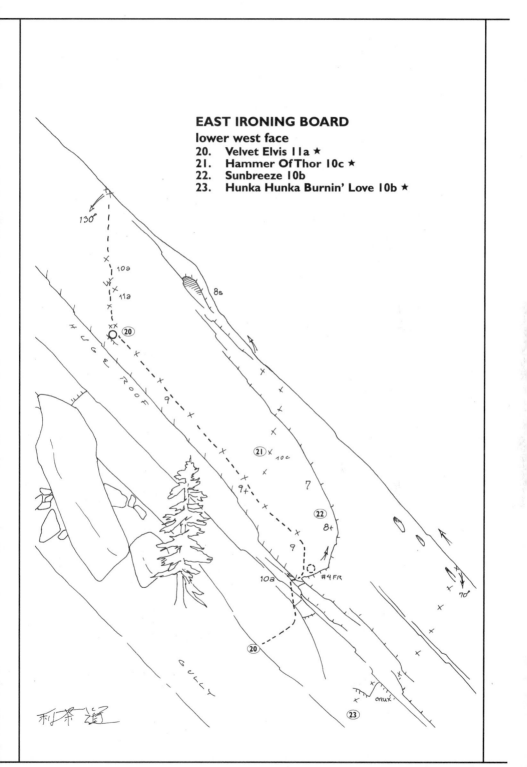

## EAST IRONING BOARD
### lower west face
20. **Velvet Elvis 11a** ★
21. **Hammer Of Thor 10c** ★
22. **Sunbreeze 10b**
23. **Hunka Hunka Burnin' Love 10b** ★

### 16. THE STARS AT NOON 12D ★
FA: PAUL PIANA AND PETE DE LANNOY, 1988.
Stem about halfway up the dihedral of The Raven, then move right (crux) and up the arête. The short traverse to the arête is the crux. Bring RPs.

### 17. HYPERPOLYSYLLABIC 9
FA: JIM ERICKSON AND JOHN BEHRENS, 1977.
Climb the overhanging, left-facing dihedral right of The Raven. Rack up to four inches.

### 18. SINATRA'S WORLD 13 ★
FA: PAUL PIANA, 1989.
Climb the, arête just right of Hyperpolysyllabic. Six bolts to a two-bolt anchor.

### 19. SLAVE TO THE RHYTHM 13B ★
FA: DAN MICHAEL, 1987.
Begin this power test immediately right of Hyperpolysyllabic (100 yards down the gully from Green Thumb). Move right past solution holes, then crank the bulging wall. Eight bolts to a two-bolt anchor.

### 20. VELVET ELVIS 11A ★
FA: PAUL PIANA AND BRETT RUCKMAN, 1987.
The lower west face forms an unbroken overhang about 300 feet long. Begin at the low end of the overhang, 75 feet below the giant boulder jam. Climb past a piton to a ledge (10b). Optional belay requires a #3.5 and/or a #4 Friend. Traverse left barely above the lip of the roof to a two-bolt anchor and belay (9+, 120 feet). There are seven bolts along this traverse. Now climb straight up (crux) for 60 feet passing 3 bolts to another two-bolt anchor and belay. This point is just above the crux of Que Rasca. Rappel 130 feet back to earth.

### 21. HAMMER OF THOR 10C ★
Begin with the second pitch of Velvet Elvis. Climb to the second bolt, then climb more or less straight up the headwall. Five bolts to a two-bolt anchor.

### 22. SUNBREEZE 10B
FA: ROB WOOLF AND RICHARD ROSSITER, 1988.
This route follows the left-arching corner above the ledge at the start of Velvet Elvis. The initial roof is the crux. Rappel 130 feet west, or climb the crux pitch of Que Rasca (8s) and rappel from the anchor on Velvet Elvis.

### 23. HUNKA HUNKA BURNIN' LOVE 10B ★
Begin 35 feet down and right from Sunbreeze. Seven bolts to a two-bolt anchor.

### 24. SOUTH FACE 7 VS ★
FA: RICHARD ROSSITER AND ROB WOOLF, TANDEM SOLO, 1988.
This route climbs the beautiful red face at the bottom of the ridge and provides a direct start to Que Rasca. Begin at the southwest corner of the wall. Smear straight up the wall and pass a roof at a left-facing flake, which places one atop the lesser of two huge blocks. To escape the route, make a precarious move and enter the gully just east of a giant chockstone. Scramble through a tunnel and emerge on the southwest side, about 150 feet above the start of the route. To continue, climb over the chockstone and up the next block. Join Que Rasca.

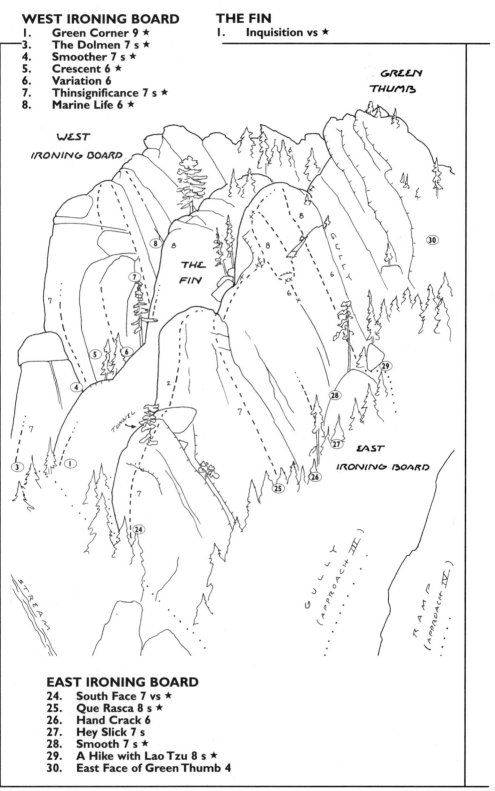

The following routes are on the east face of the East Ironing Board.

## 25.  QUE RASCA 8 s ★
FA: ROGER BRIGGS AND KRISTINA SOLHEIM, 1973.

Begin about 200 feet up along the east face and 25 feet left of a long wide crack. Climb two runout pitches to the top of the second big block in the ridge (7, 300 feet). Pass a notch and climb the crest for about 80 feet to a belay at a bolt. Move up and right past an old french piton, then friction up and left to the ridge crest (8s). Belay from bolts at the top of Velvet Elvis. Follow the crest north for about 90 feet to an old bolt anchor below the vertical step in the ridge. Rappel 60 feet west.

## 26.  HAND CRACK 6
FA: PAUL PIANA, SOLO, 1987.

Climb a hand crack to the right of the offwidth mentioned above. When the crack fades, continue to the ridge crest.

## 27.  HEY SLICK 7 s
FA: PAUL PIANA, SOLO, 1987.

Climb the face to the right of Hand Crack. Two long pitches with vague pro.

## 28.  SMOOTH 7 s ★
FA: PAT AMENT AND GORDY RYAN, 1967.

Begin from a huge boulder that sits against the bottom of the east face. Follow a crack to until it fades, then move right to another crack and follow it for 50 feet to the same fate. Climb about 15 feet above the crack and belay at a bolt, or climb another 40 feet and belay at two bolts below a bulge. Climb around either side of the bulge and run it out to the ridge crest. The left option takes the crux of Que Rasca (8 s).

## 29.  A HIKE WITH LAO TZU 8 s ★
FA: RICHARD ROSSITER, SOLO, 1988.

This line ascends the vast crystal-studded expanse to the north of Smooth. Begin at a J-shaped tree 70 feet north of the huge boulder below Smooth. Climb directly up to a shallow hole that is visible from the gully and belay (6 s, 200 feet). Above here the wall steepens like a huge wave approaching shore. Move 15 feet right along a channel, then climb up and slightly right to the crest of the ridge (8 s, 140 feet).

## 30.  EAST FACE OF GREEN THUMB 4

Begin at no particular place along the east face of Green Thumb. Climb a couple of hundred feet of undistinguished rock to the ridge crest, then go north to the summit.

# THIRD FLATIRON

"The Third," as it is known locally, rises dramatically and unmistakably from the dense forests of Green Mountain and is beyond doubt the most popular of all the Flatirons. Visible from almost anywhere in Boulder, it has a peculiar prominence from the University of Colorado campus, and as a consequence, has been the scene of some pranks and foolery. For example, it is the only flatiron to have been defaced by graffiti. A 100-foot-high "CU" has remained painted on the upper third of the east face for decades. Though painted over and camouflaged on various occasions, it was repainted in dazzling white during the early 1980s, after which it was again painted over. Now, hundreds of pounds of exterior latex hang there like cake frosting, and it is possible to climb 100 feet of the east face without touching rock. Of greater interest, the Third Flatiron offers varied and exceptional climbing on the gigantic east face, the steep west buttress, and the long south and southwest faces.

The Third Flatiron, the Ironing Boards and the surrounding area are closed to the public from February to August due to "wildlife closures" imposed by Boulder Mountain Parks.

**Approach I**—This approach leads to the very bottom of the east face and 1911 Gully. Hike the Royal Arch Trail for about 0.3 mile to a point just before it crosses to the left (south) side of Bluebell Canyon. Follow a steep path up to the southwest, passing near a subsidiary buttress (Third Flatironette), then passing to the left of some large boulders, and soon arrive at the bottom of the great face. One may scramble up to the north from this point to reach the East Bench or climb 400 feet up and right (2) to the second eyebolt on the Standard East Face. This bolt is on a blunt rib in the middle of the face. Another option is to climb the Third Flatironette (Class 4).

**Approach II**—Use this approach for the Standard East Face, the north face, and the West Bench. Hike up Kinnikinnic Road to Bluebell Shelter and find the Third Flatiron Trail just southwest of the shelter. Follow this trail past a junction with the Second Flatiron Trail (stay left) and continue to the junction with the East Face Trail, which breaks left and leads to the East Bench and the bottom of the Standard East Face. Staying right, the trail leads up the slope beneath the north face to the West Bench.

**Approach III**—The Outside Route climbs the forested gully between the East Ironing Board and the low cliff band of the Inside Route (below). It may be used to reach the east face of the East Ironing Board and the West Bench of the Third Flatiron. Hike the Royal Arch Trail 150 yards past W.C. Fields Pinnacle to the point where it begins to climb south out of Bluebell Canyon. Look for a large boulder with a painted sign that reads "Royal Arch" with an arrow pointing left. Leave the main trail and hike west (right) on a footpath up Bluebell Canyon. Cross the draw and hike up the wooded gully between the East Ironing Board and the cliffband of the Inside Route. At the top of the gully scramble east over some big boulders and arrive at the West Bench and the steep west face of the Third Flatiron.

**Approach IV**—The Inside Route climbs a ramp formed by a low cliff band along the base of the Southeast Ridge of the Third Flatiron. This approach leads to the West Bench from the south and provides access to all south face routes. Hike the Royal Arch Trail to a point across from W.C Fields Pinnacle. Drop down and cross the stream, then head west around the left side of the pinnacle and gain the long ramp that climbs for 1000 feet beneath the Southeast Ridge. There are three short scrambles along the way. The first and most difficult, the Crux Slab, is met 500 feet above the stream crossing and ascends a northeast-facing bulge from a grassy alcove (Class 4). 200 feet farther along, pass a V- shaped section of slickrock below the Southwest Chimney. A final slab leads to the West Bench (Class 3).

**Descent**—From the summit, make three rappels from large eyebolts. The direction and length of each rappel is stamped in a metal ring around the bolts.

1. Rappel 45 feet south from the summit to the South Bowl.
2. Rappel 50 feet south to Friday's Folly Ledge. Note that there are TWO eyebolts on this ledge.
3. Rappel 140 feet south from the eastern bolt and land near the top of Approach IV.
3. Or move west on the ledge and rappel 72 feet west from the western bolt to the West Bench.

It is also possible to downclimb the Southwest Chimney route: From the summit, downclimb the east face for 75 feet, then move south and west into the South Bowl. Go south through a hole called Fatman's Frenzy, then southeast down Slip-Slide Ledge for 150 feet. Carefully climb south down a steep chimney to the upper section of Approach IV. One may also rappel this route from eyebolts along Slip-Slide Ledge.

### 1.   1911 GULLY 4

A third of this route is a grunge-crawl up a hanging valley full of poison ivy and bracken ferns. That the remainder of the route justifies suffering this gnarly passage is subject to doubt. At any rate, use Approach I. The climb begins to the left of the east face, between the south face of the Third Flatiron and Queen Anne's Head. Climb through slabs and house-sized boulders on the left and enter 1911 Gully. Once above the fern garden, climb a nice chimney for about 450 feet and join the Southwest Chimney.

## South Face

The following four routes ascend the vertical south-facing wall that forms the north side of 1911 Gully. Use approach I and scramble into a "hanging garden" of ferns and poison ivy (the poison ivy can be avoided). A cleaner approach is to begin the Standard East Face, then angle up and left across the east face and rappel 150 feet from a two-bolt anchor at the top of Shoyu State.

### 2.   SOUTH FACE 10D S ★

FFA: ROGER AND BILL BRIGGS, 1986.

Begin in 1911 Gully below an arching roof/dihedral high on the wall. This was an old aid route.

### 3.   SHOYU STATE 11A ★

FA: RICHARD AND JOYCE ROSSITER, AND ROB WOOLF, 1988.

This 150-foot pitch provides fine, vertical face climbing on pebbles and tiny edges, unlike anything on the Third Flatiron. Begin on a ramp that is below the arching roof of South Face and left of a large diagonal slot. Master a bulge and follow seven bolts up and left to a two-bolt anchor. The crux is in getting established above the roof.

### 4.   BLAZING BINERS 10A ★

FA: RICHARD AND JOYCE ROSSITER AND ROB WOOLF, 1988.

This route ascends the exquisite green wall above the diagonal slot, down and right from Shoyu State. Begin from the fern garden in 1911 Gully. Make a few moves to get into a six-foot slot, place pro in a one-inch crack beneath the roof and swing onto the face at a good hold (8). Move right, then straight up past three bolts to a narrow ledge. Rappel 75 feet from slings around a horn.

### 5.   SAYONARA 11 ★

FA: BRET RUCKMAN AND BRUCE HILDENBRAND, 1989.

This route ascends the steep face to the right of Blazing Biners. Six Bolts.

## East Face

The following routes are located on the expansive, 1500-foot-high east face of the Third Flatiron.

### 6.   THIRD WORLD ZONE 6 ★

FA: RICHARD AND JOYCE ROSSITER, 1988.

This route teeters above the vertical south face and has good pro. Begin at the bottom left side of the east face. Climb a narrow left-facing dihedral along the very south edge of the east face, all the way to the top of the Dog's Head.

### 7.   EAST FACE LEFT 5 OR 7 ★

This superb route is the longest in the Boulder area. Use Approach I and begin at the very bottom of the east face, on a blunt rib that angles up to the right. When the rib levels off, climb toward the left side of the main overhang and pass it on the left (or climb a good crack straight through it, 7). Move right a bit and head straight up the face. Merge with the Standard East Face at the top of The Gash.

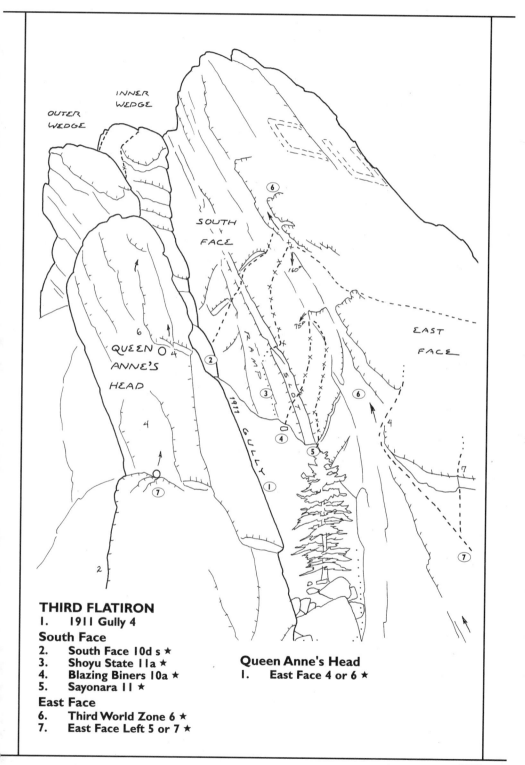

**THIRD FLATIRON**

1. 1911 Gully 4

**South Face**

2. South Face 10d s ★
3. Shoyu State 11a ★
4. Blazing Biners 10a ★
5. Sayonara 11 ★

**East Face**

6. Third World Zone 6 ★
7. East Face Left 5 or 7 ★

**Queen Anne's Head**

1. East Face 4 or 6 ★

## 8.  STANDARD EAST FACE 2 ★

FA: FLOYD AND EARL MILLARD, 1906.

This is one of the best beginner routes in North America. Ninety years of Boulder climbing history, 1000 feet of solid rock, six eyebolts sturdy enough to winch up a jeep, and a picturesque summit worthy of a picnic. One would be hard-pressed to find a better outing on a fair spring day. Keep in mind, however, that the east face is enormous, the eyebolts are about 120 feet apart, retreat is difficult, and escape from the summit requires rappels. For the beginner, this climb is a serious challenge. Use Approach II. Rope up on the East Bench (the rocky shelf at the lower north edge of the east face). The climbing line is not entirely obvious. 1. Climb straight up for eight feet, then diagonal up and left past the first eyebolt (0). Move south across a water polished trough, mount the far side and climb a blunt rib 35 feet to a second eyebolt. Belay. 2. Climb straight up for 100 feet, angle up to the left on a ramp, and belay at a flake. The third eyebolt is 20 feet out to the right from this belay but lacks a good stance. 3. Climb straight up for 120 feet to the next eyebolt (Class 4), or climb out to the right above the third eyebolt and ascend a very clean, blunt rib along the edge of the trough (2). 4. Climb up and left for 120 feet to the fifth eyebolt (0), or climb up and right past large solution holes and belay at a one-inch crack that slants up to the right (0). 5. From either belay, head directly toward the upper right end of the painted letter C and belay at the sixth and last eyebolt (Class 4, 120 feet). You are now near the bottom of the huge chimney known as The Gash. 6. **Standard Finish**. Climb up and left, pass a bulge (2), then go up and right along a ramp and belay at its top, 100 feet. 7. Step left and climb straight up for another 100 feet, move right, and belay on a large chockstone near the top of The Gash (0). One can escape the route at this point by scrambling west into the South Bowl. 8. To reach the summit, cross The Gash to the north and continue for 10 feet out onto Kiddy Kar Ledge. Climb 40 feet up to a wide horizontal crack, make a move to the left, and break for the top. The protection is a little lean here but the climbing is truly magnificent (2, 100 feet).

### GREENMAN'S CRACK 3

From the top of The Gash get into a groove or chimney that angles up along the left side of the summit block. The crux (3) is near the top and requires some interesting body language.

### THE GASH CLASS 4

From the sixth bolt, one may also reach the summit or the South Bowl from the Gash: Climb around to the right and enter the huge chimney that splits the upper face. Climb past a couple of large chockstones and join the Standard Finish 100 feet from the top.

### DIRECT FINISH 4 ★

From the sixth bolt, cross The Gash to the north and climb straight to the summit in two, long aesthetic pitches. This takes a line between The Gash and a parallel groove about 40 feet to the north (3). Recommended.

The author free soloing *Saturday's Folly* (5.8+), circa 1987, Third Flatiron. Photo by Jim Sanders.

THIRD FLATIRON
from the northeast
East Face
7.   East Face Left 5 or 7 ★
8.   Standard East Face 2 ★
10.  College Drop Out 7 s ★
10a. PhD Roof 10c ★

South Bowl

Dog's Head

West Bench

Outer Wedge

10A

8

10

7

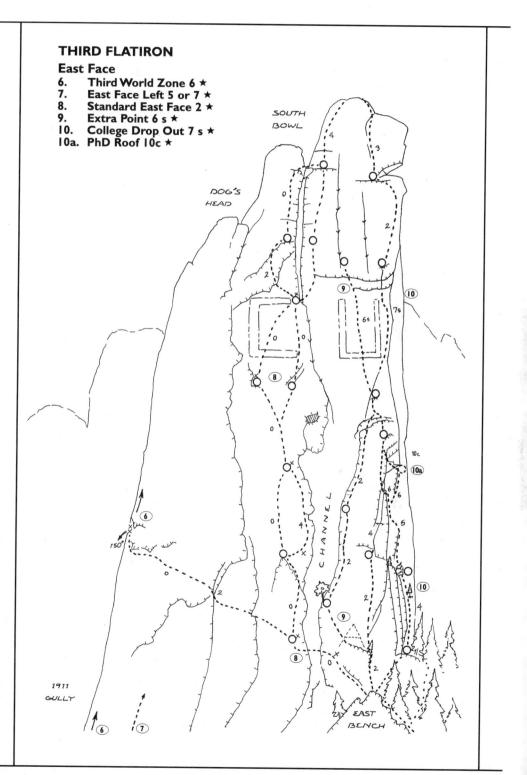

# THIRD FLATIRON

## East Face

6. **Third World Zone 6 ★**
7. **East Face Left 5 or 7 ★**
8. **Standard East Face 2 ★**
9. **Extra Point 6 s ★**
10. **College Drop Out 7 s ★**
10a. **PhD Roof 10c ★**

SOUTH
BOWL

DOG'S
HEAD

CHANNEL

1911
GULLY

EAST
BENCH

### 9.   EXTRA POINT 6 s ★

FA: PAT AMENT, MID-1960s.

Begin as for the Standard East Face. Climb straight up past a small tree, stay near the middle (or along the left edge) of the broad buttress, and arrive at a large, sloping ledge system in about three pitches. Climb up and slightly left through the middle of the huge, painted letter U (crux), and charge to the summit after two long pitches.

### 10.   COLLEGE DROP OUT 7 s ★

FA: RICHARD AND JOYCE ROSSITER, TANDEM SOLO, 1982.

This route offers an unorthodox alternative to the standard east face curriculum. Begin from a ledge with trees 75 feet up and right from the East Bench. Climb 75 feet up a large right-facing dihedral and belay at a small tree. Continue up the corner for about 100 feet and exit at a flake on the left (6), or continue up the dihedral and climb the well-protected PhD Roof to gain the main east face. Follow the right edge of the face past the right side of the "U" to the summit. One may also begin by climbing straight up from the East Bench. Use Approach II.

### 10A.   PhD ROOF 10c ★

FA: RICHARD AND JOYCE ROSSITER, 1990.

On the second pitch of College Drop Out, continue up the big right-facing dihedral to the right side of a large roof. Work up and left into a short crack and pull around onto the main east face.

## North Face

The following routes ascend the steep and dark north face of the Third Flatiron. Use Approach II.

### 11.   KOR ROUTE 10

FA: LAYTON KOR, 1960s FFA: CHRIS REVELEY AND BOB WADE, 1973.

This is an old aid route with some bolts on the steep north face above the PhD Roof and below Northwest Passage. No details are available, but the bolts are still there.

### 12.   DIRECT NORTH FACE 10

FA: ROGER BRIGGS AND JOHN BRAGG, 1973.

Not terribly direct, this route climbs the north face of the large ramp that runs up along the north side of the Third Flatiron, then continues up the first pitch of Jackson's Ledges, and takes the last pitch of Northwest Passage.

### 13.   JACKSON'S LEDGES 9 +

FA: DALLAS JACKSON, JOHN MUSSER, 1954. FFA: ART HIGBEE, BRIAN DANIELS, 1978.

Climb a crack in a left-facing corner that leads to the second belay on Northwest Passage. To continue, follow the rock strata up and right to the top of the west face.

### 14.   THIRD KINGDOM 7 A2 OR PAPILLON 12A ★

FA: BILL BRIGGS AND LUKE STUDER, 1972. FFA: ROB CANDELARIA.

Begin at a couple of tall trees below the upper end of the north face ramp. Proceed as indicated in the topo. Candelaria eliminated the aid on the last pitch and named it Papillon. This takes the right- leaning, overhanging roof/dihedral above the last pitch of Northwest Passage.

### 15.   NORTHWEST PASSAGE 10A ★

FA: TOM HORNBEIN, DICK SHERMAN, BOB RILEY, 1949. FFA: ROGER BRIGGS, 1972.

This is the most popular of the north face routes. Begin at the west end of the north face. Climb the left of two corners and belay on a broken ledge after about 75 feet. Make an arching traverse across a steep slab with several old pitons (Skid Row) and belay on a good ledge. Angle up and left under the big roof, jam out into space, heel-hook, and crank onto the east face, one pitch below the summit.

## West Face

The following routes ascend the dramatic west face above the West Bench. Use Approaches II, III or IV.

### 16. WEST FACE 10c ★
FFA: ROGER BRIGGS AND JOHN BRAGG, 1973.

Begin from the north side of the West Bench. Climb a corner and wide crack just right of Northwest Passage, traverse right under a roof, then turn the roof at a finger crack and join Friday's Folly Direct.

### 17. SATURDAY'S FOLLY 8+ ★
FA: GERRY ROACH, STAN SHEPHERD, 1958. FFA: PAT AMENT, GORDY RYAN, 1967.

The classic. Begin 12 feet left of Friday's Folly, near some chopped bolts. Climb up and right through a couple bulges to a thin crack with pin scars. Step right and climb a vertical wall via minor rugosities, then go up and left at a roof to finish in an easy corner. Arrive at Friday's Folly Ledge; continue upward or rappel.

### 18. FRIDAY'S FOLLY 7 ★
FA: TOM HORNBEIN AND HARRY WALDROP, 1950.

Even more classic. Begin just left of the arête formed by the right edge of the west face. Follow a crack up (7) and around the corner onto the south face, and zigzag up obvious terrain to Friday's Folly Ledge. The original finish to Friday's Folly goes up beneath the huge block that hangs 50 feet above the east end of the ledge and reaches the South Bowl via Fat Man's Frenzy (a hole that connects the South Bowl with the top of Slip-Slide Ledge). This second pitch is not popular.

### 19. FRIDAY'S FOLLY DIRECT 7 ★

From Friday's Folly Ledge one can rappel or continue straight up to the summit. From the west eyebolt, climb cracks and corners to a right-leaning, right-facing dihedral. Climb the dihedral to the South Bowl or go up and left to an exposed arête and reach the South Bowl. A final short pitch to the summit is called the West Door (7) and was soloed by Layton Kor in the middle 1960s.

## Upper Southwest Face

The following routes ascend the steep wall to the right (southeast) of the West Bench. Use Approach IV.

### 20. PENTAPRANCE 10D s ★
FA: ROGER BRIGGS, TOM RUWITCH, 5.8 A3, 1967. FFA: ROB CANDELARIA, 1975. CRUX LED FREE BY JIM ERICKSON, 1974.

This route ascends the huge left-facing dihedral down and right from Friday's Folly. See topo.

### 21. WAITING FOR COLUMBUS 10c ★
FA: RICHARD AND JOYCE ROSSITER, CRAIG "BIRD" OLSON, 1989.

This long, sustained pitch ascends the dead-vertical buttress at the right of Pentaprance. Begin on a ledge 30 feet above the gully and 150 feet down and right from the West Bench. Climb short cracks, pockets, a cool roof, et cetera. Belay from a horn on Slip-Slide Ledge. 165 feet., 5 bolts. Light SR.

## Southeast Ridge

The following routes ascend the southwest face of the long, blocky ridge that runs from the top of Slip-Slide Ledge to the bottom of W.C. Fields Pinnacle.

### 22. FALCON'S FRACTURE 8+

Begin up on a ledge a few yards right of Waiting For Columbus. Climb a left-facing dihedral with a wide crack to Slip-Slide Ledge. Jim Erickson soloed a (9) finger crack below the ledge as a direct start in 1976.

**THIRD FLATIRON**

North Face
12. Direct North Face 10
14. Third Kingdom 7 A2 or Papillon 12a ★
15. Northwest Passage 10a ★

West Bench

## THIRD FLATIRON

### North Face
11. **Kor Route 10**
12. **Direct North Face 10**
13. **Jackson's Ledges 9 +**
14. **Third Kingdom 7 A2 or Papillon 12a ★**
15. **Northwest Passage 10a ★**

### West Face
16. **West Face 10c ★**
17. **Saturday's Folly 8+ ★**

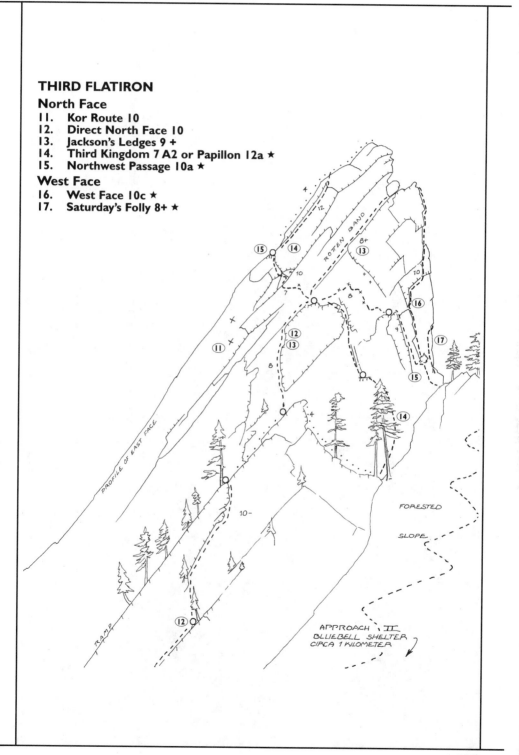

**THIRD FLATIRON**

**West Face**
17. Saturday's Folly 8+ ★
18. Friday's Folly 7 ★
19. Friday's Folly Direct 7 ★

**Upper Southwest Face**
20. Pentaprance 10d s ★
21. Waiting for Columbus 10c ★

South Bowl

Dog's Head

West Bench

Approach III

Approach IV

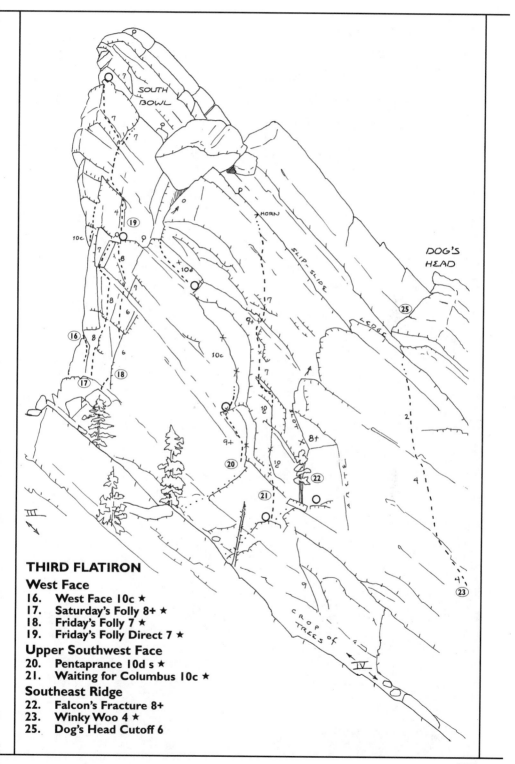

## THIRD FLATIRON

### West Face

16. West Face 10c ★
17. Saturday's Folly 8+ ★
18. Friday's Folly 7 ★
19. Friday's Folly Direct 7 ★

### Upper Southwest Face

20. Pentaprance 10d s ★
21. Waiting for Columbus 10c ★

### Southeast Ridge

22. Falcon's Fracture 8+
23. Winky Woo 4 ★
25. Dog's Head Cutoff 6

The author on *Waiting For Columbus* (5.10c), Third Flatiron.
Photo by Gerry Roach.

### 23. WINKY WOO 4 ★
FA: CLEVE MCCARTY, RICHARD WINK, AND ROBERT KULSTAD, 1957.

Begin about 100 feet down along the inside approach ramp from Falcon's Fracture, a few feet left of the bottom of the Southwest Chimney. Climb the 200-foot, vertical wall via huge bucket holds.

### 24. SOUTHWEST CHIMNEY 2 ★
This is the easiest downclimb from the summit and is actually an interesting route on its own. Begin two hundred feet down the Inside Route (Approach IV) from the West Bench. This is about 150 feet above the "crux slab" of the approach. Climb a large, left-facing dihedral/chimney to an eyebolt on Slip-Slide Ledge. To reach the summit, scramble up Slip-Slide Ledge, go through the hole called Fatman's Frenzy and gain the South Bowl. Go east into the top of The Gash, turn left and traverse out onto Kiddy Kar Ledge then climb the final pitch of the Standard East Face. One may also reach the summit via Dog's Head Cutoff (4), or even the improbable Veinbrenner's Viggle (8).

### 25. DOG'S HEAD CUTOFF 6
FA: RONALD IVES, 1934.

The south side of the east face tops out with a blunt pinnacle called the Dog's Head. The upper end of this feature overhangs the bottom of Slip-Slide Ledge and is separated from the main rock by a seven-inch chimney, 55 feet long. This is the route. The wall to the left may be climbed to avoid the chimney (4). Step right at the top and angle up to the right for 145 feet to the top of The Gash.

### 25A. VEINBRENNER'S VIGGLE 8
Start up Dog's Head Cutoff, but traverse out right beneath the lip of the immense overhang and turn the roof.

### 26. RITE OF SPRING 9 ★
FA: RICHARD ROSSITER AND ROB WOOLF, 1988.

This route ascends the 230-foot south face of the Inner Wedge. Scramble past the "crux slab" to the grassy alcove at the base of the South Chimney and begin eight feet left of a cave. Climb 60 feet and belay on a ramp beneath an overhang with a bolt. Master the bulge (9) and climb a "plated wall" to a shallow left-facing corner that can be seen from the ground. Jam up the corner, step left into a short, thin crack, pass a bulge (8), and face climb up and left to the top of the buttress (165 feet).

### 27. SOUTH CHIMNEY 5 ★
The South Chimney is actually a huge fault between the Inner and Outer Wedges and goes all the way through from the south side to 1911 Gully. Begin in a huge right-facing dihedral 30 feet above the "crux slab" of Approach IV. Stem straight up the steep dihedral for 50 feet (5) and enter a slot (right side in). Wiggle up the slot (5), pull around to the left, and belay on a good ledge. Bridge up the classic chimney to where it narrows, stem past the crux on the outside (5), re-enter as it widens, and belay on a ledge inside the fault. Climb west up a steep slab with a bolt, then up and right over a bulge (4), and on to the summit of the Inner Wedge. This is 20 feet southeast from the top of the Southwest Chimney. One may also begin this climb in a right-facing dihedral 30 feet right of the South Chimney.

### 28. INNER SANCTUM 9 ★
FA: RICHARD ROSSITER AND ROB WOOLF, 1988.

Begin in a left-facing corner 15 feet right of the South Chimney and climb to a ledge. Step left and climb a right-facing corner through a bulge, then go up and right over fine rock to the summit of the Outer Wedge.

### 29. THIN CRACK 11c
Begin 20 feet of the right of the South Chimney. Climb a clean, overhanging crack to a rock horn with some slings around it.

**THIRD FLATIRON**

**South Face**
3. Shoyu State 11a e

**Upper Southwest Face**
21.   Waiting for Columbus 10c ★

**Southeast Ridge**
23.   Winky Woo 4 ★
24.   Southwest Chimney 2 ★
26.   Rite of Spring 9 ★
27.   South Chimney 5 ★
30.   Fail Safe 10 ★

West Bench

Queen Anne's Head

Approach III

Approach IV

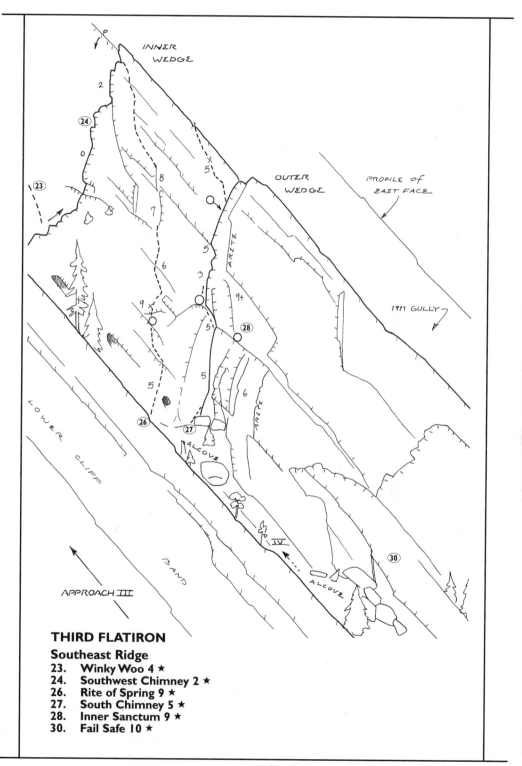

P

INNER WEDGE

2

24

0

23

8

7

6

9

5

7

5

26

27

ALCOVE

OUTER WEDGE

PROFILE of EAST FACE

ARETE

5

3

9+

5

28

5

6

ARETE

1971 GULLY

IV

ALCOVE

30

LOWER CLIFF

BAND

APPROACH III

**THIRD FLATIRON**

**Southeast Ridge**

23. **Winky Woo 4** ★
24. **Southwest Chimney 2** ★
26. **Rite of Spring 9** ★
27. **South Chimney 5** ★
28. **Inner Sanctum 9** ★
30. **Fail Safe 10** ★

### 30. FAIL SAFE 10 ★

FA: PAT AMENT AND GORDY RYAN, 1967.

Immediately below the "crux slab" of the approach is a grassy alcove with an overhanging wall on the north side. Climb the obvious hand and fist crack up the wall to the crest of a minor ridge and rappel. SR to 4 inches.

### 31. DOKTOR MERKWURDIGLIEBE 8

FA: JIM ERDICKSON, SOLO, 1972.

Find a 20-foot crack about 150 feet up Approach IV from W.C. Fields Pinnacle. This may be the crack in a small dihedral just below the boulder jam below Fail Safe.

### 32. SOARKS 10

FA: TOM HIGGINS AND PAT AMENT, 1977.

This route is said to ascend the overhanging arête of the first pinnacle up the approach gully from W.C. Fields Pinnacle (p. 203), and is supposed to have a rock-driven bolt "half way up in a rotten band."

### 33. HOLIER THAN THOU 11B ★

FA: BRET RUCKMAN AND TIM COATS, 1989.

Begin just right of Soarks. Climb an overhanging wall with solution holes. Five bolts and a pin to a two-bolt anchor.

### 34. FACE WITH TWO BOLTS 11

This is a fine-looking route on the vertical south-facing wall, 70 feet up the approach gully from the top of W.C. Fields Pinnacle (p. 203). If the two visible bolts are the only pro, the upper half of the route will be very runout.

## QUEEN ANNE'S HEAD

This elegant tower forms the lower south side of 1911 Gully. It is the second pinnacle up from the bottom of the 1000-foot Southeast Ridge. The east face of Queen Anne's Head is several hundred feet high and leans back at a 55-degree angle. The west face is only about 50 feet high, but overhangs at an angle parallel to the east face. Approach via the Royal Arch Trail. The point at which to leave the trail will be obvious once near the objective. To descend from the summit, rappel 105 feet north into 1911 gully, or rappel 50 feet to a ramp that may be downclimbed to the same fate. The slabs at the bottom of 1911 Gully are best negotiated via a 40-foot rappel from a tree.

### 1. EAST FACE 4 OR 6 ★

Begin at the left side of the east face. Climb a long, undercut, left-facing dihedral to a good stance (4, 150 feet). Continue upward until it is easy to move right (east) onto the east face and belay on a good ledge (Class 4, 120 feet). Climb to the south end of a small overhang and belay from a bolt (4, 120 feet). Move right ten feet, master the roof, and follow a flared crack to the summit (4, 150 feet. Or from the belay at the south end of the overhang, climb straight up the small, left- facing dihedral (6) to the summit. See topo page 187.

### 2. NORTH FACE 9

FA: JIM ERICKSON AND JOHN BEHRENS, 1980.

From 1911 Gully, work up onto a ramp and climb a short, right-facing flake that leads to the north edge of the east face.

## W.C. FIELDS PINNACLE

This unique spire is located at the bottom of the Southeast Ridge of the Third Flatiron, 100 feet south of Queen Anne's Head. It is characterized by a narrow east ridge that mushrooms into a bulging summit block with several imposing overlaps. Approach via the Royal Arch Trail and break off at a point just southeast of the pinnacle. Descend by downclimbing the West Face or by rappelling 70 feet off the west side.

### 1. WEST FACE 4

Hike up along the southwest side of the pinnacle until directly under the summit. The route is obvious from here.

### 2. A VERY AMENT SLAB 8 ★

FA: Pat Ament and Tom Avery, 1969. FFA: Pat Ament, Bob Hritz, Tom Menk, 1969.

Begin at the bottom of the narrow east face. Climb straight up for 120 feet to a fixed pin. Move right over a steep step (5) to a bolt belay at the base of the bulging summit block. Climb up and left to a bolt (4) and up a crease (8), then go up to another bolt. Move up and right to the final overhang, move left, then pull up over the bulge (5), and scramble to the summit (80 feet).

**SECOND FLATIRON AND FIRST FLATIRON**, from the east

Sunset
Flatironette

First Flatiron

Deviations

South
Block

Pullman Car

Second Flatiron

First
Flatironette

Spy

# FIRST AND SECOND FLATIRONS AREA

. . . . . . . . . . . . . . . . . . . . . . . . . . .

This chapter covers the Second Flatiron, First Flatiron and adjacent crags. Climbs in this area receive a good deal more traffic now than in the past due to the standing "wildlife closure" of the Third Flatiron and Ironing Boards. Approach all crags from Chautauqua Park.

## SECOND FLATIRON

The Second Flatiron is the large, irregular formation between the First and Third Flatirons. The peculiar summit block , called the Pullman Car, has attracted most of the climbing activity; however, the comparatively enormous South Block or South Wing sports a classic Flatiron route along its southeast ridge. To reach the bottom of the east face use a connecting trail that runs between the Third Flatiron Trail and the First Flatiron Trail. The connecting trail may be reached from either end. To descend from the summit, downclimb the west side of the Pullman Car (class 4). The First Flatiron Trail descends from the saddle between the First and Second Flatiron.

### I.   SOUTHEAST RIDGE 7 ★

FA: LAYTON KOR, SOLO, 1959.

Begin at the south side of an east-facing slab beneath the massive southeast overhang. Climb the slab and belay beneath the first tier of the roof. Climb through this tier to the small slab above (crux), go around the second tier on the left and gain the scenic (and much easier) southeast ridge. From the top of the South Block, scramble northwest to the gully next to the Pullman Car. Exit left to hiking terrain or finish with the South Side route on the Pullman Car.

### 2.   SOUTHEAST OVERHANG A4

FA: LARRY DALKE AND TERRY O'DONNELL, 1963.

Climb the middle of the red slab and aid out over the massive roof.

### 3.   FREE FOR ALL 6 ★

Begin in a broad, tree-filled gully up and left from the low point of the face. Scramble all the way to the south side of the Pullman Car. Or begin at the low point of the face and climb pleasant slabs until it is obvious to cut up and slightly left to the northeast base of the Pullman Car. Climb steeper rock (6) heading for the East Face Overhang, but at the last minute, traverse left, then up into the gully on the south side of the Pullman Car. Finish up with the Southside (6).

### 4.   FREEWAY CLASS 4 ★

This excellent scramble is 800 feet long, but does not lead to the summit. Begin at the nadir of the face. Climb slabs for 300 feet to the crest of a blunt ridge. Follow the ridge northwest to a high point. Go west, then north into the gully between the First and Second Flatirons.

## Pullman Car

The following routes ascend the long and narrow summit block.

### 5.   SOUTHWEST CRACK 7

FA: CARL KELLOG AND KATHY OLSON, EARLY 1970S.

Climb a crack on the southwest side of the Pullman Car.

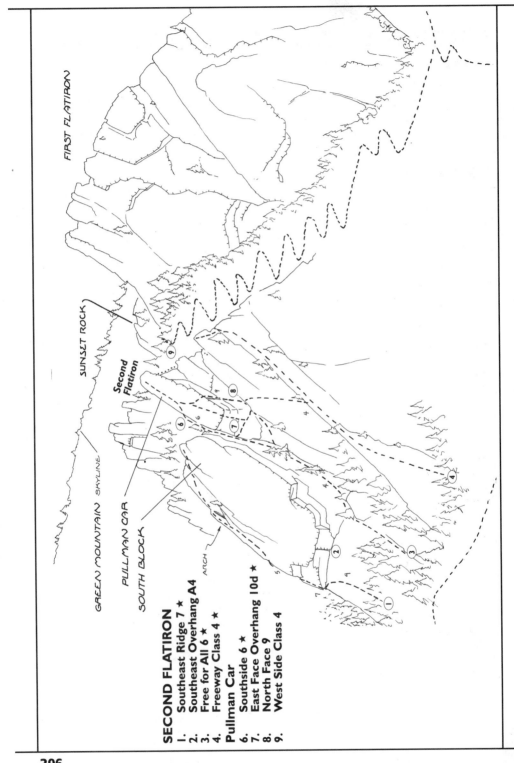

SECOND FLATIRON
1. Southeast Ridge 7 ★
2. Southeast Overhang A4
3. Free for All 6 ★
4. Freeway Class 4 ★
Pullman Car
6. Southside 6 ★
7. East Face Overhang 10d ★
8. North Face 9
9. West Side Class 4

FIRST FLATIRON

SUNSET ROCK

Second Flatiron

GREEN MOUNTAIN SKYLINE

PULLMAN CAR

SOUTH BLOCK

ARCH

### 6. SOUTHSIDE 6 ★

FA: CARL KELLOG AND KATHY OLSON, EARLY 1970S.

This is the logical finish to Free for All and the Southeast Ridge. Begin 40 feet up from the low (east) end of the south face of the Pullman Car. Climb 30 feet of tricky rock and gain the east face. Scramble to the summit.

### 7. EAST FACE OVERHANG 10D ★

FFA: JIM ERICKSON AND DIANA HUNTER, 1973.

Begin with Free for All and continue all the way up onto the Pullman Car, but where that route goes left, continue straight up.

### 8. NORTH FACE 9

FA: DAVID HORNSBY AND HAROLD WALTON, 1948. FFA: JIM ERICKSON AND DAVE BOWERS, 1973.

Begin 75 feet up along the northeast side of the Pullman Car and spot two tongues of rock, one above the other. Start here and follow cracks up to the east face of the Pullman Car.

### 9. WEST SIDE CLASS 4

This is the easiest route to the summit and is the standard downclimb. It is also the shortest summit route to any of the Flatirons. Scramble up the northwest corner of the Pullman Car.

## SUNSET FLATIRONETTE

Also known as Sunset Rock. This small crag is located about 100 feet southwest of the First Flatiron. In reality it is not so small, as its south ridge drops about 600 feet into the draw between the Second and Third Flatirons. Approach via the Third Flatiron Trail or the First Flatiron Trail, depending on which route one is to climb.

### 1. CHASE THE SUN 4 ★

Approach via the Third Flatiron Trail and continue past the junction for the East Bench. Leave the trail and find the bottom of the ridge up behind the Second Flatiron. Begin at the low point of the south (kind of southeast) ridge. Move left around a horn, gain the crest of the ridge and continue to a notch. The next pitch follows the crest to a second notch beneath a steep headwall. Traverse right around a corner and climb steep rock into a basin. Climb out of the basin and follow easier rock for two pitches to a false summit. An exposed traverse leads to the top.

### 2. DISINCLINATION 10A

FA: JIM ERICKSON AND STEVE WUNSCH, 1976.

Begin near the north end of the ridge. Climb an overhanging crack 50 feet off the ground.

### 3. PACK RAT 7

FA: MIKE BROOKS AND JIM STUBERG, 1980.

Begin on the west side of the ridge, 30 feet south of the summit. Climb a V-slot and a corner to a tree.

## DEVIATIONS

The Deviations are small finger-like flatirons southwest of Sunset Flatironette. They provide a few east side scrambles on friable rock.

## FIRST FLATIRON

The First Flatiron, with its massive east face and castellated summit ridge, flies high above the trees on the northeast shoulder of Green Mountain. If the Third Flatiron draws more traffic, it is mainly because its Standard East Face route is easier and less committing than the same on the First. The Direct East Face route on the First Flatiron is one of Boulder's grand excursions, and the view from

**FIRST FLATIRON—East Face**
8. Kamikaze Roofs 9 s ★
9. Zig Zag 7 ★
10. Baker's Way 4
11. Fandango 5 ★
16. Direct East Face 6 s ★
18. Northeast Gully 4 s
20. North Arête 4 ★

the summit is the best of all the Flatirons. Over the last few years the First Flatiron has had a lot more traffic due to a "wildlife closure" of the entire Third Flatiron area and the Ironing Boards.

**Approach**—Begin from Chautauqua Park. Cross Kinnikinic Road (closed to cars) and pick up the Chautauqua Trail, which heads southwest across a large open meadow. Once in the trees, this trail intersects the Bluebell-Baird Trail. Go left (southeast) a short way, then right on the First and Second Flatiron Trail. This trail leads to the bottom of the east face, then climbs the wooded gully to the saddle between the First and Second Flatirons. The Spy Express trail branches right (north) from the bottom of the east face and leads beneath the First Flatironette to The Spy.

**Descent**—To escape the summit, rappel 100 feet west from a large eyebolt. Or rappel 50 feet to another eyebolt above the southwest face, then rappel 60 feet to the ground. One may also downclimb the Southwest Face.

### 1.   WEST FACE 10D

FA: GERRY ROACH AND JEFF WHEELER, 1959. FFA: MIKE MUNGER, 1976.

Begin well around to the north from the Southwest Face. Climb a steep rotten dihedral to the summit ridge.

### 2.   DIRECT 8 s

FA: RICHARD ROSSITER AND LYNN HOUSEHOLDER, 1978.

Begin at the left edge of the southwest face and climb directly up to the bowl beneath the summit. Finish as for Southwest Face.

### 3.   SOUTHWEST FACE 0 ★

This route is often used as a downclimb. Begin south of the summit, behind and right of a large pine tree. Climb straight up, then angle up and left along the rock strata. Enter a small bowl (note the steel eyebolt) and climb the west face of the final tower.

### 4.   WAY OF THE ANCIENTS 7 s ★

FA: RICHARD ROSSITER, SOLO, 1988.

This 500-foot face and friction climb is the furthest left on the east face. Begin at an easy gully 80 feet up along the edge of the face from a big roof. Belay at a juniper tree (40 feet up). Angle up to the left on a course concurrent with Hubris. Where Hubris begins to curve up to the right in a left-facing corner, continue angling up and left toward the edge of the face. Gain a small rib, pass a rappel point with a couple of old pins and head straight for the summit.

### 5.   HUBRIS 4 OR 6 s ★

FA: GERRY ROACH, SOLO, 1987.

Begin as for Way Of The Ancients. Angle up to the left and gain a long left-facing corner that is rounded and crackless. After a couple hundred feet a roof blocks the corner. Move out left into a crack and ramp system or climb over the roof onto a smooth slab (6 s) with an old bolt. From here take the line of least resistance up the right side of a wide inset that tops out just north of the summit.

### 6.   ATALANTA 4

FA: GERRY ROACH, SOLO, 1987.

Begin as for the preceding route, but continue up the gully/groove past the juniper tree to a good ledge with small trees. Belay beneath a left-facing dihedral. Climb the dihedral to a couple of large trees. Continue in the dihedral system to the summit ridge.

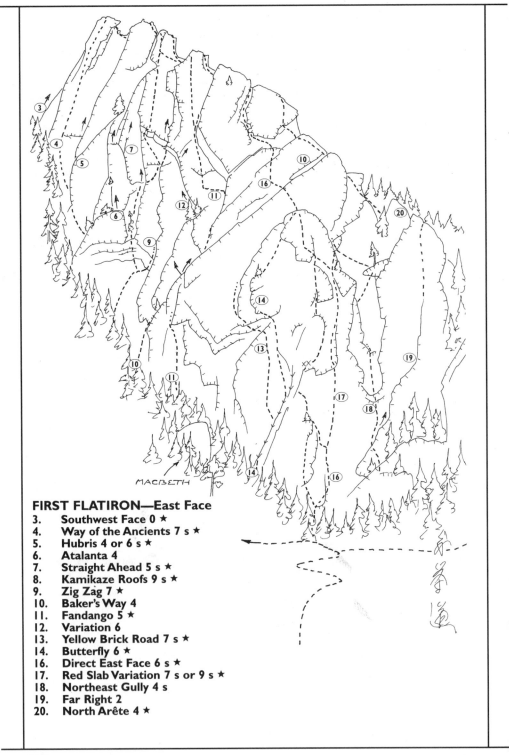

MACBETH

## FIRST FLATIRON—East Face

3.     Southwest Face 0 ★
4.     Way of the Ancients 7 s ★
5.     Hubris 4 or 6 s ★
6.     Atalanta 4
7.     Straight Ahead 5 s ★
8.     Kamikaze Roofs 9 s ★
9.     Zig Zag 7 ★
10.    Baker's Way 4
11.    Fandango 5 ★
12.    Variation 6
13.    Yellow Brick Road 7 s ★
14.    Butterfly 6 ★
16.    Direct East Face 6 s ★
17.    Red Slab Variation 7 s or 9 s ★
18.    Northeast Gully 4 s
19.    Far Right 2
20.    North Arête 4 ★

## 7. STRAIGHT AHEAD 5 s ★

FA: ROSSITER, SOLO, 1988.

Begin just right of Atalanta. Follow a shallow left-facing corner to a crack with an old Holubar piton. Above the piton the crack fades out. Climb straight ahead up the blank slab to the left end of the upper roof on Kamikaze and belay. Climb a left- facing dihedral to easier terrain and join the "false summit pitch" on the North Arête.

## 8. KAMIKAZE ROOFS 9 s ★

FA: ROSSITER, SOLO, 1988.

Begin as for Zig Zag at the bottom of a slab, directly below a huge overhang (Lower Kamikaze Roof). Climb through the right side of the roof and enter a channel with some stunted trees (the Bonsai Garden). This is 30 feet to the left of the Zig Zag dihedral. Follow the channel up and right, round a bulge, and climb a left-facing corner to a point just short of the left end of a six-foot roof (Higher Kamikaze Roof). One may also reach this roof in the following manner: traverse further to the right from the top of the channel and belay as for Zig Zag, turn a roof formed by some overlaps, and climb straight up the middle of a clean slab. Turn the six-foot roof at either of two points left of center (8 s or 9 s) and fly up the face to the skyline ridge.

## 9. ZIG ZAG 7 ★

Several hundred feet down to the right from the Southwest Face route, a very large roof leads out across the east face, then drops straight down to form a left-facing corner. Begin near the bottom of this corner, climb a slab up toward the right side of the roof and belay. Move out through the right side of the roof (crux), then follow a left-facing, zigzag dihedral to the summit ridge, at one point going behind a giant flake.

## 10. BAKER'S WAY 4

Begin about midway along the south edge of the east face, beneath two small pines 40 feet above the ground. Climb past a bulge (4) and follow a right-angling ramp or ledge all the way across the east face to the skyline ridge. At this point the climb joins the North Arête and tackles several interesting and exposed pinnacles en route to the summit.

## 11. FANDANGO 5 ★

Directly out to the right from the start to Baker's Way, a large roof caps a slab. Begin 80 feet below the left side of the roof. Climb the slab, cross Baker's Way and belay. Go part way up a left-facing corner, then work left to a belay niche. Climb over a small roof, up a slab and enter a massive left-facing dihedral that leads to the summit ridge at the notch below the "quartz crystal pitch." From the bottom of the dihedral, one may also climb straight up the slab on the left (6s).

## 12. VARIATION 6

Climb straight up from the junction with Baker's Way and belay at the big trees 35 feet left of the regular line. Take a left-leaning, left-facing dihedral to its junction with Zig Zag, then angle up and right to join the last pitch of Fandango.

## 13. YELLOW BRICK ROAD 7 s ★

FA: RICHARD ROSSITER AND RALPH BALDWIN, TANDEM SOLO, 1977.

200 feet up and left along the south margin of the east face is a huge boulder called Macbeth. Begin to the right of this boulder. Climb up the middle of a diamond-shaped slab via pale yellow rock that has a cobblestone appearance. Belay at the upper left edge of the diamond-shaped slab, below the right end of a big roof. Move out left and climb the roof with poor protection, then continue up a slab to join the last independent pitch of the Direct East Face.

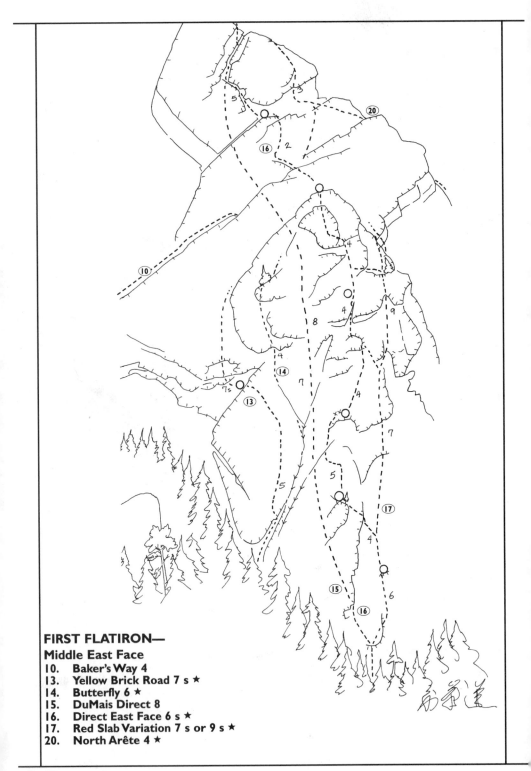

**FIRST FLATIRON—**

**Middle East Face**

10.   Baker's Way 4
13.   Yellow Brick Road 7 s ★
14.   Butterfly 6 ★
15.   DuMais Direct 8
16.   Direct East Face 6 s ★
17.   Red Slab Variation 7 s or 9 s ★
20.   North Arête 4 ★

## 14. BUTTERFLY 6 ★

FA: GERRY ROACH AND JEFF WHEELER, 1956.

Begin just right of Yellow Brick Road. Climb just left of a prominent groove and belay beneath a bulging headwall. Angle up to the right and eventually merge with the Direct East Face. One may also angle up to the left (6).

## 15. DuMAIS DIRECT 8

FA: RICHARD DuMAIS, ET AL.

Begin at the low point of the face. Climb the wall a short way left of Direct East Face, but to the right of Butterfly. Climb through a very steep section about halfway up (crux) and gain the big ledges at midface. Work up and left to the left of Direct East Face, then join Direct East Face in the last 75 feet below the ridge crest.

## 16. DIRECT EAST FACE 6 S ★

FA: PAT AMENT AND LARRY DALKE, ABOUT 1960.

This is among the very best of the Flatiron slab routes, combining great length and superb rock with scenic grandeur. The face is about 1,000 feet high and some ten pitches are required to reach the summit. Begin from the nadir of the face. Climb up and right into a shallow left-facing corner, past a bolt and continue on to a belay on a narrow shelf. Move up and left to a good ledge with a tree and belay. Climb straight up a slab, then left into a crack and up to a belay with two bolts. Angle right, then straight up the headwall on good holds. From the huge ledge at the top of the headwall angle up and left toward a slot at the left side of a roof. Bridge and stem up the slot, then take the left or right side of a gully to the skyline ridge and finish as for North Arête.

## 17. RED SLAB VARIATION 7 S OR 9 S ★

From the first belay, climb straight up a red slab , over a small roof, and up an intimidating wide groove (9). The groove can be eliminated on the left.

## 18. NORTHEAST GULLY 4 S

Also known as East Face Gully. Begin about one hundred feet up to the right from Direct East Face. Climb up and left into a groove that leads into a broad gully. Climb straight up the gully, then move left into a large right-facing corner, then cross right to a tree. Climb up and left across the gully and join Baker's Way or Direct East Face.

## 19. FAR RIGHT 2

Also known as East Face North Side, this pleasant climb takes the long, narrow face to the right of the Northeast Gully and finishes near the beginning of the North Arête.

## 20. NORTH ARÊTE 4 ★

This excellent route follows the castellated skyline ridge. To reach the traditional start, hike the Spy Express around to the north end of the First Flatiron and mount the ridge from the west as it rises out of the trees. Several steep steps and false summits are encountered enroute to the top: a roof that is passed on the left, the "quartz crystal pitch," the "false summit pitch" and finally the summit tower itself.

The following two crags are approached from the Spy Express trail that leads north from bottom of the First Flatiron.

# FIRST FLATIRONETTE

This crag lies 150 feet north from the low point of the First Flatiron. The Spy Express trail runs beneath its base. To exit the top of this rock, walk west then north to The Spy. Hike up around the top of The Spy, then down along its north face to the Spy Express trail.

Sharon Sadleir climbing the First Flatiron. Photo by Richard Rossiter.

### 1.  EAST FACE 2

From the low point of the east face, hike up to the right past two gullies to the bottom of the larger piece of the face. Climb 350 feet of good rock to the summit.

### 2.  NORTH RIDGE 2

Begin at the low point of the rock. Gain the ridge and continue past some notches to the summit.

## THE SPY

The Spy is a distinctive fin of rock at the far north end of the First Flatiron. The east ridge is 370 feet long and only ten feet wide near the top. The Spy Express leads directly to its base. To escape from the summit, jump off to the west.

### EAST RIDGE 4 ★

Begin at the bottom of the east ridge and climb 120 feet to a five-foot vertical step. The step may be passed on the left (3) or the right (4). Continue for 100 feet and pass a smooth bulge on the right (crux). Climb 100 feet of easier rock to the summit. Climb down and back up to a west summit and take the jump. Hike back down around the north side of the rock.

THE AMPHITHEATER,
from the northeast

Flagstaff Mountain

Fourth Pinnacle

Third Pinnacle

Second Pinnacle

Ginseng Pillar

First Pinnacle

West Bench

East Bench

# THE AMPHITHEATER

Gregory Canyon Amphitheater is a popular enclave of towers and adjacent crags several hundred yards south of the Gregory Canyon parking area off Baseline Road. The Amphitheater consists of two large towers connected at a low point called the West Bench and three more pinnacles in a row to the west . The area features many routes of moderate difficulty as well as enjoyable bouldering. On any fair day the pinnacles are typically besieged by climbing schools, outing clubs, and masses of unaffiliated climbers, especially inside the Amphitheater. This is not a good place to bring your dog.

Routes on the Amphitheater are listed counterclockwise beginning with South Face Left on the First Pinnacle and finishing with the West Bench Dihedral, a few feet to the left. Use the Amphitheater Trail to reach the east side and the Amphitheater Express (trail) to reach the north side.

Due to very heavy climbing use of the Amphitheater, additional permanent anchors are needed above the south and north faces of the First Pinnacle, as well as the east wall of the West Bench.

## FIRST PINNACLE

This massive tower forms the north and east sides of the Amphitheater. The east arm is called the East Bench, and the small pinnacle at its base is T-Zero. To escape from the summit, downclimb the West Ridge to the West Bench, or rappel 110 feet east from an eye bolt. One may also rappel 45 feet southeast to the top of the East Bench and rappel another 60 feet north from slings. Another eye bolt is oddly located ten feet below the top of the Northeast Chimney route. Three permanent anchors are needed at strategic points just below the rim of the south face.

### 1.    SOUTH FACE LEFT 11 (TR)
Begin just right of the West Bench Dihedral. Climb the steep face up and right past a curved face hold and continue up the left side of the wall. It is a bit easier to join the upper part of South Face Center.

### 2.    SOUTH FACE CENTER 10 vs ★
This excellent route is normally toproped and no free ascent has ever been recorded. Begin ten feet left of the regular line. Step off a block, then face climb to a triangular hole followed by a thin crack and gain a narrow ledge at mid-face. Climb a short crack to a left-leaning, left-facing dihedral and finish on the ridge crest just left of the big block.

### 3.    INSIDE SOUTH FACE 9 s ★
FA: BILL EUBANKS, BRAD VANDIVER, 1946. FFA: LARRY DALKE, PAT AMENT, 1960.
This route is normally toproped from two bolts on the ridge crest. Begin atop a pedestal toward the right side of the face, angle up and left to a narrow ledge, lieback up a blunt flake to a left-facing corner, and continue via easier terrain to the summit. Or from the narrow ledge at mid-face, move up to the right and climb an insecure, left- leaning, left-facing groove/corner.

The following routes ascend the upper east side of the First Pinnacle, but begin from the East Bench above the East Bench Dihedral.

### 4.    LEFT VARIATION 4
From the top (north end) of the East Bench, traverse 15 feet left and follow a shallow dihedral to the summit.

# GREGORY CANYON AMPHITHEATER

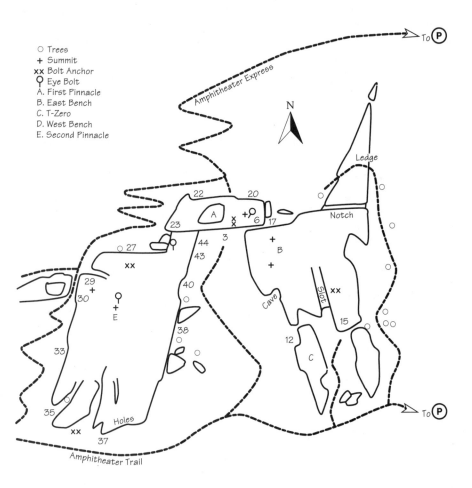

○ Trees
+ Summit
xx Bolt Anchor
○ Eye Bolt
A. First Pinnacle
B. East Bench
C. T-Zero
D. West Bench
E. Second Pinnacle

## 5.   McCrumm's Crack 4

From the top of the East Bench, step left and climb a concave wall with flakes and potholes into a crack that leads to the summit.

## 6.   Southeast Arête 5 ★

Begin from the top of the East Bench. Climb a shallow trough with a bolt just left of the blunt southeast arête. Short but excellent.

## 7.   Juniper Crack 5

From the top of the East Bench, move out right to a stance on the narrow east face beneath a juniper tree. Climb past the right side of juniper and up a crack to where it fades, then continue up the face to the top (crux).

## 8.   Pizza Pie Crack 5

Begin as for Juniper Crack but continue to the right for another 10 feet and climb the next crack.

## 9.   Northeast Traverse 5

Traverse past Pizza Pie Crack to the right edge of the east face and climb along the exposed northeast arête to the summit.

# East Bench

This ridge extends from the north end of the First Pinnacle to the little tower called T- Zero and forms the east wall of the Amphitheater. To descend, downclimb the East Bench Dihedral or the Inside West Face, or rappel 60 feet north from slings, just east of the top.

## 10.   East Bench Dihedral 2

Climb the 90-degree dihedral formed by the inside south face and the inside west face of the Amphitheater.

## 11.   Inside West Face Class 4

About 50 feet downhill to the south of East Bench Dihedral is a smoke-blackened cave. Begin 15 feet west of the cave, at a patch of poison ivy. Angle up and north to within 15 feet of the East Bench Dihedral, cut back to the south beneath a steep red wall, then back north to finish in the upper part of the dihedral. One may also climb straight up from the right side of the red wall (4).

T-Zero— This is the miniature tower at the south end of the East Bench that forms the southeast corner of the Amphitheater.

## 12.   Finger Crack 5 ★

Climb a short crack with piton scars along the left side of the west face.

## 13.   Overhang 11 ★

A primer in modern face climbing. Set a toprope and work out the moves on the overhanging west face.

## 14.   North Ridge 0

This is the easiest way to the top and provides the descent.

## East Bench (outside)

The following routes are located on the outside (south and east sides) of the East Bench.

### 15. P.S. I'M BLONDE 12A ★

FA: PAUL PIANA, BRET RUCKMAN, FRED KNAPP, 1989.

Begin just around to the right from T-Zero and right of a rotten red slot. Climb in from the left (#2 Friend) or climb straight up for 50 feet (small gear), then follow five bolts up a narrow left-leaning wall. Gain a two-bolt anchor and lower off.

### 16. OUTSIDE EAST FACE 9 s ★

FA: PAUL MAYROSE AND PAT AMENT, 1964.

The location of this route is not certain. It appears to begin a few feet right of the preceding route, along the south margin of the east face. The original description places it "downhill and to the south of the Northeast Chimney." Climb a steep wall near its left edge.

### 17. NORTHEAST CHIMNEY 3

On the north side the Amphitheater, a steep chimney divides the East Bench from the First Pinnacle. Climb the chimney past three chockstones and arrive at the top of the East Bench.

### 18. DIVERSION 7

This pitch ascends the narrow east face of the First Pinnacle beginning with the Northwest Chimney. Climb past the first chockstone, then move out right onto the steep wall and climb past an overhang (7). Finish with Juniper Crack.

### 19. NORTH FACE LEFT 10 (TR)

FA: (?) RICHARD AND JOYCE ROSSITER, 1988.

Climb a very steep crack with knobs and holes along the left side of the north face. Near the top, swing around onto the east face and continue to the summit.

### 20. DIRECT NORTH FACE 7

Begin about 15 feet right of the preceding route. Climb straight up via solution holes and knobs, move a few feet right, and then go up and right to a belay stance. Climb a right-angling groove, then continue more easily to the ridge crest of the First Pinnacle. Belay from two bolts.

### 21. VARIATION 9

FA: JIM ERICKSON, SOLO, 1975.

Climb an overhanging, right-facing dihedral, then traverse down and left to join the main line (?).

### 22. D-A's ROUTE 9

FA: PAT AMENT, LARRY DALKE, 1961. FFA: JIM SOUDER, SCOTT WOODRUFF, 1979.

Begin at the west side of the north face, just before the wall curves around toward the West Bench. Climb a steep crack (with piton scars) to a roof, then hand traverse up and left to a sloping belay stance. A narrow slot leads to the top. The free version of this route climbs in from the right and avoids the poorly protected moves at the bottom of the piton crack.

### 23. WEST RIDGE CLASS 4 ★

Begin from the north end of the West Bench. Scramble east to the summit of the First Pinnacle passing a large block on the right (south).

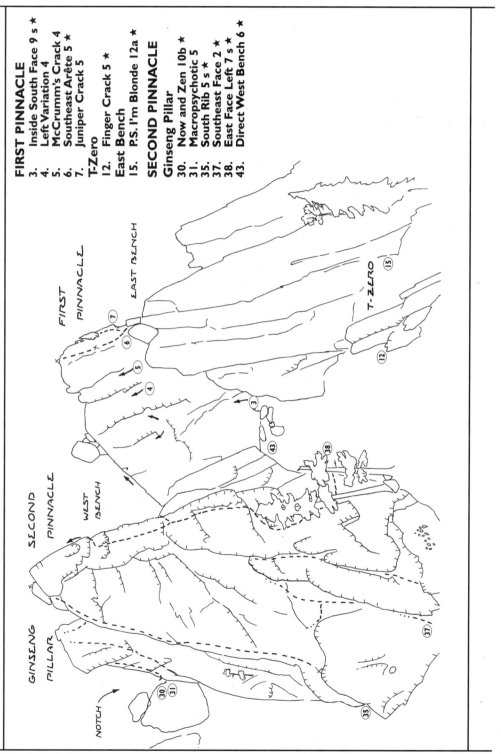

## FIRST PINNACLE

3. Inside South Face 9 s ★
4. Left Variation 4
5. McCrumm's Crack 4
6. Southeast Arête 5 ★
7. Juniper Crack 5

**T-Zero**

12. Finger Crack 5 ★

**East Bench**

15. P.S. I'm Blonde 12a ★

## SECOND PINNACLE

**Ginseng Pillar**

30. Now and Zen 10b ★
31. Macropsychotic 5
35. South Rib 5 s ★
37. Southeast Face 2 ★
38. East Face Left 7 s ★
43. Direct West Bench 6 ★

## SECOND PINNACLE

This commanding tower forms the west side of the Amphitheater and has a very impressive east face. To descend from the summit, downclimb the Northwest Corner (4), or from an eyebolt on the summit, rappel 75 feet northwest and arrive at the same spot. One may also rappel 160 feet down the east face to the inside of the Amphitheater.

## West Bench (outside)

The following three routes begin from the top of the West Bench. Belay at a large eye bolt in a tilted block.

### 24. UPPER EAST FACE 5 TO 9

From the eyebolt, traverse left across the east face to a ledge and join one of the east face routes.

### 25. RED GULLY 8

FA: PAT AMENT AND PAUL MAYROSE, 1964.

Begin from the top of the West Bench. Traverse 20 feet left into the bottom of a right-facing dihedral. Climb to the top of the dihedral, exit left, and follow a slab to the summit.

### 26. NORTH FACE 6 S ★

Also known as the Northeast Inset, this line takes the prominent right-leaning groove that leads to the summit from the south end of the West Bench. An exciting and insecure lead.

### 27. RED WALL 10c ★

FA: PAUL PIANA AND SUZANNE JACKSON, 1989.

Begin beneath a north-facing red wall just right of the West Bench. Climb up to an obvious wide crack, then break left and continue up the steep face past four bolts to a two-bolt anchor. Bring a #1 Friend.

### 28. NORTHWEST CORNER CLASS 4 ★

The easiest and shortest downclimb from the summit. As an ascent, begin 40 feet right (west) from the top of the West Bench. Climb into an obvious narrow chimney, then move up into the notch between the main summit and Ginseng Pillar (on the right) and scramble 30 feet (eastward) to the top.

## Ginseng Pillar

The next four routes climb to the summit of Ginseng Pillar, the steep little spur that forms the northwest corner of the Second Pinnacle. To escape from the summit, scramble down to the east and downclimb the Northwest Corner route.

### 29. SIBERIAN NORTH FACE 10B ★

FA: STEVE ILG AND RICHARD ROSSITER, 1988.

Begin just right from the bottom of the Northwest Corner. Hand traverse up and left along a flake/crack to a narrow stance. Clip a bolt and go straight for the top.

### 30. NOW AND ZEN 10B ★

FA: RICHARD ROSSITER AND STEVE ILG, 1988.

Begin in the gap between Ginseng Pillar and a large balanced rock. Climb the steep west face just right of the arête, turn a small roof, and work up the slab to the left side of an overhang. Stretch up around the arête and clip a bolt, then swing out onto the north face and climb straight up to the summit. A few of the larger sized Friends are needed before reaching the bolt.

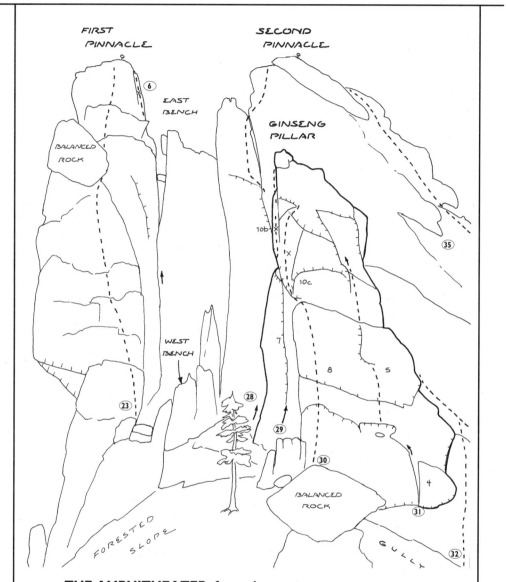

## THE AMPHITHEATER, from the west
## FIRST PINNACLE
6.     Southwest Arête 5 ★
23.   West Ridge Class 4 ★
## SECOND PINNACLE
28.   Northwest Corner Class 4 ★

### Ginseng Pillar
29.   Siberian North Face 10b ★
30.   Now and Zen 10b ★
31.   Macropsychotic 5
32.   Upper West Face 0
35.   South Rib 5 s ★

### 31. MACROPSYCHOTIC 5

FA: ROSSITER, SOLO, 1988.

Begin about 20 feet down and right of the preceding route. Climb a short, clean crack that widens as it goes up, then step up onto a white pedestal, climb the face above (5), and take an easy chimney to the summit.

### 32. UPPER WEST FACE 0

Just to the right of Macropsychotic, climb up a shallow gully and right-facing corner to the trough that leads up to the notch between Ginseng Pillar and the main summit...climb either or both.

### 33. SHORTCUT 4

About halfway up along the west face (between the Amphitheater Trail and Ginseng Pillar) a short cliff with good holds allows entry to the inner sanctum of the southwest face. From here, follow a large gully (see Southwest Face) northward to arrive at the notch between Ginseng Pillar and the true summit. One may also join the upper South Rib (5 s).

### 34. SOUTHWEST FACE 0

Begin just up and left from the bottom of the south ridge, a few paces from the trail. Scramble into the left of two prominent chimneys and pass beneath two large chockstones. Emerge into a broad basin reminiscent of desert slickrock and belay from a massive eyebolt. Continue north over easy rock and climb a short wall below a tree. Scramble 100 feet up an easy gully and gain the notch between Ginseng Pillar and the summit of the Second Pinnacle. Climb the steep west face 30 feet to the summit.

### 35. SOUTH RIB 5 s ★

Climb to the big eyebolt as for the preceding route, then move up and right and follow the exposed south rib directly to the summit of the Second Pinnacle. An excellent climb.

### 36. OFF FENCE 9 s

Begin around to the right of the crest at a large overhang. Step off the south end of a buck and rail fence, then climb up and left to join the South Rib route.

### 37. SOUTHEAST FACE 2 ★

This route avoids the exposure and runouts of the South Rib by following slots and chimneys off to the right. Thirty feet or so to the right of the chockstone chimney, a wider chimney leads up into the basin with the eyebolt. Begin 15 feet to the right of this. Step off a pedestal and climb a short slab into a three-foot-wide slot. Arrive at the broad basin described above. At the far right (east) side of this basin is another sturdy eyebolt that could be used as a belay anchor. Move up and right, eventually finishing with a south-facing chimney. One could begin this or one of the preceding two routes with the big chimney left of the three-foot-wide slot.

### 38. EAST FACE LEFT 7 s ★

Begin this superb route 100 feet up along the east face of the Second Pinnacle, 15 feet right of two large trees. Hand traverse left along a crack and climb onto a block. Move straight up behind a tree (8+ s) or left a bit to avoid the branches, and angle back right (7 s) to belay on a good ledge. Traverse right along the ledge, then stem across into a left-facing corner. Climb straight up (4) until it is possible to step around to the right, into a right-facing red dihedral (Red Gully). Climb the dihedral, or better, climb the beautiful face to the left of the dihedral (7 s) straight up to the summit overhang, skirt around to the right and continue to the top. One may also climb through the summit overhang (9). The variation that goes left to avoid the tree limbs was climbed by Cleve McCarty and Paul Lessig, 1968. The direct version on the upper face was soloed by R. Rossiter, 1988.

### 39. DIRECT EAST FACE 9 vs

FA: LARRY DALKE AND PAT AMENT, 1963. FFA: MIKE YOKEL, 1969.

This route would be a lot of fun if it had some protection. Just up and right from the preceding route, angle up and right along a flake, move right and climb a slot through a roof. It is also possible to climb straight up the arête left of The Inset to the roof. Climb through a second roof, and finish with the Red Gully. Another variation climbs through the roof on the left after the initial flake (Jim Erickson, solo, 1972).

## West Bench

The low connecting ridge between the First and Second Pinnacles is called the West Bench. On its west side it barely rises above the slope of the hill, but on the east it drops steeply for 100 feet to the floor of the Amphitheater and is the most popular venue in the area. To descend from the top of the bench, downclimb the Standard Inside East Face route or rappel 100 feet east from an eyebolt in a large block. One may also hike around the Second Pinnacle and back up into the Amphitheater. These routes are all toproped from the lone eye bolt. It would be highly useful to have additional permanent anchors along the top of the wall.

### 40. THE INSET 5 s

Begin about 45 feet downhill to the left from the West Bench Dihedral and just left of a low overhang. Climb up the right side of the wide trough and finish up to the right. Or climb directly up a thin crack (7).

### 41. ROOF 9+ s ★

FA: LARRY DALKE EARLY 1960s.

This obstacle is just right of the wide inset and is about 12 feet above the ground. The left side is quite difficult and the center is a lot harder than that.

### 42. SLOT 6 ★

Climb the 12-inch crack just right of The Roof and finish with a steep finger crack at the top of the face.

### 43. DIRECT WEST BENCH 6 ★

Begin five feet right of Slot. Climb steep rock up to a left-angling crack, then go straight up, finishing in a finger crack with piton scars (as for Slot).

### 44. STANDARD INSIDE EAST FACE CLASS 4 ★

This route is the easiest downclimb and has served as the maiden voyage to many a climber (going up of course). Climb the crack system that begins a few feet left of the West Bench Dihedral.

### 45. WEST BENCH DIHEDRAL 4

Jam and stem up the junction between the east and south inside faces of the Amphitheater.

## THIRD PINNACLE

The Third Pinnacle is located about 150 feet west of the Second Pinnacle and appears as a small flatiron with a dramatic summit tower. To approach the east face, by hike up to the notch with the balanced rock just west of Ginseng Pillar, then walk around to the west. To escape from the summit, downclimb the east side of the summit tower, then scramble north and west to hiking terrain.

### 1. WEST OVERHANG 7

This miniature route is a good primer in climbing upside-down. Hike around to the west side of the rock and climb a short crack to the summit.

### 2. RED TIDE II TR

Begin up along the overhanging west face, 50 feet above the Amphitheater Trail. Climb past a large, left-pointing flake and finish just right of a big block on the ridge crest.

### 3. SOUTH RIDGE 6

Find the foot of the ridge beside the trail, 150 yards past the Amphitheater. The first 80 feet are the most difficult. Continue over a false summit and on to the west side of the pinnacle.

### 4. HALLS OF IVY 2

Begin below the middle of the east face. Climb a short slab up past a tree, tackle the roof band, and jam a wide crack to the summit.

**The following three routes ascend a slab and pass a roof band on the right side of the east face.**

### 5. THIN CRACK 4

Climb a crack past a tiny fir tree and continue through the left side of a roof band. Finish as for Halls Of Ivy.

### 6. TRIDENT 7

Climb up the center of the slab and turn a three-foot roof in the right of three cracks. Join Halls Of Ivy high on the face.

### 7. WIDE CRACK 4

Begin at the right side of the east face. Climb a tiny flatiron up to a tree, then continue up a wide crack past another tree and join Halls Of Ivy near the summit.

## FOURTH PINNACLE

Second highest of the group, this rock stands about 200 feet to the west of the Third Pinnacle. Approach via the Amphitheater Trail and break off to the northwest after passing the south ridge of the Third Pinnacle. Descend from the summit by downclimbing a wide crack on the west side.

### 1. HALLS OF POISON IVY 4

This route ascends the large left-facing dihedral that tops out just left of the summit. Begin about 30 feet left of East Face. Climb slabs beneath an overhang, then veer up and left to a ledge with poison ivy. Follow a crack in the east-facing wall of the dihedral and exit right at the top to reach the summit.

### 2. EAST FACE 6

The right side of the east face forms a broad buttress with a hanging gully above a steep head wall. Climb the head wall at an old bolt ladder to get up into the gully, then continue more easily to the summit.

## GREGORY FLATIRONETTE or FIFTH PINNACLE

This large buttress is located 200 yards west of the Amphitheater and climbs from Gregory Canyon to a tiny pointed summit a short way west of the Fourth Pinnacle and a short way east of the Saddle Rock Trail and Amphitheater Trail junction. To reach the base of the rock in Gregory Canyon and the beginning of the North Ridge route, start up the Saddle Rock Trail, then break south at an appropriate point and hike up the steep forest slope to the objective. To reach the South Ridge route, hike the Amphitheater Trail about 200 yards past the Amphitheater. The bottom of the Fifth Pinnacle is on the right (north) across the trail from a small cave. To escape from the summit, downclimb the South Ridge to a level spot in the crest where it is easy to climb off to the west. Or scramble north for 100 feet and exit east.

### 1.   NORTH RIDGE 4

Begin at the low point of the ridge. Climb for 100 feet, then gain the main east face just right of the crest and work back and forth, following the line of least resistance, for about 300 feet to the upper end of the rib. Continue along easier ground to the pointed summit, the highest of the Amphitheater crags.

### 2.   SOUTH RIDGE 3

Begin from the Amphitheater Trail, across from a small cave. Scramble up the elegant ridge past a few very Zen trees, climb a steep section, then continue northward past a notch to the tiny summit.

## SADDLE ROCK

As the north ridge of Green Mountain drops steeply into Gregory Canyon, a pleasing granite buttress rises out of the trees. Perhaps more popular at earlier times, it still draws the eye of the climber and offers a few brief passages in a beautiful setting.

**SACRED CLIFFS, from the west**

*Pebble Beach*

Arch →

# SACRED CLIFFS

The Sacred Cliffs are a series of spectacular buttresses and towers along the jagged south ridge of Green Mountain. From the summit, the ridge descends to a broad, sandy col, climbs to an 8073-foot summit, and then descends again into Bear Canyon. The east side of the ridge consists of steep slabs that drop into the seldom-visited jungles of Skunk Canyon. The west side presents an array of superb formations featuring nearly 50 routes on solid Fountain Formation sandstone. Many climbers developed the routes in this area, most of which required at least some fixed protection. Due largely to the period in which they were established, there are very few pure "sport climbs." The late Bill DeMallie played a major role in the development of the Sacred Cliffs and it is partly in his honor that I have chosen to publicize this area. Note: Though no raptors are reported to nest on the Sacred Cliffs, these crags are closed to the public from February to August.

**Approach**—Hike the West Ridge Trail past its junction with the Ranger Trail and continue to the first sharp switchback. Leave the trail and follow a vague game trail southward for about 200 yards to where the first features are encountered. To reach the main cliff, follow a vague path southward to a broad, sandy saddle of Zen-like beauty, then continue for another 100 yards to where the path leaves the ridge crest and contour along the base of some west-facing cliffs. The first significant buttress is Pebble Beach, upon which the best routes were destroyed by "trad" climbers, who ironically later took up drilling their own "sport routes." All the bolts on this crag should be replaced. The path continues beneath more spectacular west-facing cliffs where the remainder of the routes appear to have all fixed gear in tact. This area may also be reached from the west end of Bear Canyon— bit more of a stroll.

## Name Game Area

This group of small buttresses and boulders is located about 200 yards south from the summit of Green Mountain on the west side of the ridge crest.

### BULLET HOLES 12

Climb the overhanging southwest arête of a large block just north of Name Game. Toprope only.

## NAME GAME ROCK

This is really a large boulder with a vertical north face and an overhanging west face. All but one of the routes are on the smooth north face. Toprope only.

**1.   SALATHE 12A**
Toprope the left side of the south face.

**2.   DON'T TOUCH THE NUDE 11B**
Move up and left past an overlap, then straight up the face to a bolt anchor (removed).

**3.   NUDE MONODOIGT 11A**
Climb the face right of center passing two overlaps. Originally had three bolts.

# GREEN MOUNTAIN, SACRED CLIFFS

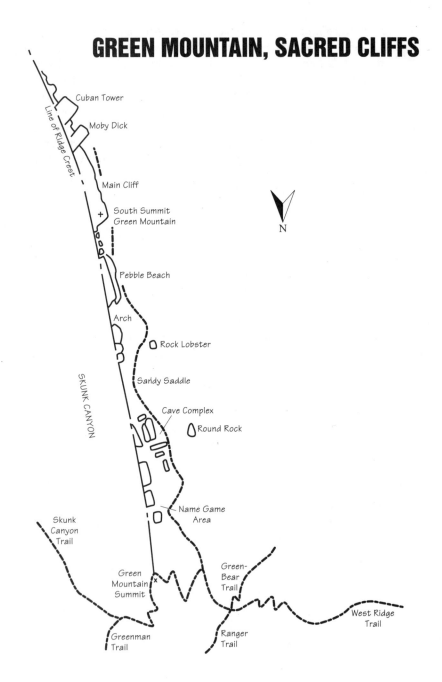

Cuban Tower

Moby Dick

Line of Ridge Crest

Main Cliff

South Summit
Green Mountain

N

Pebble Beach

Arch

Rock Lobster

SKUNK CANYON

Sandy Saddle

Cave Complex

Round Rock

Name Game
Area

Skunk
Canyon
Trail

Green
Mountain
Summit

Green-
Bear
Trail

West Ridge
Trail

Greenman
Trail

Ranger
Trail

**4.   CLOSE TO THE EDGE 10D**

Climb the right edge of the north face. Bolt anchor removed.

**5.   SLAVE TO THE STARS 12B/C**

Face climb on the south side of the block. Originally had five bolts.

## CAVE COMPLEX

About 50 yards south of Name Game is a chaotic jumble of boulders and cliffs defying logical description. Hidden within this miasma are two caves, one having an old wood-burning stove.

**1.   LAST WALTZ 12?**

This route is located on the west end of the next rock south of Name Game and east of a cave. Climb a severely overhanging red wall with fluorescent green lichen. Six bolts chopped. Never redpointed.

**2.   MY CAVE OR YOURS 11B**

Climb the smooth, triangular north face across the alcove from Last Waltz. Three bolts chopped.

**3.   MIRROR, MIRROR 12B/C**

Locate a large block just west of the first cave. Climb quartz pebbles up the gently overhanging west face. Bolts chopped.

**4.   EATERS OF THE DEAD 9**

Climb an overhanging off-width crack in a 30-foot block just west of the second cave.

**5.   ROUND ROCK 11**

Locate a "fantastic pebbled monolith" 100 yards downslope (west) from the second cave. Many interesting problems up to 35 feet high on the northeast and west sides. Two bolts on top (may still be in place).

## Pebble Beach Area

The following routes are located on the first series of buttresses south (southeast) of the sandy saddle. The initial cliff (before the larger buttress called Pebble Beach) is pierced by an improbable tunnel that connects with the steep upper reaches of Skunk Canyon.

### ROCK LOBSTER B1

Locate this odd leaning cube on the right as the trail climbs and pulls away from the ridge line. Climb a shallow groove up the northeast corner. More climbing to left up overhanging jugs and fins.

## PEBBLE BEACH

This large buttress is located just south of the tunnel and may be identified by its vertical north face, split by a hand crack.

**1.   98 POUND WEAKLING 9+**

Begin at the lower left corner of the buttress. Turn a bulge, then continue up the right side of a smooth face. Three bolts, chopped.

**2.   PERFECT HAND CRACK 9+ ★**

Begin up and left from the preceding route. Climb the obvious crack in the north face. Rappel from two bolts.

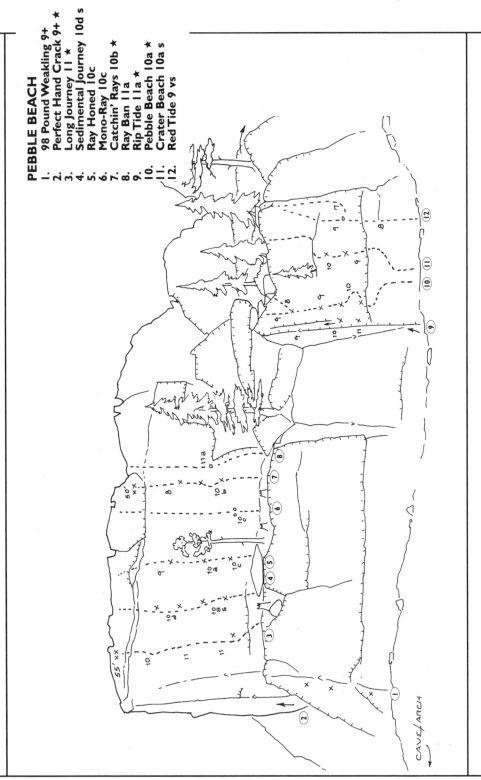

## PEBBLE BEACH

1. 98 Pound Weakling 9+
2. Perfect Hand Crack 9+ ★
3. Long Journey 11 ★
4. Sedimental Journey 10d s
5. Ray Honed 10c
6. Mono-Ray 10c
7. Catchin' Rays 10b ★
8. Ray Ban 11a
9. Rip Tide 11a ★
10. Pebble Beach 10a ★
11. Crater Beach 10a s
12. Red Tide 9 vs

CAVE/ARCH

### 3.  LONG JOURNEY 11 ★ TR
Climb the left side of the upper west face, just right of the arête. A poor bolt was placed a short way up this pitch. Toprope.

### 4.  SEDIMENTAL JOURNEY 10D S
Climb the middle of the pebbly and steep west face. Four bolts.

### 5.  RAY HONED 10C
FA: GREG HAND, KENT LUGBILL, VICTOR CREAZZI, CHARLIE ROLLINS, JEFF MCWHIRTER, STEVE GLENN, RAY SNEAD, 1989.
Begin just left of a tree. Climb the vertical west face past three bolts, then traverse left and up to a two-bolt anchor. SR.

### 6.  MONO-RAY 10C TR
Begin to the right of the tree and climb straight up the wall to a two-bolt anchor. Toprope, 40 feet.

### 7.  CATCHIN' RAYS 10B ★
FA: RAY SNEAD AND KENT LUGBILL, 1989.
Follow three bolts up the right side of the west face. Lower off, 40 feet.

### 8.  RAY BAN 11A TR
Begin just right of the preceding route. Climb straight up past the left end of a small roof. Toprope, 40 feet.

The following routes are located on a subsidiary buttress at the lower right side of the main rock. All bolts chopped. These routes are excellent and should have all fixed gear replaced.

### 9.  RIP TIDE 11A ★
Climb the arête and a shallow dihedral along the left side of the buttress. Two bolts, chopped.

### 10.  PEBBLE BEACH 10A ★
Turn a roof, then climb pebbles up the steep face just right of Rip Tide. Four bolts, chopped.

### 11.  CRATER BEACH 10A S
Turn the roof and climb the middle of the face. Two bolts, chopped.

### 12.  RED TIDE 9 VS
Climb right side of face past a large cobblestone.

## MAIN CLIFF
This section begins 75 yards south of Pebble Beach with the South Summit of Green Mountain and a forms a continuous west-facing cliff for nearly a half-mile. There are many interesting features, including the leaning monolith of Moby Dick and the Cuban Tower at the southeast end of the crest. Beyond the Cuban Tower, the cliff fades and the slope drops into Bear Canyon. Many of the routes were established on the lead and much of the fixed pro is of poor quality and oddly positioned.

## SOUTH SUMMIT
The towering South Summit is the most prominent feature on the south ridge of Green Mountain. It has a large, flat north face similar to Pebble Beach, a steep west face with a huge overhang, and notch on the south that separates it from the continuation of the Main Cliff. To escape from the top, rappel 80 feet from a two-bolt anchor just north of the summit, or rappel 140 feet from a two-bolt anchor on the far side of the notch to the south of the summit.

SACRED CLIFFS, South Summit and Main Cliff

South Summit
Green Mountain

234

### I. POULTRY IN MOTION 10c/d ★

FA: KENT LUGBILL AND RAY SNEAD, 1989.

Begin at the northwest corner of the buttress. Climb a dihedral with a two-inch crack or scramble up a gully on the left and belay at a tree. Climb a thin crack through a roof and continue straight up the middle of the north face past a bolt and fixed pin. Lower off from two-bolt anchor (80 feet).

### 2. NORTH FACE CRACK 10

FA: CHIP CHASE AND KENT LUGBILL, c. 1980.

Climb to the roof as for the preceding route. Traverse right beneath the roof, then follow a crack up the right side of the north face.

### 3. THIN CRACK 11 s ?

Begin up in an inset at the lower right side of the north face. Climb an elegant thin crack in the smooth wall to a two-bolt anchor beneath a roof. Two knifeblades and two bolts. Gear needed.

### 4. CALL ME A CAB 11A ★

FA: JIM LESUER AND DAVE SCHUELING.

Just right of the lower north face is a smooth west-facing wall with a roof. Climb the wall just right of center. Five bolts to a two-bolt anchor on a ramp.

### 5. GUANO MASTER 7

Climb a left-facing dihedral and a chimney with a wedged block. Finish in the notch just south of the summit block. Rappel 140 feet from bolts.

### 6. PILLARS OF FRENZY 10D s ★

Climb the first 40 feet of Guano Master, then step right to the arête. Climb the narrow segmented column past five bolts to the notch south of the summit block. Blind #2 Friend placement above third bolt. Rappel 140 feet from a two-bolt anchor.

### 7. GREEN CORNERS 8

Climb the dihedral system just right of the Pillars Of Frenzy.

### 8. BEAR ESSENTIALS 10D

Begin at a right-facing dihedral about 20 feet right of the Pillars Of Frenzy. Start up the dihedral, then move left and climb straight up to a bulge. Climb the crack on the left (8) or pull over the right side of the bulge (10d). Belay in a chimney and continue with the following route.

### 9. GRIZZLIES FROM HELL 10c ★

Climb straight up the right-facing dihedral and belay at the bottom of a chimney (10c). Climb the chimney through a big overhang and belay beneath a higher roof (8). Climb a four-inch crack through the roof and continue up a dihedral. Move right and rappel 100 feet from a three-bolt anchor.

### 10. ANOTHER MINDLESS CRACK 10

Begin beneath a right-facing dihedral that forms the left side of an inset. Climb the corner to an incut band and belay. Jam a four-inch crack and crank over a wedged block in a bomb bay chimney.

### 11. LE GEEK 10A ★

Begin beneath the arête at the right side of a big inset. Start up the right side of the arête, then move left and climb to the top of a black slab. Four bolts to a one-bolt anchor on a big ledge. Scramble right and rappel 70 feet from a tree.

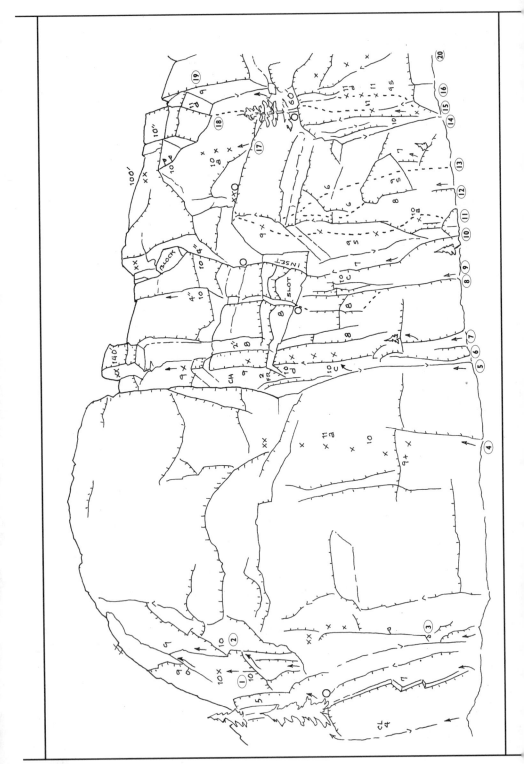

## THE SACRED CLIFFS
## SOUTH SUMMIT

1. Poultry In Motion 10c/d ★
2. North Face Crack 10
3. Thin Crack 11 s ?
4. Call Me A Cab 11a ★
5. Guano Master 7
6. Pillars Of Frenzy 10d s ★
7. Green Corners 8
8. Bear Essentials 10d
9. Grizzlies From Hell 10c ★
10. Another Mindless Crack 10
11. Le Geek 10a ★
12. Death Flake 9 vs
13. Dead Men Tell No Tales 9 vs
14. Gumby Groove 5
15. Pebble Of No Return 11a ★
16. Leave The Lats At Home 11d (9 s) ★
17. Beached Whale Impersonation 10c ★
18. High On Crack 11d ★
19. Just Say No 9 ★
20. Swab The Deck 10c ★
21. Walk The Plank 10b/c

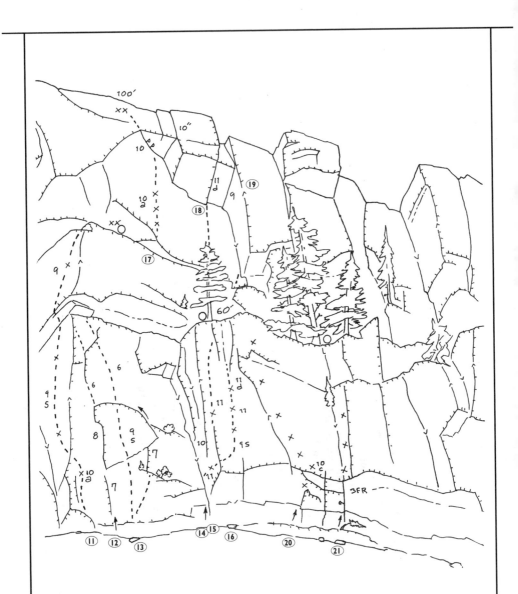

## SOUTH SUMMIT
11. **Le Geek 10a** ★
12. **Death Flake 9 vs**
13. **Dead Men Tell No Tales 9 vs**
14. **Gumby Groove 5**
15. **Pebble Of No Return 11a** ★
16. **Leave The Lats At Home 11d (9 s)** ★
17. **Beached Whale Impersonation 10c** ★
18. **High On Crack 11d** ★
19. **Just Say No 9** ★
20. **Swab The Deck 10c** ★
21. **Walk The Plank 10b/c**

### 12. DEATH FLAKE 9 VS

Lieback along the left side of a big flake, then continue up the right side of the arête and finish with Le Geek.

### 13. DEAD MEN TELL NO TALES 9 VS

Climb up the middle of the flake (9 vs), then continue up the face and finish as for the preceding route. One may also climb along the right edge of the flake (7).

### 14. GUMBY GROOVE 5

Climb the left-facing dihedral that leads to the rappel tree. Rappel 70 feet or traverse right 20 feet and climb a left-facing dihedral to the top of the ridge. Traverse 50 feet north to a three-bolt anchor and rappel 100 feet to the ground.

### 15. PEBBLE OF NO RETURN 11A ★

Climb the first 10 feet of Gumby Groove, then up and right beneath a small overhang and up the right side of the arête to tree. Two bolts. Bring a selection of small nuts.

### 16. LEAVE THE LATS AT HOME 11D (9 S) ★

Begin as for the previous route, but go right around the arête from the first bolt. Climb straight up the wall to the tree. Four bolts.

The following three routes ascend the head wall above the ledge with a tree mentioned in the preceding routes. To escape from the ridge crest, traverse 50 feet north to a three-bolt anchor and rappel 100 feet to the ground.

### 17. BEACHED WHALE IMPERSONATION 10C ★

Up and left from the tree, follow bolts up a slab and crack through a roof with two pins. Two-bolt belay anchor.

### 18. HIGH ON CRACK 11D ★

Climb the left side of the inset roof directly above the rappel tree. Strenuous and technical. SR.

### 19. JUST SAY NO 9 ★

Follow a left-facing dihedral up through the right side of the inset roof.

### 20. SWAB THE DECK 10C ★

FA: JOE DESIMONE AND JIM GUERIN, 1989.

Begin beneath a blunt arête that leads up and left to the rappel tree mentioned above. Work up and right over a black-streaked bulge, the up and left along the right side of the arête. Seven bolts.

### 21. WALK THE PLANK 10B/C

FA: JOE DESIMONE AND MIKE BILDERBACK, 1989.

Begin 15 feet right of Swab The Deck. Climb the overhanging wall past a fixed pin, place a #3 Friend in a wide section and pull over the lip. Move out right past a bolt and climb the left side of an arête past two more bolts to a big ledge. SR.

## MOBY DICK

Moby Dick is the striking, leaning monolith near the south end of the Main Cliff. Two routes are recorded on the steep north face. To escape from the summit, rappel 100 feet from a two-bolt anchor.

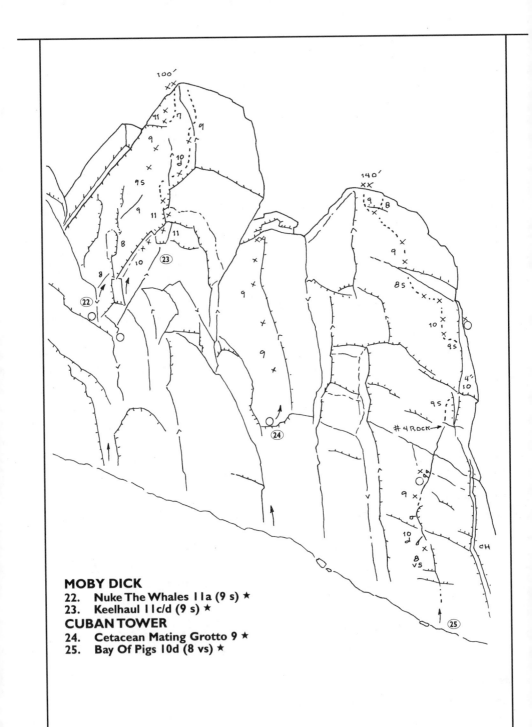

## MOBY DICK
22. **Nuke The Whales 11a (9 s)** ★
23. **Keelhaul 11c/d (9 s)** ★

## CUBAN TOWER
24. **Cetacean Mating Grotto 9** ★
25. **Bay Of Pigs 10d (8 vs)** ★

Main Cliff

Moby Dick

Cuban Tower

**SACRED CLIFFS, MAIN CLIFF**

### 22. NUKE THE WHALES 11A (9 S) ★

To begin, scramble 15 feet to a ledge and belay at left. Start up corner at edge of face, then traverse up and right along a crack. Climb past right side of block, right again along a short crack, then straight up the wall past four bolts. Crux at the top. SR with 10 QDs.

### 23. KEELHAUL 11C/D (9 S) ★

To begin, scramble 15 feet up to a ledge and belay beneath the right edge of the north face. Climb up and right beneath an overlap to an exposed stance on the overhanging northwest arête (two bolts, 10d). Climb along the edge of the north face past five more bolts, then pull around onto the west face and head for the summit. SR with 12 QDs, double ropes recommended.

## CUBAN TOWER

Just south of Moby Dick is the Cuban Tower, the last significant crag on the south ridge of Green Mountain. It features a short, steep slab on its north face and a very steep and impressive west face with one superb route. Approach time is about one hour. To escape from the summit, rappel 140 feet west from a two-bolt anchor.

### 24. CETACEAN MATING GROTTO 9 ★

Scramble up to the notch between Moby Dick and the Cuban Tower. Climb the smooth north face past four bolts. Belay from a bolt by a big block. Rappel.

### 25. BAY OF PIGS 10D (8 VS) ★

Bill DeMallie wrote of this route, "If this were the only climb on the ridge, it would still be worth the walk." Begin just right of a large block at the bottom of the west face. 1. Climb through a bulge (8 vs), then work up and right past assorted pins and bolts to a sling belay at two-pin and bolt (10d). 2. Climb up and right into an alcove (9 s, blind stopper placement), then jam an overhanging crack (of varying width up to four inches) and belay from a bolt near the top of a pedestal (10). 3. Step down from the belay and traverse left to a bolt (9 s), then up pebbles past two more bolts to a roof (10). Make a long traverse left (8 s), up past a large cobblestone, then angle up and left to the summit (9, seven bolts).

# Rated Route Index

# Route Name Index

# ACCESS: It's every climber's concern

**The Access Fund,** a national, non-profit climbers' organization, works to keep climbing areas open and to conserve the climbing environment. Need help with closures? land acquisition? legal or land management issues? funding for trails and other projects? starting a local climbers' group? CALL US!

Climbers can help preserve access by being committed to leaving the environment in its natural state. Here are some simple guidelines:

• **STRIVE FOR ZERO IMPACT** especially in environmentally sensitive areas like caves. Chalk can be a significant impact on dark and porous rock—don't use it around historic rock art. Pick up litter, and leave trees and plants intact.

• **DISPOSE OF HUMAN WASTE PROPERLY** Use toilets whenever possible. If toilets are not available, dig a "cat hole" at least six inches deep and 200 feet from any water, trails, campsites, or the base of climbs. *Always pack out toilet paper.* On big wall routes, use a "poop tube" and carry waste up and off with you (the old "bag toss" is now illegal in many areas).

• **USE EXISTING TRAILS** Cutting switchbacks causes erosion. When walking off-trail, tread lightly, especially in the desert where cryptogamic soils (usually a dark crust) take thousands of years to form and are easily damaged. Be aware that "rim ecologies" (the clifftop) are often highly sensitive to disturbance.

• **BE DISCREET WITH FIXED ANCHORS** *Bolts are controversial and are not a convenience*—don't place 'em unless they are *really* necessary. Camouflage all anchors. Remove unsightly slings from rappel stations (better to use steel chain or welded cold shuts). Bolts sometimes can be used pro-actively to protect fragile resources—consult with your local land manager.

• **RESPECT THE RULES** and speak up when other climbers don't. Expect restrictions in designated wilderness areas, rock art sites, caves, and to protect wildlife, especially nesting birds of prey. *Power drills are illegal in wilderness and all national parks.*

• **PARK AND CAMP IN DESIGNATED AREAS** Some climbing areas require a permit for overnight camping.

• **MAINTAIN A LOW PROFILE** Leave the boom box and day-glo clothing at home—the less climbers are heard and seen, the better.

• **RESPECT PRIVATE PROPERTY** Be courteous to land owners. Don't climb where you're not wanted.

• **JOIN THE ACCESS FUND!** To become a member, make a tax-deductible donation of $25 or more.

# The Access Fund

*Preserving America's Diverse Climbing Resources*
PO Box 17010 Boulder, CO 80308
303.545.6772 • www.accessfund.org

# More Climbing Guides from Falcon and Chockstone Press

# FALCON GUIDES ®Leading the Way™

**FALCON GUIDES** ® are available for where-to-go hiking, mountain biking, rock climbing, walking, scenic driving, fishing, rockhounding, paddling, birding, wildlife viewing, and camping. We also have FalconGuides on essential outdoor skills and subjects and field identification. The following titles are currently available, but this list grows every year. For a free catalog with a complete list of titles, call FALCON toll-free at 1-800-582-2665.

## HIKING GUIDES

Hiking Alaska
Hiking Arizona
Hiking Arizona's Cactus Country
Hiking the Beartooths
Hiking Big Bend National Park
Hiking the Bob Marshall Country
Hiking California
Hiking California's Desert Parks
Hiking Carlsbad Caverns
 and Guadalupe Mtns. National Parks
Hiking Colorado
Hiking Colorado, Vol.II
Hiking Colorado's Summits
Hiking Colorado's Weminuche Wilderness
Hiking the Columbia River Gorge
Hiking Florida
Hiking Georgia
Hiking Glacier & Waterton Lakes National Parks
Hiking Grand Canyon National Park
Hiking Grand Staircase-Escalante/Glen Canyon
Hiking Grand Teton National Park
Hiking Great Basin National Park
Hiking Hot Springs in the Pacific Northwest
Hiking Idaho
Hiking Maine
Hiking Michigan
Hiking Minnesota
Hiking Montana
Hiking Mount Rainier National Park
Hiking Mount St. Helens
Hiking Nevada
Hiking New Hampshire

Hiking New Mexico
Hiking New York
Hiking North Carolina
Hiking the North Cascades
Hiking Northern Arizona
Hiking Olympic National Park
Hiking Oregon
Hiking Oregon's Eagle Cap Wilderness
Hiking Oregon's Mount Hood/Badger Creek
Hiking Oregon's Three Sisters Country
Hiking Pennsylvania
Hiking Shenandoah National Park
Hiking the Sierra Nevada
Hiking South Carolina
Hiking South Dakota's Black Hills Country
Hiking Southern New England
Hiking Tennessee
Hiking Texas
Hiking Utah
Hiking Utah's Summits
Hiking Vermont
Hiking Virginia
Hiking Washington
Hiking Wyoming
Hiking Wyoming's Cloud Peak Wilderness
Hiking Wyoming's Wind River Range
Hiking Yellowstone National Park
Hiking Zion & Bryce Canyon National Parks
The Trail Guide to Bob Marshall Country
Wild Country Companion
Wild Montana
Wild Utah

■ *To order any of these books, check with your local bookseller
or call FALCON ® at **1-800-582-2665**.
Visit us on the world wide web at:
www.FalconOutdoors.com*

FALCON®

# FALCONGUIDES® Leading the Way

Come to America's wilderness areas and enjoy some of the most pristine hiking conditions you'll ever experience. With FalconGuides® you'll be able to plan your trip, including learning how to get there, getting a permit, if necessary, and picking your campsites. Types of trails, difficulty ratings, distances, maps, elevation charts, and backcountry regulations are covered in detail. You'll also learn "leave no trace" principles, safety tips, and other essential information specific to the wilderness area you visit. The following titles are currently available, and this list grows every year. For a free catalog with a complete list of titles, call FALCON toll-free at 800-582-2665.

---

Hiking the Beartooths
Hiking the Bob Marshall Country
Hiking Colorado's Weminuche Wilderness
Hiking Oregon's Central Cascades
Hiking Oregon's Eagle Cap Wilderness
Hiking Oregon's Mount Hood & Badger Creek Wilderness
Hiking Wyoming's Cloud Peak Wilderness
Hiking Wyoming's Wind River Range
Wild Montana
Wild Utah

Wilderness area FalconGuides® are
published in cooperation with
*The Wilderness Society*

*To order any of these books, check with your local bookseller,*
*Or call FALCON at 1-800-582-2665.*
*Visit us on the world wide web at:*
*www.FalconOutdoors.com*